One Guyana

From Division and Bankruptcy to Unity and Prosperity

Mohamed Irfaan Ali

HANSIB

First published in 2025 by Hansib Publications
76 High Street, Hertford, SG14 3TA, United Kingdom

info@hansibpublications.com
www.hansibpublications.com

ISBN 978-1-0682437-5-2
ISBN 978-1-0682437-6-9 (Kindle)
ISBN 978-1-0682437-7-6 (ePub)

A CIP catalogue record for this book is available from the British Library

Produced and printed in Great Britain

Founded in London in 1970, Hansib Publications has played a crucial role in documenting the Caribbean experience and bringing Caribbean perspectives to a wider audience. It is renowned for its extensive catalogue of Caribbean fiction and non-fiction, spanning a diverse range of genres, including historical novels, biographies, poetry anthologies, political commentaries and social narratives. It has also made significant contributions to Caribbean scholarship by publishing insightful works on history, culture, politics and social issues.

Today, Hansib Publications remains a significant force in the world of Caribbean publishing and continues to publish books that reflect the vibrant diversity of the Caribbean region and the global Caribbean diaspora. Its legacy of promoting Caribbean voices and perspectives has made it an invaluable resource for those seeking to understand and appreciate the rich cultural heritage of the Caribbean.

Contents

Glossary of Terms

ACCC	Arthur Chung Convention Centre
AFC	Alliance for Change
AIFLD	American Institute of Free Labor Development
AML/CFT	Anti-Money Laundering and Countering the Financing of Terrorism
APNU	A Partnership for National Unity
ANUG	A New and United Guyana
BIM	Building Information Modeling
BIFDI	Baishanlin International Forest Development Inc.
BGTUC	British Guiana Trades Union Congress
BOG	Bank of Guyana
CANU	Customs Anti-Narcotics Unit
CARICOM	Caribbean Community
CCJ	Caribbean Court of Justice
CIA	Central Intelligence Agency
CIO	Chief Immigration Officer
CJIA	Cheddi Jagan International Airport
CLI	Civil Liberties Index
CMAG	Commonwealth Ministerial Action Group
COI	Commission of Inquiry
CSO	Community Service Officers
CXC	Caribbean Examination Council
DBIS	Demerara Berbice Interconnected System
DEA	Drug Enforcement Administration
DMS	Distribution Management System
DPP	Director of Public Prosecutions
EOI	Expression of Interest
FBI	Federal Bureau of Investigation
FDI	Foreign Direct Investment
FPSO	Floating Production Storage and Offloading
ERC	Ethnic Relations Commission
ERP	Economic Recovery Programme
FAO	Food and Agriculture Organization
GAIBANK	Guyana Agricultural and Industrial Development Bank
GAWU	Guyanese Workers' Agricultural Union
GBA	Guyana Bar Association
GBC	Guyana Broadcasting Corporation
GC	*Guyana Chronicle*
GCMFB	Guyana Mortgage Finance Bank
GDF	Guyana Defence Force
GDP	Gross Domestic Product
GECOM	Guyana Elections Commission
GFC	Guyana Forestry Commission

GI	Gini Index
GNBS	Guyana National Bureau of Standards
GNCB	Guyana National Co-operative Bank
GNI	Guyana News and Information
GOAL	Guyana Online Academy of Learning
GPF	Guyana Police Force
GPS	Guyana Prison Service
GPSU	Guyana Public Service Union
GRL	Guyana Refrigerators Ltd
GROW	Guyana Reinvestment in Opportunities for Work
GSDS	Green State Development Strategy
GT	*Guyana Times*
GtE	Gas-to-Energy project
GuySuCo	Guyana Sugar Corporation
GWI	Guyana Water Incorporated
HDI	Human Development Index
HIES	Household Income and Expenditure Survey
HIPC	Highly Indebted Poor Country
ICAHR	Inter-American Commission on Human Rights
ICJ	International Court of Justice
iN	iNews Guyana
IMF	International Monetary Fund
IWRM	Integrated Water Resources Management
KN	*Kaieteur News*
LJP	Liberty and Justice Party
LSMS	Living Standard Measurement Survey
MPI	Multidimensional Poverty Index
MIR	Mortgage Interest Relief
MOFA	Ministry of Foreign Affairs
NAC	National Aquatic Centre
NBS	New Building Society
NDC	Neighbourhood Democratic Council
NQI	National Quality Infrastructure
NR	News Room
NRR	National Register of Registrants
NRRDB	National Register of Registrants Database
NTC	National Toshaos Council
NTDS	Neglected Tropical Diseases
OAS	Organization of American States
OBGYN	Obstetrics and Gynaecology
OGDI	One Guyana Digital Initiative
OLE	Official List of Electors
PSA	Prostate-Specific Antigen
PRIMIS	Police Record Management Information System
PRO	Public Relations Office
PTA	Parent Teacher Association
RDC	Regional Democratic Councils
RLE	Revised List of Electors
RSV	Respiratory Syncytial Virus
SDG	Sustainable Development Goal
SN	*Stabroek News*
SOPs	Statement of Polls
TB	Tuberculosis
TCI	The Citizenship Initiative
TNM	The New Movement
TUC	Trade Union Council
TVET	Technical and Vocational Education and Training
UAE	United Arab Emirates
UF	United Force
UM	University of Miami
UNDP	United Nations Development Programme
URP	United Republic Party

USA	United States of America
PAHO	Pan American Health Organization
PNC	People's National Congress
PPP	People's Progressive Party
PPP/C	People's Progressive Party Civic
PRI	Political Rights Index
PSA	Production Sharing Agreement
PSIP	Public Sector Investment Programme
UWI	University of the West Indies
VAT	Value Added Tax
WMO	World Meteorological Organization
WPA	Working People's Alliance
WRSM	Women's Revolutionary Socialist Movement

Foreword

Guyana is a small but complex country. Until recently, known on the world stage only for the 1978 massacre at Jonestown, it has been catapulted into the global limelight on account of massive discoveries and development of oil and gas resources. The runaway explosion of economic growth has, in one fell swoop, lifted the society out of the doldrums of underdevelopment to heights of prosperity once deemed impossible. Much the same may be said of political development. A country once hobbled by authoritarian rule has gradually wended its way into democratic consolidation. This is true notwithstanding new *populist* threats to democracy that are emerging from the WIN political party led by Azruddin Mohamed.

One Guyana: From Division and Bankruptcy to Unity and Prosperity provides a comprehensive account of the challenges and triumphs of a nation as it pushes its way from the ashes of colonialism into the era of global modernity.

In 1947, a handful of Guyanese patriots, led by Dr Cheddi Jagan, formed the Political Action Committee, the precursor to the People's Progressive Party (PPP). The PPP was founded as a multi-racial and nationalist movement in January 1950, dedicated to the emancipation of the Guyanese people from colonial rule. The struggle for independence was paramount. The dynamics of the Cold War, however, encroached on the momentum for national sovereignty. By 1955, external architects had engineered the split in the PPP. The People's National Congress under L.F.S. Burnham emerged as an alternative to the PPP. By 1964, the PNC (in coalition with the conservative United Force) took office through electoral subterfuges hatched in London with full support from 'across the pond'.

The die was cast, and Guyana entered a nearly three-decades-long saga of decline and humiliation, marked by economic stagnation, electoral banditry, political violence, and perhaps most tellingly, a sapping of the energies of the people who voted with their feet. They left by the hundreds of thousands, an exodus triggered by the slow-motion despotism that swept this land from Lethem to Lesbeholden, from Leonora to Linden, and everywhere in between. No one, excepting elites with the then-ruling PNC, was spared.

If the logic of the Cold War underpinned the installation of the PNC, then the end of that era also presented an opportunity to escape economic strangulation and political authoritarianism. The Atlanta-based Carter Center entered the annals of Guyanese history by convincing President Hugh Desmond Hoyte to hold free and fair elections. In October 1992, the first free and fair elections in decades took place under the watchful eyes of international observers. The PPP won those elections and immediately began the task of reconstructing a nation that had been devastated by mismanagement.

You will see, however, that democracy once won, must always be defended. In 2015, the PNC-led APNU-AFC coalition won the elections. Despite a successful no-confidence motion in the National Assembly in December 2018, which required new elections to be called within three months, this did not happen until March 2020. However, much like the decades preceding it, the APNU-AFC dragged the nation through months of electoral agony. The shocking disregard for electoral decency is fully outlined in this book.

Successive PPP governments since 1992 have been guided by a set of fundamental principles. These are as follows: (1) that democracy and development are indivisible; (2) that there must be the right balance between long-term investments in infrastructure and medium and near-term consumption priorities; (3) that human development must always be the objective of economic policies; (4) that economic development must be environmentally sustainable; (5) that foreign investment and international partnerships must be configured around national priorities and; (6) that inclusive development is critical to racial harmony and cultural advancement.

The very first iteration of the *National Development Strategy* (which was led by Bharrat Jagdeo) expressly emphasised inclusive governance and development. The multi-volume document stated that "... we could considerably assist in removing the scourge of racism from our land, if we developed and put into practice inclusive systems of governance in which all would feel that they have a stake." Further "... that a considerable degree of harmony would prevail in our country if we were able to formulate and implement social and economic policies which would lead not only to significant economic growth, but also to the widest distribution of the benefits of such growth among the population..." (*National Development Strategy* 2001-2010).

The stress on inclusive governance cannot be overstated. This is because Guyana has had some serious challenges on account of the electorally driven weaponisation of identity. The public sphere is rent with claims of marginalisation and discrimination, often with little or no substantiation. It is imperative that we never forget that the racialisation of this country's politics is a direct result of foreign intervention.

The administration of President Mohamed Irfaan Ali is focused on using the new revenues from the oil and gas sector, not only to tackle the abiding socio-economic challenges in the society, but to embark on a long-term process of structural and institutional transformation. Nothing expresses this more than the "One Guyana" symbol adopted by the president. One Guyana signifies emphasis on building a society based on mutual respect for all the cultural traditions in this land of "six races".

But more than that, *One Guyana* points to a commitment to equitable development. While egalitarianism is a benchmark in democratic governance, we must take cognisance of the historical record, and specifically of the differential opportunities that were hatched and reproduced in conquest, slavery, indentureship and colonial rule. *One Guyana* is, therefore, mindful of the structural underpinnings of regional and other disparities, and dedicated to bridging the gap.

Inclusive governance is real and forms an integral dimension of development policies and budgetary priorities. It is this context, for instance, that fifteen per cent of the 'revenues' from carbon credits sales are handed over to the two hundred and forty-two Amerindian villages. In the years to come, these resources are likely to increase through initiatives such as the Global Biodiversity Alliance, which was recently launched here in Guyana.

The Irfaan Ali administration has invested heavily in education, healthcare, housing, jobs creation, and an ever expanding system of social services to benefit the elderly, the disabled and the indigent. Further, special measures, such as the Local Content Act (2021) have been put into place to ensure that the Guyanese people are given priority in service sectors linked to the hydrocarbon industry.

One Guyana: From Division and Bankruptcy to Unity and Prosperity offers a historically-grounded and data-driven analysis of the political and economic development of Guyana in the modern era. It is rare that perspectives on the political economy of development benefit from an admixture of scholarly rigour and the first-hand experience of a sitting head of state and government. This book, therefore, provides a truly remarkable opportunity for readers in Guyana, the Caribbean, and elsewhere in the developing world, to get an insider's view of how a country moves from structural underdevelopment and authoritarian rule, to one of hope, prosperity and perhaps even national unity.

As President Ali moves into a second term with a more robust manifesto, and with the solid record of the PPP/C keeping election promises, the expectations of rapid development are high. Notwithstanding all the challenges old and new, Guyana's future looks assured.

Randolph B. Persaud, PhD
Fellow, IHRSSF (University of Guyana) &
Professor Emeritus, SIS, American University, Washington DC

1

The Genesis of a Fragmented Society

We meet at a time of grave crisis. The Coalition's domestic and foreign policies have landed Guyana into a morass. CHEDDI JAGAN

Since its independence, Guyana has been plagued by perpetual economic and social hardships until 1992, primarily due to the polarising brand of politics practised by the People's National Congress (PNC). During the elections of 1957, the seed of divisive politics was sown by the PNC, where racism and segregation were introduced as the main pillars of the campaign. The practice of racial divisions as a means of political gain has remained a central strategy of the PNC, now rebranded as A Partnership for National Unity (APNU), since the 1950s.

The party has demonstrated its incompetence in pursuing visionary and transformative policies that serve the broader interests of the populace, both during its tenure in government and while in opposition. Furthermore, its reluctance to become a government for the people had led it to become overly reliant on its sole and crude strategy of *divide and rule*. During the period 1966-1992, while in Government, the PNC expelled minorities from rural communities, committed hate crimes, and even proposed to divide the country into two separate "ethnic nations" - one for African and one for East Indian citizens (Smith, 1995). Even after being in opposition for over two decades, the party resorted to the same divisive politics when it returned to power in 2015. Between 2015 and 2020, the PNC, as the main party in the APNU&AFC coalition government, fired over 2,000 (Amerindian) Community Service Officers (CSOs) and approximately 7,000 sugar workers without providing any viable alternative employment options. The party initiated a series of forensic audits with the aim of discrediting leaders of the PPP and public officials who served the country during the PPP/C administration. While in opposition, the PNC consistently stoked social discord by propagating unfounded claims that non-supporters of the People's Progressive Party (PPP) are victimised and marginalised. This false narrative often fuels fears of ethnic tension and insecurity, which often lead to violent conflicts. The divisive politics practised by the PNC have scarred the social fabric of our country and driven a wedge between our people, which has prevented them from living together in peace and harmony. This chapter chronicles the divisive politics of the PNC, from its formation in the mid-1950s through its rise to power in 1964 with the support of external forces.

History of violent political conflicts

In the lead-up to independence, a new constitution was introduced to replace the Legislative Council with the House of Assembly, paving the way for the historic 1953 elections. The elections were contested by the multi-cultural People's Progressive Party (PPP), led by Cheddi Jagan and Forbes Burnham, which won by a significant margin. However, just after 133 days in office, the PPP was removed from office by a combination of British emergency orders and heavily armed British troops due to concerns about constitutional subversion and the perceived threat of a communist regime. In response, the constitution was suspended, a state of emergency was declared, and a *transitional government* was established to administer the country until new elections could be held.

In 1957, elections were called. This time, the People's National Congress (PNC), led by Forbes Burnham, and the People's Progressive Party (PPP), under the leadership of Cheddi Jagan, contested the elections. The PPP secured a decisive victory, reaffirming its political dominance at the national level and preference among the people. Dissatisfied with the results, the opposition PNC issued a new call for constitutional reform before the next elections, culminating in the 1961 general elections being held under a first-past-the-post electoral system. Again, the PPP emerged victorious, winning almost 60 per cent of the legislative seats. Jagan was elected to office for the third time and was set to become the first Prime Minister of an independent Guyana (Smith, 1971). This marked the beginning of a crucial turning point in Jagan's tenure in office – one characterised by increasing geopolitical tensions, racism, violence, segregation, and foreign interventions.

In 1961, the PNC mounted a new wave of attacks by challenging the legitimacy of Jagan's government. This time, they have conspired with the United Force (UF), urging the British government to hold new elections using a proportional representation system. The system was viewed as a biased instrument to facilitate an outcome favourable to the colonial authority (Mars, 1990). To bolster their destabilisation campaign, the PNC joined forces with the Trade Union Congress to launch a mass protest against the PPP government, which culminated in riots on February 16, 1962. Numerous buildings were destroyed, damaged, and looted in Georgetown (Ishmael, 2004). Over the next two years, anti-government street demonstrations and industrial strikes continued, with external assistance from the PNC, UF, and the Trade Union Council (TUC). In 1963, for instance, the TUC launched a strike that lasted for 80 days. The strike came to an end after nine citizens lost their lives and several others were injured (SN,07/10/2009). However, this event seems pale compared to riots in the Wismar during 1964, where many properties were destroyed, and persons killed, raped, and assaulted. This deadly riot was followed by the bombing of the Sun Chapman boat that claimed the lives of forty-three citizens. As part of the diabolical X-13 plan, engineered by the PNC, Freedom House, along with twelve buildings in Georgetown, were bombed. Given these dreadful events, the British Colonial Office delayed the granting of independence and amended the electoral laws, allowing for a system of proportional representation.

The country went back to the polls in 1964 under the new electoral system. Two themes from the 1961 elections resurfaced during the elections campaign. First, Jagan was branded as a socialist, while Burnham and Peter D'Aguiar were promoted as proponents of the mixed-economy concept and laissez-faire capitalism, respectively. Second, the anti-government strikes and demonstrations that took place during 1962-1963 provoked racial tensions that led to the polarisation and division of our citizens.

None of the contesting parties won a majority of seats in the 1964 elections. The PPP obtained 46 per cent of the votes, the PNC 40 per cent, and the UF 12 per cent. A coalition was necessary to determine the winner. In 1964, the system of proportional representation was introduced and adopted to enable a coalition between the People's National Congress and the United Force (UF). Soon thereafter, the PNC, under Forbes Burnham's leadership, formed a coalition government with the United Force (UF), resulting in Peter D'Aguiar being appointed Minister of Finance. With the ousting of Jagan, Schlesinger surmised that "with much unhappiness and turbulence, British Guiana seemed to have passed safely out of the communist orbit" (Third World Traveler, 1968).

In the years following Guyana's independence, Burnham focused on strengthening the Guyana Defence Force (GDF) and the Guyana Police Force (GPF) with the assistance of the United States and Britain. The National Security Act was enacted, which gave the government considerable power to suppress dissent. Another piece of legislation that helped strengthen Burnham's grip on power was the National Registration Bill.

From December 1964 to October 1992, Guyana was governed by the People's National Congress (PNC) as a virtual one-party state. During this period, the PNC nurtured racial antipathies and projected an image that asserted socialism as its ideological guide. In the early 1970s, Burnham was conferred with the José Martí Award, Cuba's highest honour, and then welcomed into the People's Republic of China during Mao Zedong's regime as a fellow comrade. In Guyana, progressive-to-radical leaders such as Fidel Castro were invited to witness the country's socialist transformation. On the ground, the economic landscape rapidly transformed into one characterised by strong state control and ownership. Some of the leading foreign companies were nationalised, resulting in government control of the economy exceeding 80 per cent.

During the twenty-eight years of the PNC dictatorship, citizens were constantly engaged in anti-government demonstrations and strikes. These events reflected the struggle of workers and citizens for basic human rights, including the right to elect their representatives in free and fair elections.

Table 1 below shows the frequency of violent political events between 1947 and 1970. The period 1947-1954 was characterised by state repressive violence when the British government was busy preventing what it perceived to be a "communist" PPP ascendance into office. During this period, there were nine anti-government demonstrations and sixty strikes. These events were accompanied by an average of one case of extreme conflict (see Table 1).

In the decade that followed (1954-1964), anti-government demonstrations and strikes were driven by the destabilisation campaign of the PNC and its allies to remove the PPP. During this period, the PNC planted the seed of divisive politics. The most violent period was 1962-1964, which saw mass demonstrations, riots, and terrorist attacks resulting in citizens being killed and several hundred properties destroyed. These events culminated in the accession of the PNC to office.

The period between 1967 and 1970 witnessed a significant increase in anti-government demonstrations and strikes. These actions were a manifestation of

Table 1- Frequency of political violent events (1947-1970)

Period	Anti-Government Demonstrations	Strikes	Insurrectionary Events/Riots, etc.
1947-50	4	34	1
1951-54	5	26	0
1955-58	3	42	0
1959-62	3	46	2
1963-66	6	130	3
1967-70	1	143	1
Annual Average for Period 1947-70	4	70	1

Sources: Mars, P. (1990, page 78)

the citizens' struggle against the practice of the People's National Congress (PNC), which utilised the state as a weapon to suppress political rivals and those who did not support the party's agenda. This practice is rooted in the strategy of 'divide and rule,' which was introduced by Burnham after he left the People's Progressive Party (PPP) to form the PNC. At the parliamentary level, the exclusionary politics practised by the PNC was conspicuous, with 68 per cent of its parliamentary representatives being from one ethnic group.

In what followed, the People's National Congress (PNC) party was able to establish authoritarian control over the nation by strategically altering its ideological and foreign policy stances to align with the interests of the United States and the United Kingdom. The party's leadership, under the guidance of its leader Forbes Burnham, facilitated this shift in policy, which ultimately led to the consolidation of power by the PNC. This calculated move enabled the party to assume a dominant position in the country's political landscape, effectively suppressing opposition and consolidating its hold on the nation.

Burnham aligned himself with socialism during a time when the country was seeking independence from British control. At that time, socialism was viewed as less dangerous than communism, which was embraced by Dr Jagan, the leader of the PPP. By joining forces with the United Force to remove the

PPP, Burnham signalled that his party was pro-Western and amenable to capitalism. The shifting ideological posturing by Burnham allowed his party to mobilise the support of the United States and the United Kingdom. However, his political trajectory was marked by notable inconsistencies. For instance, between 1969 and 1977, his party pursued socialism, and from 1978 to 1982, it pivoted to a mixed economic model. Some commentators considered these changes as indicators of opportunism driven by his desire to acquire, consolidate, and retain political power.

The ousting of Jagan with the support of external forces

In 1955, Forbes Burnham severed ties with the PPP after a failed attempt to take control of the party. The attempt failed, and Jagan and his wife, Janet nee Rosenberg, took control of the leadership. In 1960, Britain began preparing for the transfer of an independent British Guiana to the PPP (Fraser, 2000). In the United States, however, the Kennedy administration was less enthusiastic. According to the Central Intelligence Agency (CIA) report submitted to the US Intelligence Board (GNI, 06/2000):

> [Jagan] would proceed forthwith with an effort to establish an avowed Communist regime...[and] that an independent Jagan government would seek to portray itself as an instrument of reformist nationalism which would gradually move in the direction of [Fidel] Castro's Cuba. Such a regime would almost certainly be strongly encouraged and supported by Castro and the [Soviet] Bloc.

The British, however, were keen on leaving the country's affairs as gracefully and honourably as possible. The United States, on the other hand, was much more concerned about the country's prospects in a post-independence world, particularly with respect to joining forces with Cuba and challenging US influence in the Americas, a risk considered too significant to ignore. The Kennedy administration made it clear to the British that it had unsettled sentiments about the Jagans and Cuba ties. To the British, this was less of a concern. In fact, they were unwilling to undertake or allow the United States to intervene and prevent Jagan's victory since they perceived Jagan as 'salvageable'.

In 1961, the Governor of British Guiana related to the CIA in Washington that the British could work with the Jagans and that Burnham was racist and untrustworthy. However, the US Secretary of State Rusk had different plans. He was concerned that Jagan's accession to power would have grave foreign policy ramifications for the US and even cause acute embarrassment due to the inevitable disruption to Anglo-American relations. In a telegram from the Department of State to the Embassy in the United Kingdom, Secretary Rusk urged intervention to prevent the likely eventuality, even if it meant interfering in the electoral process to justify the need for fresh elections. However, in response, Foreign Secretary Home urged that little could be done, and the best way to preserve Western influence might be to work with Jagan (GNI, 06/2000):

> Your people and ours have looked very carefully into the possibilities of taking action to influence the results of the election [...] I am convinced that there is nothing practical-i.e., safe and effective that we could do in this regard and that if we tried anything of this kind, we should only make matters worse [...] the choice before us in situations like this is either to allow the normal process of democracy and progress towards self-government to go ahead and do our best to win the confidence of the elected leaders, and to wean them away from any dangerous tendencies, or else to revert to what we call "Crown Colony rule." It is practical politics to take the latter course only when it is quite clear that a territory is heading for disaster. We have done this once already in British Guiana-in 1953. But since the restoration of the democratic process in 1957, the elected government has behaved reasonably well and we have had no grounds which would justify a second attempt to put the clock back [...] No one can say for certain how Jagan will behave if he is returned to power [...] But he has learnt a good deal in the last eight years; he has not, since 1957, proved as difficult to deal with as he was earlier [...] and, if we in the West show a real willingness to try to help, we think it by no means impossible that British Guiana may end up in a position not very different from that of India.

However, the Kennedy administration was reluctant to support Jagan and instead instructed the US consul general in Georgetown to gather information on the two leading opposition parties: the United Force (UF) and the People's National Congress (PNC). The PNC's support base lay predominantly in urban areas among the working- and middle-class black communities. The UF primarily represented the middle class and the business community, particularly the Europeans. The UF also represented Christian-dominated Amerindian communities. The British, on the other hand, were working to ensure that a strong opposition was in place to help keep the PPP in check (Fraser, 2000). However, despite various antics and subterfuges by the British, including the redrawing of electoral district boundaries, the PPP won 20 seats, while the PNC obtained 11 and the UF 4, allowing the PPP to secure a legislative majority. The results of the elections were a sober reminder of the opposition parties' inability to unseat the PPP, even with the electoral boundaries redrawn in their favour.

Unpalatable by the outcome of the elections, the US Secretary of State decided to take up the offer to support the British policy in handling Jagan's victory. A meeting was subsequently proposed by the Department of State for representatives of the two governments to sit down and discuss the situation (Fraser, 2000). A request that was later revealed to be driven by ulterior motives.

In a memorandum from the President's Special Assistant (Schlesinger) to President Kennedy, the State Department proposed four recommendations for addressing the Jagan's predicament. The first was for the United States to offer economic and technical assistance to British Guiana and then help with the country's admission to the Organization of American States (OAS) and Alliance for Progress. The third was for Jagan to be given a friendly reception on his visit to the U.S. and have an audience with President Kennedy. The fourth recommendation, however, was more sinister. It proposed the implementation of a clandestine program aimed at exposing and dismantling all forms of communism in British Guiana and, if possible, seeking an alternative to Jagan himself.

After the meeting in London, the United States remained sceptical of the British assessment of Jagan and was determined to have him removed from office. However, though reluctantly, the United States decided to collaborate with the British, as British Guiana inched closer to independence. To help attenuate the U.S.'s concern of him being labelled a pro-communist, Jagan reassured the Kennedy administration of his willingness to cooperate with the

U.S. He also promised to adhere to the rules of parliamentary democracy and join the Alliance for Progress to assure the U.S. that an independent Guiana under his leadership would not become a threat to the United States. Appointments of several cabinet members from other ethnic groups were also made to counter the perception that the People's Progressive Party (PPP) represented the interests of the Indo-Guyanese community solely. His actions garnered him new support, including that of groups that have traditionally opposed the PPP, such as the British Guiana Trades Union Congress (BGTUC).

During Jagan's visit to the U.S., the Kennedy administration followed through with their plan to offer development aid to British Guiana. While Jagan viewed the aid as an opportunity to counter the narrative advanced by his political opponents, who labelled him a communist and anti-American, the aid to Jagan was part of a coordinated strategy by the U.S. to keep British Guiana within the Western bloc. The disbursement of the aid ultimately proved to be a major challenge. With differences in the scale and timing of the aid, the U.S. was only willing to provide a fraction of the requested amount. In fact, Jagan was required to provide several iron-clad guarantees that would ensure his government desist from joining forces with the Communist bloc.

The Kennedy administration's approach to providing aid in measured amounts – despite Jagan's request for substantial support – proved to be more of a setback than help for his government. Instead of satisfying his full request, the U.S. government offered a modest US$5 million for development and a team of advisors to help develop a "realistic development program" (Fraser, 2000). At a meeting with the Agency for International Development (AID), Jagan expressed his disappointment, having expected a more robust commitment from the agency. His initial request ranged between US$60 million and $250 million. Given the gap between his request and the AID mission offer, Jagan signalled his intention to seek assistance from alternative sources. The AID interpreted this response as an indication of his willingness to turn to the Soviet Union for support – a preconceived and prejudicial assumption that had long shaped U.S. perceptions of his political ideology. In the end, he left the U.S. empty-handed, with the Kennedy administration offering to send an economic mission to Georgetown to assist in formulating a formal aid proposal.

Though the Kennedy administration was not forthcoming with the aid, it had not yet decided to oust the PPP government from office. In an interview with the Russian newspaper, Kennedy made it clear that the United States was willing to work with a Marxist-led government if the electoral process was fair, citing Jagan's victory in British Guiana as an example. To show his willingness to work with the Jagan administration, Kennedy, through the State Department, authorised US$1.5 million in technical assistance to the British Colony and promised to deploy an economic mission the following year (Fraser, 2000).

In British Guiana, the situation on the ground was becoming increasingly tense, and the opposition was seeking any reason, however frivolous, to justify the incitement of political violence. For instance, the fiscal budget introduced in 1962 under the PPP had called for mandatory savings and higher taxes. Though mired in economic prudence, the PNC, the British Guiana Trades Union Congress (BGTUC), and UF utilised this budget to instigate strike action, which eventually led to riots and arson in Georgetown, partly due to the police force's reluctance to cooperate with the government. It was further revealed that the Central Intelligence Agency (CIA) also provided support for these strikes, which were intended to bring down the Jagan government (Rabe, 1999).

In numerous memorandums to Kennedy, Schlesinger repeatedly referred to these initiatives as anti-Communist clandestine capabilities. Fearful that Guyana would become a Communist state under Jagan, the Kennedy administration proposed that the British delay independence and hold new elections under a proportional representation electoral system to deny Jagan power.

The British complied with the U.S. request and postponed independence. To help delay the granting of independence, a Commission of Inquiry (COI) was set up to investigate the cause of the recent disorder in British Guiana. According to the findings of the COI, the riots started as a result of fear of Communist tendencies, mainly due to the PPP government being in office. Other major causes were omitted from the report, including the underlying racial tensions and evidence of a coordinated plot to overthrow the government. The role of the CIA was also deliberately omitted. According to Ishmael (2004), the riot:

> [...] was comparable to an act of spontaneous combustion when some highly fermented substance is subjected to long pressures. The mass of discontented and idle workers on strike was inexorably driven by

> the sheer force of bored monotony to find release in rowdyism and rioting. The false rumour of a child's death caused by the deleterious effects of tear gas furnished the immediate stimulus to violence.

In the eyes of the U.S., Burnham was seen as a preferred alternative to Jagan. To help improve his public image, the U.S. State Department credited Burnham for obtaining U.S. scholarships for the people of Guiana. The American Institute for Free Labor Development (AIFLD), an organisation funded by the U.S. government through AID, also came on board to publicly endorse Burnham. At that time, the only concern of the State Department was whether the CIA could manipulate the elections in favour of Burnham without causing a backfire. It was believed that if elections were held under proportional representation, the opposition party would be able to secure victory. Later, in *A Thousand Days* (Swan-Ambrose, 2011, 52), Schlesinger writes:

> An independent British Guiana under Burnham (if Burnham can commit himself to a multilateral policy) would cause us many fewer problems than an independent British Guiana under Jagan. And the way was open to bring it about because Jagan's parliamentary strength was larger than his popular strength. He had won 57 per cent of the seats on the basis of 42.3 per cent of the vote. An obvious solution was to establish a system of proportional representation. (Schlesinger, 1965, p.779).

In March 1963, the PPP introduced a Labour Relations Bill, which allowed workers to choose their union representation through secret voting. The aim was to replace the Manpower Citizens' Association (MPCA) - a major source of support for the opposition parties, whose ties with the British and U.S. trade unions allowed it to solicit aid from Jagan's opponents residing overseas– with the PPP-controlled Guyana Agricultural and Industrial Workers' Union (GAWU). The opposition parties responded by calling for a strike by most of the unions they controlled, including the Civic Service Association. The British government and trade unions financially supported the strike, providing between $50,000 and $70,000 per week. The Public Service International, ostensibly a CIA front, was also part of the strike (Fraser, 2000).

Later that year, a state of emergency was declared, and Jagan tendered "his resignation on the condition that elections were held under the existing electoral system and that the winner be given the independence" (Fraser 2000, 605). During that period, Jagan turned to the Soviet Union and Cuba for food and fuel. This move incensed the Kennedy administration, causing disagreement between the U.S. and Great Britain since the aid from Cuba and Russia was shipped under the protection of an elite British Ship. The situation in Guiana had become a major concern for the Kennedy administration, as the U.S. was determined for Britain not to transfer power without first removing Jagan from office. Kennedy feared that a British Guiana ruled by Jagan could likely determine the outcome of the next presidential election in the U.S., as it would appear that the Soviet Union had leapfrogged Cuba and landed in the Western Hemisphere. To address the differences between the U.S. and Britain, both countries agreed on a joint strategy to oust Jagan.

After the strike, the British urged Jagan and Burnham to discuss a coalition government to evade criticism of the *coup de grâce* imposed on Jagan. However, three months later, the PPP and PNC were still at odds, as the PNC was demanding proportional representation, while the PPP was reluctant to accept it. The PNC was also demanding an equal number of cabinet posts under a coalition government despite having a lower share of the popular vote.

The failure of the talks between the PNC and the PPP led to new talks being held in London. However, this, too, ended in a deadlock. At this point, it became clear that the plan was to force Jagan into a perpetual deadlock, thereby facilitating the entry of the British government to deal the final blow. As planned, a joint letter by Burnham and Peter D'Aguiar was subsequently sent asking "the British Government to settle on their authority all outstanding constitutional issues, and [with a commitment] to accept their decisions" (UN, 1963). The solution was a new constitution and proportional representation, followed by elections and, subsequently, independence, in line with the U.S.'s plan and the PNC's demands. The ground was laid for the removal of Jagan through constitutional process. Having realised the insidious plan afoot, Jagan accused Britain of subservience to the U.S. and of using division and differences sown by the PNC to institute constitutional changes and manipulate the electoral process. What was once thought of as a key strategy to remove the PPP from office remained the only known strategy and eventually became the ultimate symbol of the PNC: violence and racial tension. The following year, sporadic violence re-emerged in British Guiana as the nation prepared for elections. However, Jagan failed to mobilise support from the United Nations, and the British Labour Party was of no help. In December 1964, with the support of the United States, the newly formed PNC-UF coalition assumed office, paving the way for the country's independence in May 1966.

Burnham-Peter D'Aguiar Government: 1964-1968

As discussed above, the Burnham-Peter D'Aguiar coalition acceded to power during the 1962-1964 period of internal strife with the assistance of external forces, that surreptitiously imposed the proportional representation voting system to ensure the electoral defeat of the PPP government. The first task of the coalition was to repress the PPP organisation. PPP activists were confined to jail without trial. In just a few years thereafter, the vibrant PPP grassroots organisation became enfeebled because of systematic incarceration, victimisation, and harassment. Under the new dispensation, the working class remained divided along ethnic lines.

The Burnham-Peter D'Aguiar union was a rocky one. Burnham was embarrassed that Peter D'Aguiar was a remnant of Guyana's colonial plantocracy, a privileged colour-class group. Burnham's discomfort grew even greater with the constant reminders from the PPP of his ideology while serving as Prime Minister against the United Force. However, he was willing to pay the price in return for solidifying his power, although he agreed that the philosophical and social objectives of the PNC were not aligned with those of the UF (see Griffith, 1991; Fraser, 2000). The relationship between the two political parties grew increasingly bitter, and in mid-1968, elections were called once again. This time, some members from the UF crossed the parliamentary floor, allowing the PNC to secure a majority and evict the UF from the coalition arrangement. With the UF out, the PNC attained total government control for the first time.

In 1968, through a highly controversial election, the PNC claimed victory with 68 per cent of the votes. The Burnhamite state, after 1968, demonstrated independence in crafting political decisions and embarked on a large-scale nationalisation policy. Though the British and U.S. played an instrumental role in the ascendency of the PNC into government, the new PNC regime increasingly distanced itself from all foreign economic controls. The regime was also known for its authoritarian style of ruling through coercive forces to maintain political control. The latter was fortified through the passage of the National Security Bill and a sharp increase in military expenditure. This led to the marginalisation of the opposition by the PNC regime and a shift in the pattern of protest and violence from a political to a more economic type of conflict, especially between ethnic groups. For instance, during the 1969 Rupununi Uprising, a group of Amerindians staged an armed rebellion against the authoritarian PNC regime, seeking to secede from the region in which they resided in an effort to escape political marginalisation.

Notwithstanding, the new government under Burnham immediately went to work to fortify and solidify its position in government. The election commission was staffed with PNC sympathisers, and changes were made to the election administration process. In the elections that soon followed, 1968, Burnham put the political rigging machine to work, where tens of thousands of fictitious votes were cast in favour of the PNC, allowing the party to win at the polls. His final move was to evade legal challenges by the Privy Council in England by declaring Guyana a republic. To ensure control and quell retaliation, Burnham often dispatched the army and police force to polling stations and throughout communities. Burnham remained in office because of repeated electoral fraud from 1968 until he died. His accession to power, however, sparked immediate protests from the opposition. The UF's supporters also initiated a series of boycotts, resulting in a decline in private investment and mass migrations of its supporters who possessed significant capital and skills. The Burnham regime simultaneously introduced restrictions on the importation of spare parts of agricultural machinery to stifle the agriculture sector and punish citizens who were believed to be supporters of the opposition.

1978 Onwards: Challenges to the Burnham Regime

To strengthen his support base, Burnham made changes to the pillars of the PNC power, defying the International Commission of Jurists' recommendations to remove racial imbalances in the public service. Specifically, the civil service, police, the defence force, and the Trade Unions' Council were purged of all potential opponents, most of whom were non-African. The pattern was more pronounced in the Guyana Police Force and the Guyana Defence Force.

Apart from the spate of nationalisation, the PNC regime was confronted with increased difficulties from both the splinter groups, such as the WPA and the PPP. The PPP repeatedly criticised the Burnham regime for its bureaucratic state capitalism. To compound these difficulties, the country faced out-of-control inflation, high unemployment, widespread shortages of essential items, and a breakdown in public utilities. These changes eventually became the symbols of Guyana. Everyone suffered from the state of affairs, including Afro-Guyanese, leading to the general disenchantment of the institutional power structures (the public service unions, the army, and the police). In the past, the loyalty of these groups was maintained by a supposed 'Indian majority menace. In 1977, the WPA and other civic-minded groups joined the battle against the PNC regime. Even the PNC supporters themselves, who held senior government positions, threatened to withdraw their support. In traditional strongholds of the PNC, such as Linden, party supporters mounted strikes and took to the streets in demonstrations. By 1978, Guyana's economic and political crisis had reached catastrophic and unbearable levels. In that year, Burnham altered the constitution by replacing the parliamentary model with the presidential executive. The following year, the PNC was on the brink of disaster when the WPA formally joined the race to contest the general elections. The PPP expressed sympathy with the WPA and even joined the party in boycotts, strikes, and demonstrations, united by a shared conviction that Burnham was intent on establishing a dictatorship in Guyana. The founding leader of the WPA, Dr Walter Rodney, declared that "The PNC must go. And they must go by all means necessary" (Kwayana, 1988).

Conclusion

The PNC planted the seeds of racial politics in the 1960s and has continued to practice this form of politics ever since. Prior to gaining power, the PNC popularised this type of politics via anti-government demonstrations and strikes aimed at stoking racial tensions to destabilise the PPP/C government. After gaining power with the support of external forces, the PNC continued its divisive tactics by discriminating against minorities, committing hate crimes, and even hatching the infamous X-13 plan.

During that period, the country suffered from widespread poverty, economic stagnation, and the mass exodus of our citizens, including supporters of the UF who possessed significant capital and skills. Unfortunately, this type of politics also fostered distrust and ethnic polarisation among our people.

For the country to benefit from its natural endowments and for its citizens to realise the dream of lived prosperity, it is essential to confront the divisive politics of the PNC by promoting unity, inclusiveness, and a collective vision that recognises and celebrates our diversity, rather than allowing it to be a source of division.

REFERENCES

Fraser, C. (2000). The 'New Frontier' of Empire in the Caribbean: The Transfer of Power in British Guiana, 1961–1964. *The International History Review*, *22*(3), 583-610.

Guyana News and Information (2000, June). Declassified Documents on British Guiana. Declassified Documents on British Guiana

Griffith, I.L. Ed. (1991). *Strategy and Security in the Caribbean*. Westport, CT: Praeger.

Ishmael, O. (2004). *Report of the commission of inquiry into the disturbances in British Guiana in February 1962*. http://www.guyananews.org/govt/wynnparry_report.html

Kwayana, E. (1988). "Walter Rodney: The Prophet of Self-Emancipation" *Libcom.org, 2015,libcom.org/library/walter-rodney-eusi-kwayana* .

Mars, P. (1990). Ethnic conflict and political control: The Guyana case. *Social and Economic Studies*, 65-94.

Rabe, S. G. (1999). John F. Kennedy and Latin America: The "Thorough, Accurate, and Reliable Record" (Almost) [Review of *Foreign Relations of the United States, 1961–1963, vol. 10, Cuba, 1961–1962; Foreign Relations of the United States, 1961–1963, vol. 12, American Republics, 1961–1963*, by U.S. Department of State]. *Diplomatic History*, *23*(3), 539–552. http://www.jstor.org/stable/24913679

Smith, R. T. (1995). 'Living in the gun mouth': race, class, and political violence in Guyana. *New West Indian Guide/Nieuwe West-Indische Gids*, 69(3-4), 223-252.

Smith, R. T. (1971). Race and Political Conflict in Guyana. *Race*, *12*(4), 415-427.

Stabroek News. (2009, October 7). Guyana's delayed political independence. https://www.stabroeknews.com/2009/10/08/features/guyana%E2%80%99s-delayed-political-independence/

Swan-Ambrose, G.E. (2011). Imperial Infringement or Self-destruction? The Demise of the Caribbean's Black Power Socialist Experiment.

Third World Traveler (1968). The Subversion of Undesirable Governments excerpted from the book *Intervention and Revolution The United States in the Third World* by Richard J. Barnet, World Publishing, 1968, paperback edition. https://thirdworldtraveler.com/Insurgency_Revolution/Subversion_IAR.html

FO to mission, United Nations, tel., 25 Oct. 1963, FO 371/167689.

2

Economic Meltdown: 1965-1992

But perhaps the even greater loss has been the deterioration in the physical quality of life of the population. Since 1980, average incomes have fallen by 50 per cent, unemployment has doubled to 40 per cent of the work force; health and educational services are minimal, and many of the best doctors, nurses and teachers have emigrated. THE MCINTYRE REPORT

The divisive politics practised by the PNC had detrimental effects on the economy. Once a booming and stable economy in the 1960s, "the GDP fell during the late 1970s and decreased by an estimated 6 per cent per year during the 1980s" (Country Studies, n.d) due to the PNC's divisive political strategies, failure to adhere to democratic governance and prudent fiscal policies. Unable to service its debts, the country was deemed bankrupt. The decay was visible everywhere. The economic and social infrastructure deteriorated, and poverty reached unprecedented levels. With citizens prevented from exercising their democratic rights to elect a government of their choice and the army, police, and splinter groups used by the PNC to spread fear, there was a mass exodus of Guyanese. This chapter evaluates the debilitating effects of the divisive politics practised by the PNC from independence to 1992.

Seizing control of the productive sector

After gaining power in 1966 with the support of external forces, the People's National Congress (PNC) remained in office until 1992 by manipulating the electoral process and practising racial politics (Gafar, 2005). During its 28 years in office, the PNC consolidated its power by politicising the public sector by seizing control of the country's productive assets and by implementing a slew of policies under the banner of Cooperative Socialism from 1970 to 1988. This allowed the PNC to nationalise the bauxite and sugar industries, foreign-owned banks, Sprostons Engineering Company, West Indies Oil Company, Berger Paints Limited, and Cable and Wireless Co. Ltd. (Danns, 1988), and forced private rice farmers to sell their produce to state-owned mills. The sugar and bauxite industries were also nationalised without resistance from foreign owners because of the generous commercial terms offered by the PNC government. However, the foreign-owned banks were forced to relinquish ownership. Most of these institutions yielded by selling their shares for $1 (KN, 10/02/2022). The PNC's nationalisation programme contributed significantly to the 408 per cent increase in the country's external debt between 1970 and 1977, since it involved the conversion of national assets into national debt (Danns, 1988).

The PNC also expanded the state's role into various industries, including retail, distribution, wholesaling, manufacturing, transportation, communications, forestry, and fishing (Thomas, 1982a). By 1976, the government boasted that it owned and controlled 80 per cent of the economy, taking control over 80 per cent of the import and export sectors and 85 per cent of the total investment (Gafar, 1996). These outcomes directly resulted from the PNC's desire to establish 'party paramountcy' over the state, economy, and entire population. The concept of party paramountcy was formally announced to the nation in the 1974 Declaration of Sophia (SN, 10/03/2007) and subsequently institutionalised through several key measures. Most notably, it was enshrined in the newly merged government department of the Ministry of National Development and the Office of the General Secretary of the PNC (Thomas, 1982a).

In 1978, the PNC postponed the constitutionally due elections and held a Referendum to alter the Constitution, vesting powers in the President that exceeded those of our colonial masters. The new Constitution insulated the President from any criminal or civil proceedings, granted the President veto power over the National Assembly as well as the power to appoint the Chairpersons and majority of members or all the members of the Elections Commission, Public Service Commission, Police Service Commission, Judicial Commission and Teacher's Commission (Thomas, 1982b). The President, under the new Constitution, had the power to appoint the Chief of Staff and commanders, the Commissioners of Police and deputies, the Chancellor of the Judiciary, the Chief Justice, and the Director of Public Prosecution.

With these powers, the PNC undermined the independence of the Police Service Commission, Judicial Service Commission, and Civil Service

Commission and extended its reach over the media and judiciary (Trotz and Peake, 2001). The PNC's onslaught on the independence of the courts and law manifested in various forms. According to Thomas (1982b, 112), some of the notorious examples of the attack on the courts and law included:

> ... (1) flying of the PNC flag over the Court of Appeal in order to assert its paramountcy over all state institutions; (2) flight of judges from the judiciary; (3) the introduction of legislation with retroactive effect (the so-called administration of Justice Act), designed to reverse a court decision given against the state and condemned by the legal association; (4) the use of the National Security Act with its wide powers of search and arrest to 'legally' harass its opponents; (5)the use of torture and inhumane treatment against arrested persons; (6) the arbitrary refusals to permit pickets, public demonstrations and public meeting.

During the 28 years in office, the PNC used the state to discriminate, intimidate, and inflict harm on citizens and the opposition parties. The murders of Father Bernard Darke, Vincent Teekah, Ohene Koama, Bholanauth Permanand, Jagan Ramessar, Edward Dublin, Michael Forde, and Walter Rodney are some of the atrocious examples of state violence during the 28 years. The House of Israel was also utilised by the PNC to terrorise citizens.

Because of the pervasiveness of the state and the powers vested in the self-proclaimed Supreme Leader of the party, Forbes Burnham, the PNC ruled with an iron fist and committed constitutional and human rights abuses with impunity. The PNC openly rigged elections in 1973, 1978, and 1980, denying citizens the right to elect a government of their choice. From 1966 until it was voted out of office in 1992, Guyanese lived in fear and were compelled to either display unquestioned loyalty to the party's leader or leave. There was a mass exodus of Guyanese, and those who were unable to escape from Guyana had to toe the party line to avoid state violence or gain employment locally. In Guyana, recruitment was not based on qualification and experience but on loyalty to the maximum leader and his party.

Collapse of productive sectors

The local economy collapsed during the PNC's dictatorship. From 1970 to 1990, the country registered low or negative economic growth, averaging a paltry -0.7 per cent per annum (see Figure 2.1). For eleven of the twenty-one years spanning 1970-1990, the country recorded negative growth, ranging from -0.9 per cent in 1986 to -13.2 per cent in 1982. The growth rates recorded during the PNC dictatorship (for example, 1974-1976) were driven by favourable external factors, such as the boom in commodity prices on international markets, rather than the government's economic policy. Gafar (1996) attributed the country's economic crisis during the 1970s and 80s to four types of disequilibria that emerged from the PNC's experiment with cooperative socialism, namely (1) a monetary disequilibrium (price inflation, foreign reserves depletion, accumulation of external debt and collapse of the Guyana dollar due to money creation by the central bank); (2) fiscal disequilibrium (fiscal and trade deficits and accumulation of foreign debt that resulted from excessive government spending due to political and economic mismanagement), (3) foreign trade disequilibrium (capital flight and overvalued exchange rate caused by policies to restrict imports and exports), and (4) labour market disequilibrium (acute shortage of skilled labour due to the mass exodus of Guyanese and deterioration

Figure 2.1: Real GDP and Economic Growth (%), 1970-1990

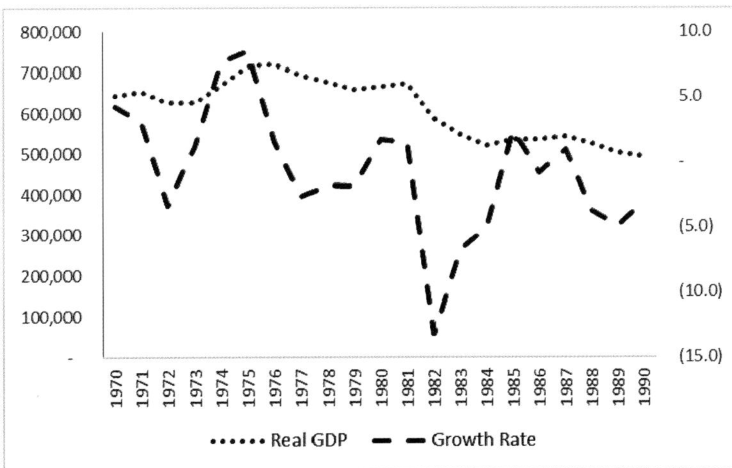

Source: World Bank and author's computation

in the educational standards and collapse in real wages). Thomas (1982a) also linked the country's economic collapse to similar factors, including government mismanagement, the migration of skilled Guyanese, and social, political, and institutional fragilities.

Due to the rapid deterioration of the domestic economy, the per capita GDP declined steadily between 1970 and 1980, despite negative population growth rates resulting from mass migration (see Figure 2.2). Indeed, the economic decline was so sharp that it outpaced the negative population growth rates, thereby causing the per capita GDP to shrink. In 1990, the per capita GDP was 26 per cent lower than in 1970, one of the lowest in the Western Hemisphere (World Bank, 1992).

Private consumption as a share of Domestic Expenditure at market prices also displayed a similar trend, declining from 63.7 per cent in 1965 to 52.1 per cent by 1990. This outcome reflected the scarcity of essential goods in the economy caused by lower domestic production and import restrictions. However, Public Investment as a share of Domestic Expenditure at market prices increased from 4.4 per cent in 1965 to 19.1 per cent by 1990. Because economic growth was negative or low for most years from 1970 to 1990, it means that the public

Figure 2.2: Population growth rates (%) and per capita GDP (G$), 1970-1990

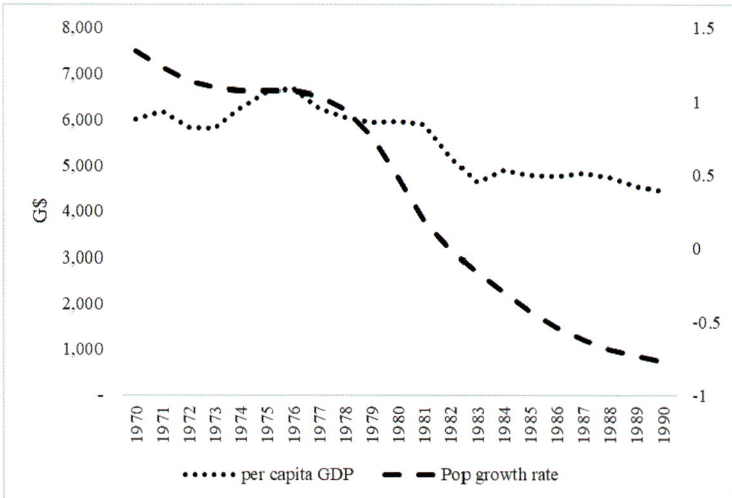

Source: World Bank and author's computation

investments by the PNC did not yield any growth dividends but instead harmed productivity and, by extension, the domestic economy. Additionally, since the expansion in public investment was accompanied by a concomitant decline in public consumption, it also means that government spending generated a negative wealth effect (Gali et al., 2007).

To mask the economic and financial hardship that ensnared the local economy, the Burnham regime saw it prudent to print more money and increase borrowing. However, as economic principles would dictate, this created a recipe for even greater disaster. For instance, between 1975 and 1977, the money supply increased by 38 per cent. Public debt, on the other hand, moved from $267 million in 1970 to $638 million in 1973 and then to $2.5 billion in the early 1980s. At the same time, foreign exchange reserves fell from $250 million in 1975 to negative $350 million by the end of 1980. To improve the country's balance of payment position and foreign exchange reserves, the Burnham guiding philosophy was to simply reduce "workers' living standards in order to reduce consumption and hence the demand for imports" (Thomas 1982b, 109) – a move that was later regarded as callous, economically regressive, and socially burdensome.

The deterioration in the local economy reflected the sharp contraction in the outputs of the key sectors, especially the sugar and bauxite industries. In 1990, sugar production was 132,007 tonnes, approximately 50 per cent lower than the 309,000 tonnes and 311,000 tonnes produced in 1965 and 1970, respectively. The nationalisation of the industry, along with the appointment of managers based on party loyalty and race rather than merit, contributed to its decline (Gafar, 1996). The sugar levy imposed by the PNC government in 1974 to support the expanding bureaucratic state machinery also crippled the industry, as it denied GUYSUCO funds that could have been utilised to upgrade and modernise its operations. During the corresponding period, bauxite production also plummeted from 2,873,000 tonnes in 1965 to 1,423,060 tonnes by 1990 (see Table 2.1). The steep decline in bauxite production was due to the nationalisation of the industry in 1971, mismanagement of the industry, and a lack of external financing and investment in the sector (Gafar, 1996).

The collapse in these industries contributed to the widening of the fiscal deficit and the accumulation of foreign debt, which, as a percentage of exports, increased from 187 per cent in 1980 to 688 per cent in 1989 (World Bank,

Table 2.1: Production and export of sugar, rice, and bauxite, 1965-1990

	Export			Production		
	Sugar ('000)	Rice ('000)	Bauxite ('000)	Sugar (Tonnes)	Rice (Tonnes)	Bauxite (Tonnes)
1965	267	95	2,033	309,000	165,000	2,873,000
1966	279	110	2,320	289,000	160,000	3,295,000
1967	293	102	2,552	344,000	130,000	3,254,000
1968	294	96	2,609	317,000	136,000	2,439,000
1969	326	74	2,890	364,000	113,000	2,748,000
1970	279	61	3,328	311,000	142,000	2,984,000
1971	337	74	3,043	369,000	120,000	3,191,000
1972	300	70	2,574	315,000	94,000	2,651,000
1973	225	48	2,565	264,915	109,980	903,000
1974	303	51	2,439	340,830	142,974	1,046,663
1975	285	82	2,461	299,880	159,988	1,091,418
1976	297	71	1,806	332,010	109,980	995,015
1977	208	66	1,839	241,920	209,996	1,424,629
1978	281	105	1,825	324,765	181,984	807,725
1979	268	86	1,724	298,305	142,034	728,234
1980	252	81	1,843	269,640	166,004	834,692
1981	267	78	1,659	300,790	165,596	1,502,413
1982	256	35	1,141	292,329	181,598	1,159,010
1983	222	40	1,175	255,900	147,591	1,048,293
1984	214	73	1,659	245,731	179,786	1,261,025
1985	215	29	1,612	246,888	156,124	1,507,557
1986	216	38	1,401	249,367	183,216	1,419,870
1987	187	69	1,372	224,542	146,758	1,332,796
1988	137	56	1,297	110,943	129,962	1,346,303
1989	170	44	1,317	130,490	93,444	1,318,604
1990	132	51	1,389	132,007	150,793	1,423,060

Source: Bank of Guyana and Bureau of Statistics

1992). In 1986, Guyana's budget deficit represented almost 37 per cent of its GDP. In the region, the only countries to have approached this level were Nicaragua, with 23.6 per cent, and Suriname, with 23.4 per cent. This, of course, led to a significant increase in total debt in 1990, reaching approximately 600 per cent of GDP, while scheduled debt service represented 99 per cent of the country's exports of goods and non-factor services.

While the rice and bauxite industries were the primary casualties of the mismanagement of the economy during the PNC dictatorship, domestic food production, as well as the services sector, also sank to unprecedented levels. Rice production declined steadily between 1965 and 1972, then rebounded for five years, culminating in 1977, when it reached a peak of 209,996 tonnes. Thereafter, it trended downward, reaching its lowest level of 93,444 tonnes by 1989. The contraction in rice production from 1977 was attributed to low paddy prices, poor drainage and irrigation, land tenure issues, inadequate agro-extension services, and a shortage of machinery to harvest the crop. Consequently, rice exports contracted sharply from 95,000 tonnes in 1965 to 51,000 tonnes by 1990 (Gafar 1998). Notwithstanding, a non-reimbursable levy of 15 per cent was introduced on rice exports as a means to boost revenue and offset the perpetual growth of the nation's debt. Also, certain essential goods saw a sharp increase in prices. For instance, the retail price of rice rose by 224 per cent in the first two months of 1989, and cooking gas by 224 per cent. The destruction of the food production system and services sectors was aptly described by Thomas (1982b, 108) thus:

> In addition to the collapse of the main producing sectors other sectors of the national economy have also been failing e.g., domestic foodstuffs, services and so on. In particular, it should be mentioned here, the system of public utilities have virtually collapsed. Electricity, water-supply, public transport, telephone services, the Post Office, all have deteriorated to levels unheard of before ...

Meanwhile, Thomas (1982b, 49) stated that:

> ... in 1976, the country was producing only eight ounces of poultry per person per week, one egg per person per eight days, three or

> four ounces of pork per person per week three to four ounces of beef per person per week and 0.8 pints of milk per person per week ...

The precipitous decline in the economy was attributed to the failure of government policies by the PNC during the 1970s and 1980s (Worrel, 2024). Indeed, according to Thomas (1993, 135), the economy "collapsed under the weight of economic mismanagement and severe political difficulties."

Economic Mismanagement

Given the bloated bureaucracy created by the PNC to exert absolute control over the economy and state, the government's recurrent expenditure expanded exponentially in absolute and relative terms. The government's recurrent expenditure grew unceasingly from $84.2 million in 1966, when it took office, to $1,252.5 million by 1986 (see Table 2.2). The total recurrent expenditure of the government represented 68.8 per cent of GDP at factor cost in 1986, compared with 24.6 per cent in 1966. The main drivers of the increase in the central government's recurrent expenditure were personal emoluments, debt charges, and defence spending (see Table 2.2).

Personal emoluments for the bureaucracy increased eleven-fold from $34.4 million in 1966 to $399.4 million in 1986 (see Table 2.2). In 1986, debt charges of $451.9 million were more than thirty-four times higher than in 1966 due to the country's massive debt overhang (World Bank, 1992). Also, spending on defence was $157.6 million in 1986, 169 times higher than $0.9 million in 1966 (see Table 2.2). The increase in defence spending was due to the militarisation of the country. At the height of the dictatorship, for every 35 persons in Guyana, one person belonged to a state security force (Thomas 1982b).

To finance the rapid growth in recurrent expenditure, the PNC imposed higher taxes on the nation. Tax revenue, which was $72.5 million (or 21.2 per cent of GDP at factor cost) in 1966, increased continuously to $2,868.4 million (or 157.5 per cent of GDP at factor cost) by 1989. Notwithstanding the imposition of higher taxes, the central government consistently reported an annual deficit in the current account for the period 1970-1990. The current account deficit also expanded from $7.9 million in 1971 (or 1.6 per cent of GDP at factor cost) to $2,266.1 million (or 16.4 per cent of GDP at factor cost) in 1990.

Table 2.2: Recurrent Expenditure, 1965-1986 ($'000)

					Administration Social Services											
Year	Personal Emolu-ments 3)	Debt Charges	Other Charges	Total	Law & Order	General	Economic Devel-opment	Medical	Education	Other	Post & Telecoms	Debt Charges	Public Works	Defence	Pensions	Other
1965	33,527	12,097	36,374	81,998	7,032	12,220	6,746	7,968	13,798	3,848	3,161	12,097	8,314	474	3,560	2,780
1966	34,397	12,989	36,768	84,154	9,093	13,904	4,513	8,245	13,900	3,630	3,518	12,989	7,351	983	3,472	2,556
1967	38,025	14,141	35,715	87,881	8,659	12,746	4,397	8,959	15,151	3,748	2,494	14,141	8,139	3,122	3,962	2,363
1968	39,762	17,874	40,572	98,208	9,018	14,728	4,719	9,367	16,216	4,253	2,560	17,874	9,383	3,432	4,242	2,416
1969	44,739	16,578	45,565	106,882	10,149	19,574	4,578	9,948	16,842	4,182	2,763	16,578	11,220	4,541	4,623	1,884
1970	49,710	17,205	56,744	123,659	10,939	25,037	4,265	10,976	19,091	4,351	3,041	17,205	13,774	6,472	5,354	3,154
1971	57,451	18,349	58,868	134,668	11,234	27,793	5,268	10,695	19,945	6,494	3,142	18,349	16,217	6,065	6,166	3,300
1972	65,762	25,290	61,568	152,620	11,325	30,455	5,873	12,169	24,555	6,269	2,884	25,290	18,193	6,992	6,304	2,311
1973	87,401	45,641	85,048	218,090	17,155	46,846	5,751	17,318	33,454	6,970	4,062	45,641	19,641	9,314	7,080	4,858
1974	88,636	57,593	107,787	254,016	17,646	48,535	7,232	19,062	39,039	9,195	4,259	57,593	21,940	15,860	9,365	4,290
1975	106,445	65,849	148,406	320,700	19,931	78,064	12,611	22,659	44,644	8,992	4,642	65,849	29,275	24,541	9,013	5,479
1976	128,345	117,250	214,277	459,872	23,073	67,655	29,516	24,901	58,009	26,562	4,164	117,250	38,047	58,077	10,889	1,729
1977	144,592	123,353	148,490	416,435	25,110	56,588	12,149	29,861	70,426	17,552	-	123,353	25,505	38,556	11,135	6,200
1978	167,031	167,973	139,512	474,516	27,357	58,378	10,670	30,767	74,089	9,653	-	167,973	34,255	42,618	12,229	6,527
1979	173,998	227,315	178,756	580,069	30,550	66,721	16,120	35,090	84,257	11,129	-	227,315	41,124	45,150	12,985	9,637
1980	186,841	299,544	222,190	708,575	35,899	81,422	26,020	42,101	94,786	11,281	-	299,544	40,455	55,872	10,794	11,091
1981	246,700	337,738	243,143	827,581	40,934	134,282	37,990	49,039	106,836	14,622	-	337,738	34,961	63,000	-	8,179
1982	233,055	401,877	196,408	831,340	44,946	99,939	27,081	47,680	88,361	16,752	-	401,877	18,346	70,000	14,530	1,828
1983	238,838	521,960	200,532	961,330	49,443	120,755	25,226	45,274	87,056	8,640	-	521,960	13,866	63,365	23,535	2,210
1984	301,226	684,839	288,403	1,274,468	53,119	212,952	27,588	49,483	99,453	1,170	-	684,839	19,711	108,098	15,120	2,935
1985	357,857	429,783	388,624	1,176,264	71,294	236,416	43,404	74,125	128,169	5,909	-	429,783	22,778	143,657	16,120	4,609
1986	399,399	451,950	401,103	1,252,452	86,090	312,111	37,367	60,225	80,373	19,035	-	451,950	23,270	157,611	19,603	4,817

Source: Ministry of Finance

While the PNC government increased capital expenditures from $36.4 million in 1966 to $1,221.7 million in 1989 (see Table 2.3), it is worth noting that recurrent expenditures consistently exceeded capital expenditures during this period. The amount expended on personal emoluments by the PNC government was higher than the total capital expenditure in the social sector and investment in public works, agriculture, and forestry. The overall deficit also expanded from $40.1 million in 1970 to $3,583.6 million by 1990 due to the sharp increase in the capital account deficit. Overall, the total deficit was partly funded by external and domestic borrowing, resulting in an increase in the country's external debt by more than eighteen-fold, from US$79.5 million in 1970 to US$1,477.4 million by 1986. By the end of 1986, Guyana's foreign debt per capita was estimated at US$1,739 (Danns, 1988), and by 1990, it had increased to more than 200 per cent of the Gross Domestic Product (GDP) (Egoumé-Bossogo et al., 2003). The total external public debt became so onerous that the government suspended payments on external debt in the early 1980s (World Bank, 1992), leading to an increase in arrears on external debt from US$34 million in 1981 to US$771.2 million by 1986. Consequently, the IMF declared that Guyana was no longer eligible for access to resources from the Fund in 1985, while the World Bank and the Caribbean Development Bank suspended loan financing for Guyana in 1986.

The total domestic public also debt increased significantly from $107.2 million in 1970 to $6,092.8 million in 1986, making the government the largest borrower of the local banking system. To put this into context, in 1970, approximately 50.4 per cent of the total deficit was financed internally. However, by 1986, this amount had increased to 85.6 per cent, mainly due to limited opportunities for external borrowing (Danns, 1988). As expected, domestic borrowing by the government, which merely accounted for 3.7 per cent of the GDP in 1970, increased sharply to 79.5 per cent by 1986. By the end of 1986, the total public debt was US$2.86 billion, with the country's total debt per capita estimated at approximately US$3,360, making it one of the most heavily indebted poor countries (HIPCs) in the Western Hemisphere.

Unable to borrow its way out of the economic crisis, the PNC resorted to printing money. The Broad Money (M2) increased from $165 million in 1970 to $9,414.3 million by 1990. The monetisation led to high inflation rates, balance-of-payments deficits, depletion of foreign reserves, and the collapse of the

Table 2.3: Capital Expenditure, 1965-1990 ($'000)

		ECONOMIC SECTOR					SOCIAL SECTOR			
Year	Total	Agriculture	Communic-ations	Forestry	Public Works	Credits	Education	Health	Housing	Other
1965	24,060	6,936	6,682	102	3,365	4,395	765	681	668	466
1966	36,386	5,913	10,402	859	6,870	8,591	997	626	1,298	830
1967	41,317	3,601	13,275	2,427	7,667	9,747	2,370	389	867	974
1968	39,652	4,250	17,142	2,493	9,705	1,803	2,438	257	293	1,271
1969	44,943	6,885	14,758	490	10,814	2,446	4,697	247	364	4,242
1970	52,129	15,105	15,298	475	7,637	4,162	4,617	506	1,114	3,215
1971	60,808	12,749	12,488	18	14,150	4,078	5,483	162	167	11,513
1972	56,387	12,725	5,092	221	12,466	10,265	4,361	379	561	10,317
1973	83,245	26,120	14,572	281	10,021	10,528	9,312	990	411	11,010
1974	104,392	20,876	21,799	195	14,827	8,435	13,148	253	258	24,601
1975	351,474	42,602	48,027	1,923	38,112	13,899	19,384	7,090	10,154	170,283
1976	288,668	45,714	66,724	454	103,497	19,097	7,347	3,272	11,517	31,046
1977	150,889	24,791	38,013	221	58,246	6,306	8,206	2,122	2,676	10,308
1978	114,815	35,933	28,567	604	33,336	3,234	4,329	1,726	1,950	5,136
1979	207,002	49,694	27,309	1,778	43,628	44,271	7,865	1,844	3,226	27,387
1980	338,000	104,016	28,536	-	65,435	74,002	16,701	7,215	3,129	38,966
1981	424,348	128,360	44,249	250	52,332	103,590	11,748	10,508	2,036	71,275
1982	790,474	364,305	22,274	-	239,301	92,228	12,232	12,325	-	47,809
1983	275,548	70,552	2,523	-	19,157	84,740	15,309	13,585	-	69,682
1984	309,614	74,528	5,439	-	24,775	107,455	13,269	13,157	-	70,991
1985	409,804	123,476	10,454	49	25,264	124,367	22,966	8,657	-	94,571
1986	1,221,566	120,234	7,619	-	37,057	967,614	17,200	2,713	-	69,129
1987	582,584	257,593	16,895	13	41,571	140,928	36,887	3,821	-	84,876
1988	949,308	136,328	29,795	39	56,299	523,324	25,690	6,070	988	170,775
1989	1,307,168	306,584	163,917	-	71,128	501,155	23,518	8,728	1,998	230,140

Source: Ministry of Finance

Guyana dollar (Gafar, 1996). During the 1970-1990 period, the country experienced double-digit inflation rates almost every year, peaking at 66.3 per cent in 1990. The gross international foreign reserves also declined from $197.3 million in 1975 to a negative $4,895.6 million by 1988 (Danns, 1992), prompting the government to impose restrictions on trade and exchange outflows, creating severe shortages of consumer goods and providing a conducive environment for the deepening and widening of the underground economy. Meanwhile, the principal exchange rate depreciated from 2 Guyana dollars ($) to US$1 in 1970 to $39.53 Guyana dollars to US$1 in 1990. According to the government's approach to financing the deficit sacrificed the 'principles of prudent fiscal policy' (Gafar, 1996). The crisis created by the PNC was fittingly described by Gafar (2005a, 150) as follows:

> ... Since independence in 1966, Guyana's economy has gone through three main phases. The first phase lasted until 1988 as the country pursued a state interventionist socialist economic policy, which proved to be a disaster. State control of the economy was characterized with excessive controls, a bloated and corrupt bureaucracy, negative economic growth, falling standard of living, widespread poverty, declining health and social indicators, mounting foreign debt, reductions in social expenditures, massive emigration of skilled workers, unsustainable trade and fiscal deficits, inflation, human rights abuses, rigged elections, and autocratic and racist rule ...

Having destroyed the economy, and in an effort to restore creditworthiness to the country, the government embarked on an Economic Recovery Programme (ERP) through the International Monetary Fund (IMF), which required the elimination of price and quantitative control, reduction in public expenditure, adoption of a flexible exchange rate, privatisation of state-owned enterprises, expansion of spending in the social sector and downsizing of government (Gafar, 2005a). Under the ERP, the government reduced the number of ministries (World Bank, 1992) and fired 17 per cent of the public sector employees in 1981/1982. The retrenched workers accounted for five per cent of the total labour force (van Dijk, 1992). Filled with resentment, the working poor took to the streets to protest tax increases, retrenchments, the removal of subsidies, and the discriminatory distribution of scarce commodities. In response, the PNC regime crushed the rebellion by (i) taking control of the workers' union through the rigging of union elections, the exclusion of the Guyanese Workers Agricultural Union (GAWU) from the Trade Union Council (TUC), and (ii) political suppression and the use of the state repressive apparatus (Ishmael, 2012).

State domination of the financial sector

Prior to 1968, the banking sector in Guyana was heavily dominated by five foreign banks. However, with the implementation of the 'cooperative socialism' policy, the government of the People's National Congress (PNC) took control over three foreign-owned banks (KN, 10/02/2022). The government also established three state-owned banks, namely the Guyana National Co-operative Bank (GNCB), the Guyana Agricultural and Industrial Development Bank (GAIBANK), and the Guyana Co-operative Mortgage Finance Bank (GCMFB).

Except for two commercial banks, the government either wholly or partially owned all major financial institutions (Ganga, 2000). The state-owned banks held 62 per cent of the banking sector's assets, while the partially state-owned banks held 38 per cent of the total banking sector assets. However, these banks were heavily politicised and often extended credit based on political affiliation, leading to most loans given by GNCB and GAIBANK becoming non-performing and unproductive. The non-performing loans of these government-owned banks were estimated to be 29 per cent of total assets at the time of their merger. In fact, when GNCB was privatised, non-performing loans accounted for 91 per cent of the bank's loan portfolio (ECLAC, 2001).

During the PNC dictatorship, credit to the private sector as a percentage of GDP trended downward from 15.1 per cent in 1970 to 12.4 per cent in 1980. In contrast, credit to the public sector increased exponentially during the same period, from 3.7 per cent of GDP (or $17.3 million) in 1970 to 27.3 per cent of GDP (or $364.9 million) in 1980. At the end of 1989, credit to the public sector reached $1,446 million (or 79.5 per cent of GDP). The decline in private sector credit, accompanied by a concomitant increase in lending to the public sector, clearly demonstrated the government's crowding out of the private sector from domestic credit markets to finance the fiscal deficit. This outcome is also due to the cooperative socialism policies that discourage private sector activities and investments.

On the monetary side, the money stock expanded sharply from $165 million in 1970 (or 31 per cent of GDP) to $850.4 million in 1980 (or 56.4 per cent of GDP), then increased further to $2,233.8 million by 1986 (or 100 per cent of GDP). The rapid growth in the money stock, in both absolute and relative terms, confirmed that the government printed money to finance the fiscal deficit. According to Ganga (2000, 203):

> The increase in money stock and deposits as a percentage of GDP was due largely to domestic credit creation to finance large fiscal deficits and an underestimation of GDP due to a growing parallel economy during the 1970s and 1980s.

During the 1970s and 1980s, monetary policy was primarily executed through direct controls, interest rate ceilings, and reserve requirements (Das and Ganga, 1997). Throughout this period, the nominal weighted average lending rate trended upward from 7.5 per cent in 1970 to 31.0 per cent by 1990, peaking at 37.5 per cent in 1989. Despite this nominal escalation, the real interest rate was also generally negative during the 70s and 80s, which is not only symptomatic of a repressed financial system but also contributed to a shortage of funds and rent-seeking activities (Gafar, 1996). To further exacerbate the situation, the government also imposed foreign exchange controls and quantitative restrictions on imports, which encouraged smuggling, thereby creating a large underground economy (Ganga, 2000). Together, the policies pursued by the government hindered the development of financial markets and institutions and, by extension, the entire economy.

Deterioration in disposable and real income

As noted elsewhere, the country recorded double-digit inflation rates during most of the 1970s and 1980s. Inflation was so high that the authorities discontinued collecting price figures after June 1989 (van Dijk, 1992). The average inflation rate, which was approximately 27.83 per cent during the period 1980-1989, rose to 103.1 per cent in 1991. Notably, the inflation rate consistently outpaced increases in wages and salaries, thereby reducing the real income of the working class (see Figure 2.3). Between 1980 and 1983, the monthly minimum wage was frozen at $270.9, while inflation soared to high double digits. Even in years when the government granted wage increases, these were outstripped by the spiralling rate (see Figure 2.3).

To curb the spiralling inflation rate, the PNC government introduced price controls. However, instead of reducing inflation, the price controls contributed to long queues, as well as rationing, shortages, the proliferation of black markets, and opportunities for rent-seeking activities in essential food items. The price controls on locally produced foodstuffs had the unintended consequence of discouraging farmers from expanding output, contributing to unemployment and poverty in rural communities. Therefore, it is reasonable to conclude that such controls facilitated a regressive redistribution of income, from economically marginalised rural producers to urban consumers.

The government also implemented measures that reduced the disposable income of citizens. These included the imposition of higher taxes, railway fees, and freight costs as well as the withdrawal of subsidies on cooking oil (Ishmael, 2012). These punitive measures were imposed at a time when unemployment had reached unprecedented levels due to the retrenchment of workers in key sectors and the government's inability to provide employment opportunities that matched the growth in the labour force (Ishmael, 2012).

Figure 2.3: Annual Inflation Rate (%) and Increase in Monthly Minimum Wage (%)

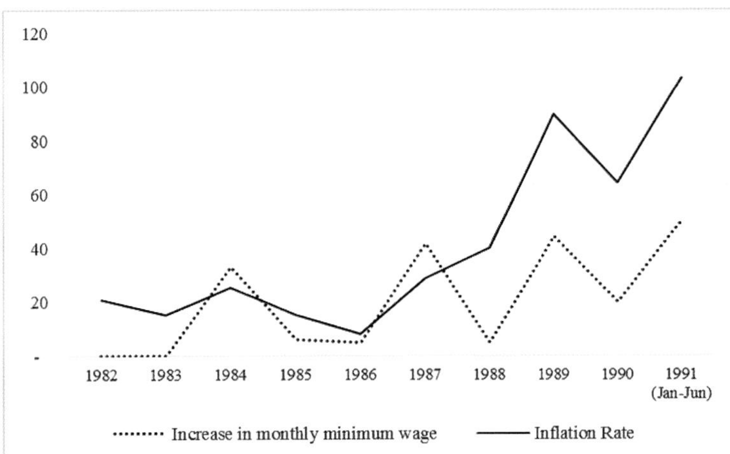

Source: IMF and Ministry of Finance

Together with the deterioration in the social sectors, the decline in disposable income contributed to the erosion of the quality of life of citizens. According to Thomas (1982b, 109-110) –

> ... the government's assault on the workers' standard of living began in 1976 and the main mechanism used were: (1) the removal of all government subsidies, most of which were long standing and introduced in order to alleviate obvious and acute hardships among the poorest sections of the community; (2) increased taxation, mainly indirect taxes which fall heaviest on the poor, in order to raise state revenue and substitute for the failure of the state enterprises to generate surpluses under their mismanagement, open corruption and alienation of the work force in these enterprises; (3) increased prices for all items sold which passed through state agencies; (4) retrenchment of workers employed in the state sector in order to reduce government spending. In 1975 state expenditure was cut by 30 percent; (5) a freeze on all wage increases in order to reduce the workers' wage and so reduce consumption and imports; (6) severe foreign exchange rationing; (7) cuts in social spending in order to reinforce the cuts in state expenditure.

The living conditions of citizens worsened with the reduction in the minimum wage from US$2.89 in 1980 to US$1.00 by 1989 (Gafar, 1996). Despite an increase in the minimum wage in 1991, the daily minimum wage was less than half a US dollar, making it the lowest in Latin America and the Caribbean (Ishmael, 2012). Furthermore, the minimum wage was woefully inadequate to purchase basic food items and well below what was required to cope with the high cost of living. According to Ishmael (2012, 281)

> The level of desperation of the workers' situation can be gauged by the purchasing power at the daily minimum wage of $64.56 in 1991. This amount could buy only about one and a half pounds beef, or six eggs, or two and a half pounds sugar. It definitely was insufficient to purchase a pound of chicken.

In his May Day 1991 speech, Joseph Pollydore vividly captured the harsh reality of workers (Ishmael, 2012, 281), which he blamed on the PNC dictatorship:

> ... workers were in a state of near destitution and incapable of buying "even basic food;" ... Government "has left children breadless and homes rice-less because of the inability of bread-winners to buy even minimum quantities for their families."

The conditions of the working class became so unbearable that citizens began to mock the government openly, labelling the Economic Recovery Programme (ERP), implemented in 1989, as the 'Empty Rice Pot' for creating more hardship (SN 04/01/2003).

Decay of social sectors

Between 1966 and 1986, the government spent more on debt service payments, personal emoluments, and defence than on the health sector. The average recurrent expenditure in the health sector during this period was merely 7.1 per cent of total recurrent expenditure. In contrast, the average spending on debt service payments, personal emoluments, and defence, law, and order represented 34 per cent, 29 per cent, and 13.9 per cent of total current expenditure, respectively, during the corresponding period. Understandably, the health sector was unable to provide reliable healthcare due to severe shortages of personnel, medical supplies, and drugs (Trotz and Peake, 2001), and the equipment in the sector was often obsolete or frequently malfunctioned (Gafar, 2005b). The number of physicians per 1,000 people declined from 0.24 in 1970 to 0.17 by 1984.

In contrast, as a share of capital expenditure, spending in the health sector accounted for an average of 5.7 per cent from 1966 to 1986, reflecting a preference for current consumption over capital spending that provides immediate and long-term benefits. The consequence of giving priority to consumption over investment, as indicated, was the long-term deterioration of the social sector under successive PNC administrations. Accordingly, health, education, housing, and other social sectors visibly collapsed before the eyes of the Guyanese people, prompting a wave of emigration as thousands sought improved prospects and living conditions for themselves and their families.

In terms of daily life, this meant health facilities lacked basic equipment. Many patients who could afford it bypassed the regional hospitals to go to the main hospitals in Georgetown or the seven private hospitals they anticipated to be better equipped. Therefore, the services provided by the regional hospitals were underutilised, and their occupancy rates were low. The country also recorded one of the highest infant mortality rates and child death rates in the English-speaking Caribbean due to poor investment in the health sector (Lakhan et al, 1990).

Spending by the PNC government in the education sector was also minimal. The education sector accounted for an average of 13.7 per cent of total recurrent expenditure and 5.5 per cent of total capital expenditure between 1966 and 1989. The performance of entry-level secondary school students and the Caribbean Examination Council (CXC) in core subjects was not only poor but also worsened during the 1980s and 1990s. School attendance rates were also low due to the rolling socio-economic crisis (Thomas, 1993).

The restricted spending on social sectors, coupled with economic decline, led to a collapse in human development and a dramatic surge in migration of Guyanese, especially those with skills and capital. Between 1970 and 1981, the cost of living rose by more than 240 per cent. Not surprisingly, the economic contraction and high cost of living led to a sharp increase in the poverty rate. During the 1970s and 1980s, the poor had limited or no access to safe drinking water, healthcare, and basic sanitation, and were forced to subsist on calorie-deficient diets (Gafar, 1996).

Using head-count estimates, Boyd (1989) argues that 65 per cent of the population in 1988 earned an income below the poverty line compared with 38 per cent in 1971. According to Boyd (1989), when the inflation rate for 1989 is taken into account, approximately 75 per cent of the population in that year was below the poverty line. Boyd (1989) also reported that the incidence of infant malnutrition was approximately 40 per cent for the years 1982-1988. Based on data from Georgetown Hospital, Clive Thomas (1993) showed that the number of patients with malnutrition increased fourfold between 1989 and 1990. The grim living conditions of citizens were vividly described by van Dijk (1992, 100), who noted the following:

Table 2.5: Current and Capital Expenditure, 1966-1986 (in percentage)

	Current Expenditure						Capital Expenditure	
Year	Personal Emolu-ments 3)	Debt Charges	Law & Order	Medical	Educ-ation	Defence	Medical	Educ-ation
1966	40.9	15.4	10.8	9.8	16.5	1.2	2.7	1.7
1967	43.3	16.1	9.9	10.2	17.2	3.6	5.7	0.9
1968	40.5	18.2	9.2	9.5	16.5	3.5	6.1	0.6
1969	41.9	15.5	9.5	9.3	15.8	4.2	10.5	0.5
1970	40.2	13.9	8.8	8.9	15.4	5.2	8.9	1.0
1971	42.7	13.6	8.3	7.9	14.8	4.5	9.0	0.3
1972	43.1	16.6	7.4	8.0	16.1	4.6	7.7	0.7
1973	40.1	20.9	7.9	7.9	15.3	4.3	11.2	1.2
1974	34.9	22.7	6.9	7.5	15.4	6.2	12.6	0.2
1975	33.2	20.5	6.2	7.1	13.9	7.7	5.5	2.0
1976	27.9	25.5	5.0	5.4	12.6	12.6	2.5	1.1
1977	34.7	29.6	6.0	7.2	16.9	9.3	5.4	1.4
1978	35.2	35.4	5.8	6.5	15.6	9.0	3.8	1.5
1979	30.0	39.2	5.3	6.0	14.5	7.8	3.8	0.9
1980	26.4	42.3	5.1	5.9	13.4	7.9	4.9	2.1
1981	29.8	40.8	4.9	5.9	12.9	7.6	2.8	2.5
1982	28.0	48.3	5.4	5.7	10.6	8.4	1.5	1.6
1983	24.8	54.3	5.1	4.7	9.1	6.6	5.6	4.9
1984	23.6	53.7	4.2	3.9	7.8	8.5	4.3	4.2
1985	30.4	36.5	6.1	6.3	10.9	12.2	5.6	2.1
1986	31.9	36.1	6.9	4.8	6.4	12.6	1.4	0.2

Source: Ministry of Finance

> 22 percent of the children suffer from malnutrition, meaning some 20,000 children; only fifty percent of the 200,000 children who should go to school seem to be attending classes. Others are absent because they have no shoes, no school uniforms, no money for transportation or exam fees, or because they must work to contribute to the family income, in 1987 Guyana consumed 55 percent of the quantity of electricity consumed in 1976, 63 percent of the volume of fuel consumed in that year and exports were only 55 percent of what they were eight years earlier...

Apart from the social sector, the public utilities system, including electricity, public transport, and telephone services, also collapsed. Electricity generated, for instance, trended downward from 220 *mwh* in 1966 to 116.2 *mwh* by 1989. Consequently, there were daily power outages (Thomas, 1982a). The deterioration of the transportation system resulted in workers taking an average of four hours to commute between work and home each day. To a large extent, the poor living conditions of citizens were due to the economic crisis. This nexus has been highlighted by many academic studies. Worrell (2024) argued that the economic situation in the 1970s and 1980s was a significant factor in Guyana's low Human Development Index (HDI) score, which was among the lowest in the Caribbean. According to Worrell (2024, 208):

> The unfortunate experiences of the late 1970s and the 1980s left Guyana with an HDI score in 1990 which was among the lowest in the Caribbean (0.548), compared with 0.732 for Barbados and 0.668 for Trinidad-Tobago, the English-speaking Caribbean's largest economy. With such a relatively low starting point, by 2019, Guyana's HDI score of 0.708 remained below the average for Latin America and the Caribbean (0.768), and a considerable distance behind.

Between 1970 and 1981, approximately 119,000 Guyanese left the country in search of a better life due to substandard living conditions. Because of the magnitude of the departure, the nation's population growth rates became negative. The migration of highly qualified professionals, which resulted in the depletion of the nation's human resources, was even more disastrous. The professionals who migrated did so because they were discriminated against for not complying with the political agenda of the PNC government and because of targeted violence combined with debilitating criminal activities in the country (Vezzoli, 2014).

At the heart of the crisis was the collapse of Guyana's production system, resulting in the deterioration of the standard of living and the real earnings of a large share of Guyanese workers. The deterioration can be attributed to the fact that the government was the leading employer in the country and failed to increase wages in line with the inflation rate. Under the Burnham regime, the guiding economic philosophy was to nationalise all units of production. This practice was evident in the 1980s when both the bauxite and sugar industries were nationalised. In contrast, the rice industry was controlled by the state marketing agency and national rice-processing facilities, the latter of which accounted for approximately 90 per cent of rice processing activities. In the words of Clive Thomas (1982b, 108)

> The control of these sectors is responsible for the government's frequent boast that it owns and controls 80 percent of the national economy. It is the real material foundation on which the PNC is seeking to constitute a ruling class.

At the national level, the state of the economy laid bare the mercy of gross mismanagement, incompetence, and lack of vision by the PNC government. For instance, from 1971 to 1980, the total annual sugar production decreased from 369,000 tons to 270,000 tons despite the sugar industry's capacity being around 450,000 tons per annum. Similarly, the annual rice production in 1980 was 160,000 tons when the actual capacity of the rice industry was 250,000 tons per annum. Dried bauxite production also fell from 2.3 million tons in 1970 to 1.6 million tons in 1980, with alumina production declining from 312,000 tons to 211,000 tons during the same period. According to Thomas (1982b, 108), "The PNC takeover of the economy has therefore been accompanied by rapid destruction." The abysmal failure of the Burnham regime to effectively manage the economy was attributed to the absence of vision, foresight, as well as economic mismanagement and wasteful spending. According to Ishmael (2012, 15):

> Prime Minister spent more than a quarter of a million dollars to repair and redecorate the building formerly occupied by the Director of Agriculture as his residence, while certain government functionaries such as Attorney General Shridath Ramphal and the High Commissioner in London, Lionel Luckhoo, were being paid abnormally high salaries and allowances.

Records indicate that a solitary plan was developed for the 1972-1976 period, which was presented in draft form in 1973, just before the national elections, and was never revised thereafter. This plan had a lofty objective to "feed, house, and clothe the nation by 1976". Despite the establishment of a state planning commission in 1978, the same old plan from 1972-1976 was lazily re-presented year after year. Gross mismanagement became the norm, and by 1976, the objectives of the plan were never achieved. In the area of housing, the plan targeted the construction of 65,000 housing units. However, only 4,167 housing units (or 6.5 per cent) of the target was achieved (Ishmael, 2012). The clothing programme under the plan, which involved the cultivation of cotton at Kimba and the processing of cotton fabric, was also a massive failure. Instead of clothing the nation, the citizens were denied access to clothing after the plan failed to deliver sufficient clothing, and the government opted to place restrictions on the importation of clothing (Ishmael, 2012). Furthermore, the nation suffered from hunger and starvation due to the anti-agricultural policies of the PNC, which resulted in the collapse of the food production system and the ban on food importation. The scarcity of essential food items forced many citizens to turn to the black market. According to Ishmael (2012, 123-124):

> Food production had declined so greatly by 1976 that consumption of food items per head of the population had dropped drastically to seriously affect the nutritional level of the young children and the population as a whole. The government's policy of banning essential imported food items compounded this situation. According to a report of the Guyana Consumers Association, in 1976 poultry production amounted to 8 ounces a week per head of the population; eggs were 1 egg per person every 8 days; fish, 14 ounces

> per person per week; beef, 4 ounces per person per week; and ground provisions, 5 pounds per person per month ...
>
> As a result of the PNC anti-agricultural policy since it led the government from 1965, almost every food commodity was in short supply in 1976. Generally every food item not produced locally was banned, although these items could be obtained at the black market at exorbitant prices.

While the average citizen punished due to the failed policies, the PNC government expanded the public sector, with political hires being the predominant recipients of new positions. These political bureaucrats became the architects of a corruption system that was unparalleled in the history of modern Guyana.

Apart from the economic and social hardship created by the Burnham regime, his party overtly assaulted the judiciary and trampled upon the rights of citizens. For instance, the PNC flag was conspicuously flaunted over the Court of Appeal to assert its paramountcy over the judiciary. The Burnham regime also made the judiciary uncomfortable, which triggered a mass exodus of judges from the legal fraternity. To curtail the judiciary, he introduced a law to reverse a contentious court decision. While incapacitating the judiciary, he also simultaneously used the National Security Act to search, arrest, and harass political opponents to suppress dissent and strike fear into the hearts of citizens.

In order to remain in power, the PNC, under Burnham and Desmond Hoyte, denied citizens the right to elect a government of their choice freely and without fear. They did this by systematically rigging elections in 1968, 1973, 1978, 1980, and 1985. The first large-scale rigging of elections occurred in 1968 when the PNC engineered a scheme for overseas voting. Two documentaries produced by Granada Television detailed how the PNC used proxy voting to rig these elections. The first documentary, entitled "The Trail of the Vanishing Votes," revealed that only 117 voters were genuine out of a sample of 551 registered voters in London, while 19 voters were found to be genuine out of a sample of 346 registered voters in Manchester. The second documentary, entitled "The *Making of a Prime Minister*," disclosed that out of 11,750 voters registered to vote in the USA, only 4,700 were genuine, while only 13,050 voters out of the 44,300 registered voters in the UK were found to be genuine. The rigging continued in 1973, but this time, the ballot boxes were hijacked and taken to army bases. In the process, two PYO members, Jagan Ramessar and Bholanauth Parmanand, were killed as they attempted to stop the hijacking of the ballot boxes. Instead of holding constitutionally due elections in 1978, the PNC held a fraudulent referendum to extend the life of the parliament and set the stage for the so-called New People's Constitution. In the new constitution, the president was vested with unlimited powers, and the ruling party took total control of state power (SN, 08/07/2022). Indeed, the amendments to the Constitution solidified Burnham's position as executive president. In the next elections, held in 1980, the PNC was similarly accused of massive election rigging. In those elections, the PNC gifted itself 78 per cent of the votes.

On the opposition side, the popularity of the WPA skyrocketed because it stood alongside the PPP and other civic-minded organisations in confronting the PNC. This engendered a new wave of threat to the PNC regime. To counter this new wave of threat from the opposition, Burnham resorted to state violence, political murder, and open terrorism, directly targeting the WPA. According to Thomas (1982b, 115), the period of repression was underlined by the murders of Father Bernard Darke, Ohene Koama, Edward Dublin, and Walter Rodney and the use of PNC thugs to attack opposition members across the country.

Burnham utilised the national security services as a critical weapon to tackle all perceived threats to his regime. All potential threats were considered "security" matters, and the security personnel were carefully selected to support the PNC dictatorship, rigged elections, and undemocratic rule. These officers were also used to spy on and harass political opponents. Apart from this, there were partisan security operatives within the security forces, such as the supporters of the House of Israel and members of the Women's Revolutionary Socialist Movement (WRSM). These groups served as an auxiliary line of defence against the opposition and the people, ensuring the perpetuity of the Burnham dictatorial regime.

To further insulate his authoritarian regime from all challenges, Burnham presented himself as the PNC, the PNC as the State, and the State as the people of the nation. This strategy aimed to represent any attack on Burnham as a direct attack on the State and its people. Consequently, to safeguard the sovereignty of the State, the PNC was constitutionally reinforced when it resorted to employing State force against its critics. The politicisation of the media played a significant role, with both state and private media outlets demonstrating allegiance to the dissemination of PNC propaganda. This allowed for the masking of the brutal violence inflicted upon the populace by the Burnham regime. According to Thomas (1982b, 117).

> Thus, it was possible to clamp the news lid on the Jonestown murders, the murders of Teekah (a Government Minister of Education), the assassinations of Rodney, Koama, Dublin and Darke. Indeed, this policy is complemented by a parliamentary process in which the speaker of the parliament can rule that none of these matters listed here were of sufficient national importance to warrant a debate in Parliament!

While the PPP passionately championed the cause of our citizens, it also acted as a responsible political party, by offering unconditional support to the PNC government on critical matters, such as "defence of national independence, sovereignty and territorial integrity" (Ishmael, 2012, 139). Rather than resorting to violence and divisive politics, the PPP promulgated *pro poor* polices to mobilise political support and unite our people, even in the face of rigged elections and violence directed at its members and supporters.

Conclusion

After gaining power in 1966, the PNC swiftly moved to seize control of the country's productive sectors under the guise of Cooperative Socialism. It then introduced the doctrine of party paramountcy, which placed the ruling party above all other state institutions, including the judiciary, military, and public service. This doctrine led to the politicisation of these state institutions and the establishment of a dictatorship, where citizens were denied the right to choose their government through free and fair elections.

During the PNC dictatorship, all the productive sectors contracted, the economy regressed, and social sectors collapsed. This resulted in pervasive poverty, mass migration as citizens fled the country in search of a better life, and long-lasting rifts in the social fabric that still plague our country today. Indeed, the persistent challenge regarding social cohesion that persists today may be attributed to the twenty-eight (28) years of PNC misrule.

REFERENCES

Boyd, D. (1989). Macro-economic Consultant Report on the Social and Economic Impact of Guyana's Economic Performance and ERP. *Washington, DC: Inter-American Development Bank.*

Country Studies (n.d.). Guyana - Economy. https://countrystudies.us/guyana/53.htm

Danns, D.E. (1988). Guyana's Debt Problem. *Social and Economic Studies*, 37(4), 79-106.

Danns, D. E. (1992). *Crisis, Adjustment and Recovery: The Lessons of Recent Experiences from the Guyana Economy for the Anglophone Caribbean.* Paper presented at the XXIV Regional Programme of Monetary Studies Annual Conference, Nassau, Bahamas, 26-29 October 1992.

Das, U.S. and Ganga. G.N. (1997). A Retrospect and Prospect on the Reform of the Financial Sector in Guyana. Social and Economic Studies, 46(2/3), 93-129.

Egoumé-Bossogo, P., E. Faal, R. Nallari, E. Weisman, 2003, Guyana: Experience with Macroeconomic Stabilization, Structural Adjustment, and Poverty Reduction (Washington: International Monetary Fund).

Galí, J., López-Salido, J. D., & Vallés, J. (2007). Understanding the effects of government spending on consumption. *Journal of the European economic association*, 5(1), 227-270.

Gafar, J. (1996). Guyana: From Cooperative Socialism to Economic Liberalization and Growth: 1976-1994. *Journal of Developing Areas*, 31(1), 41-74.

Gafar, J. (1998). Growth, inequality and poverty in selected Caribbean and Latin American countries, with emphasis on Guyana. *Journal of Latin American Studies*, *30*(3), 591-617.

Gafar, J. (2005a). The Impact of Economic Reforms on Health Indicators in Guyana. *Caribbean Studies*, 33(1), 149-176.

Gafar, J. (2005b). Do the Poor Benefit from Public Spending? A Look at the Evidence. *The Pakistan Development Review*, 44(1), 81–104.

Ganga, G. (2000). CREDIT, EXCESS LIQUIDITY AND MONETARY POLICY ISSUES IN GUYANA. *Social and Economic Studies*, *49*(2/3), 199–224.

Ishmael, O. (2012). From Autocracy to Democracy in Guyana.

Kaieteur News (2022, February 10). *Did Burnham err in nationalising the sugar industry?* https://www.kaieteurnewsonline.com/2022/02/10/did-burnham-err-in-nationalising-the-sugar-industry/

Lakhan, S., Lakhan, C., and Singh, J.B (1990). The Use of Canadian Aid to Sustain Guyana's Administrative Dictatorship. *Caribbean Studies*, 23(3/4), 69-84.

Stabroek News (2003, January 4). Desmond Hoyte (1929-2002). http://www.guyananews.org/special/hoyte/hoyte.html

Stabroek News (2007, March 10). Party paramountcy and the 1980 Constitution combined to give Burnham something close to absolute power. https://www.stabroeknews.com/2007/03/10/news/guyana/party-paramountcy-and-the-1980-constitution-combined-to-give-burnham-something-close-to-absolute-power/

Stabroek News (2022, July 8). The Constitutional Referendum of July 10th, 1978 decisively changed the course of our history. https://www.stabroeknews.com/2022/07/08/opinion/

letters/the-constitutional-referendum-of-july-10th-1978-decisively-changed-the-course-of-our-history/

Trotz, A. and Peake, L. (2001). Work, family and organizing: an overview of the contemporary economic, social and political roles of women in Guyana. *Social and Economic Studies*, 50(2), 67-101.

Thomas, C. Y. (1982a). Guyana: the IMF-World Bank Group and the general crisis. *Social and Economic Studies*, 31(4), 16-70.

Thomas, C.Y (1982b). The Current Crisis in Guyana. *Ufahamu: A Journal of African Studies*, 12(1), 107-122.

Thomas, C. Y. (1993). Lessons from experience: Structural Adjustment and Poverty in Guyana. *Social and Economic Studies*, 42(4), 16-70.

van Dijk, M. P. (1992). Guyana: Economic Recession and Transition. *Revista Europea de Estudios Latinoamericanos y Del Caribe / European Review of Latin American and Caribbean Studies*, *53*, 95-110. http://www.jstor.org/stable/25675556

Vezzoli, S. (2014). The effects of independence, state formation and migration policies on Guyanese migration. International Migration Institute.

World Bank (1992). Guyana: From Economic Recovery to Sustained Growth.

3

The Dawn of a New Era: Two Decades of Economic Progress

...I wish to see my country prosperous and developing, its people happy, well fed, well housed and with jobs to do. Second only to my passion for the independence of my people, is this dedication to their economic advancement, so that their lives may be more abundant. **DR CHEDDI JAGAN**

In 1990, when the PNC signalled its intention to hold general elections, the request was vehemently rejected by all opposition parties. Instead, a collective plea was made by all parties for the establishment of a credible electoral framework prior to the elections. This impasse led to the intervention of the Carter Center, the United Nations Development Programme (UNDP), and other agencies. As a result of these efforts, Guyana held its first genuinely free, fair, and transparent elections in 1992, in which the People's Progressive Party/Civic (PPP/C) secured a landslide victory. As a political party which prides itself on the principle of "a government of the people, by the people, and for the people", the PPP/C was tasked with the mammoth responsibility of rebuilding a shattered economy and improving the lives of the people whose living standards had been in free fall for over two decades. This chapter examines the journey of the PPP from 1992 to 2015 in repairing the damage to the economy and social sector during the twenty-eight years of PNC's misrule.

Elections 1992: an attempt to frustrate the will of the people

The collapse of the economy, coupled with internal and external pressures, forced the PNC to agree to free and fair elections after almost three decades of authoritarian rule. Free and fair elections, however, came with a heavy price tag. For instance, elections were constitutionally due by May 1990. However, beginning in 1990, a series of legal and administrative electoral reforms was undertaken in an effort to establish a credible electoral framework. In the end, elections were eventually held on October 5, 1992. The process, which lasted nearly two years, was overseen by the Council of Freely Elected Heads of Government. While the period during which the reforms occurred inevitably extended the life of the PNC government, this was the price the citizens had to pay to elect a government of their choice freely.

On election day, the PNC demonstrated its reluctance to give up power without a fight. The party began by unleashing a violent group of protestors who mounted a day-long siege on the Elections Commission. At the Guyana Broadcasting Corporation (GBC), a state-owned media outlet, rumours were being propagated that eligible voters were being denied their right to vote. In an attempt to further intimidate and disrupt the elections, the protestors threw stones and other missiles at the Election Commission building, injuring several occupants. Former U.S. President Jimmy Carter poignantly documented the severity of the unrest in his memoir *Beyond the White House: Waging Peace, Fighting Disease, Building Hope*, where he recounted the atmosphere of fear instigated by the PNC protestors (SN, 01/04/2019)

> The most personal danger I have felt since leaving the White House was in Guyana in 1992 [...]
>
> When I arrived (at the election headquarters), accompanied by three Secret Service agents, the building was surrounded by several hundred rioters, who had already broken all the windows with clubs and stones. There was only one Guyanese police officer present, a woman wearing a uniform but without sidearms [...]
>
> We went upstairs and found that all the computers had been transferred to one of the more isolated hotels for safekeeping. I phoned the hotel manager, who told me that the computers could not be operated there unless 'a battalion of troops is sent to protect us against the mobs trying to stop the vote count.

In Georgetown, a group of protestors that broke away from those who stormed the Guyana Elections Commission (GECOM) embarked on a violent rampage through the streets, looting stores and violently attacking people indiscriminately. These concerted efforts were intended to derail the election process and instil widespread fear and intimidation. Despite various efforts by international observers to convince voters that the elections were free and fair, the transition from an authoritarian regime to a democratic government was not seamless. It took four days before the PNC conceded and allowed the new government to be sworn in. After the watershed elections, Cheddi Jagan took the oath as president, thereby ushering in a new era of democratic rule. The PPP/C secured 162,058 (or 53.4 per cent) of the 303,186 votes cast.

Since taking office in 1992, the PPP/C government has introduced and maintained well-functioning democratic structures by institutionalising free and fair elections, undertaking constitutional reform to promote greater inclusivity, strengthening the Judiciary, as well as enhancing governance and an anti-corruption framework. Due to these efforts citizens are allowed to freely elect a government of their choice, while political parties are permitted to participate in elections without fear or discrimination. Additionally, the government is now required to operate in an open and transparent manner.

The transformation of our country from an authoritarian state under Burnham to a strong democracy is evident in the evolution of the Civil Liberties Index (CLI) and Political Rights Index (PRI) from 1974 to 2014. The CLI, for instance, improved from a score of 7 in 1974, indicating the lowest level of freedom, to a score of 2 between 1993 and 2004, after which it stabilised at a score of 3 until 2014 (see Figure 3.1). Similarly, the PRI improved from a weak score of 7 in 1974 to 2 from 1993 to 2014, reflecting a robust level of political freedom (see Figure 3.1).

Rebuilding the economy from ground zero

Following its election victory in 1992, the PPP/C government also promptly began rebuilding the nation's economy, which was in a state of near bankruptcy. The PPP inherited a country with an external debt of US$2.1 billion when the minimum salary in the public sector was a mere $3,000 per month. At the *per capita* level, the size of the external debt was equivalent to "$349,518 for every man, woman and child" (Ministry of Finance, 1993, 3). To make matters worse, when the domestic debt was added to external debt, the total debt burden per

Figure 3.1: Civil Liberties Index (CLI) and Political Rights Index (PRI), 1974-2014

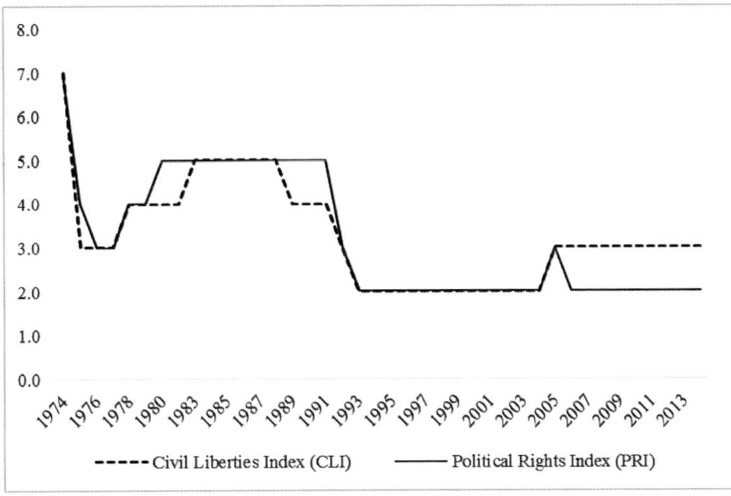

Source: Freedom in the World - Comparative and Historical Data, 2018

capita in 1992 was roughly $355,088. As a share of GDP, the total debt was almost 750 per cent, of which almost 94 per cent of the country's revenue was used to service it, one of the highest rates in the world. However, there were signs that the domestic economy was doomed to perpetual failure had the economic system that as introduced, though unknowingly due to gross incompetence, did not change. For instance, in 1989, the Minimum Holdings of Liquid Assets by Banks (Temporary Provisions) Bill was introduced, targeting the sterilisation of excess liquidity in the banking system by restricting commercial banks' lending *vis-à-vis* their deposits. Part of the process involved ensuring that the commercial banks' excess reserves were converted into medium-term debentures. This aligned with the government's strategy to defer interest payments through the issuance of medium- and long-term debt instruments. This, of course, eventually proved futile in addressing the root cause of the fiscal imbalance. In fact, what actually transpired was that the debt crisis was merely postponed, leading to the deepening of the debt trap and further increasing repayment burdens. The 81 per cent increase in interest obligation outstripped the 15 per cent in revenue by almost five-fold, further confirming not only the government's inability to execute prudent fiscal planning but also a deepening reliance on unsustainable borrowing. In the words of the then Minister of Finance, Carl Greenidge:

> "Basically, we have been seeking to convert short-term debt or liabilities (namely Treasury Bills) into medium and long-term debt and liabilities. This would enable the Government to transfer the burden of interest payments to sometime in the future [...] Additionally in 1986 special two-year debentures were issued and both of these measures impacted favourably on the quantum of payments the Government needed to make in the respective years. However, these measures have clearly not been enough, for, without further action, the Central Government would be required to find an additional amount of $266m in 1987 to meet its interest obligations. I might add that this 81 per cent increase in interest contrasts with increases in Central Government revenues of a mere 15 per cent" – National Assembly (1986, 43).

The heavy debt burden was not the only problem inherited by the PPP/C government. When the new government assumed office, poverty was pervasive throughout the country. According to the Household Income and Expenditure Survey (HIES) and the Living Standards Measurement Survey (LSMS), in 1992, more than 43 per cent of the population lived in absolute poverty, while 29 per cent lived in extreme poverty. These surveys revealed that the incidence of extreme poverty was more pronounced in the rural interior (70.1 per cent) and rural coastal 27.9 per cent) as well as among the "working class, construction workers, public sector workers in lower grade levels, and agricultural farmers" (Government of Guyana, 2000, 12). According to the World Bank, in 1992, an estimated 85 per cent of the population in Guyana lived on less than US$5.50 per day. At that time, Guyana was ranked as the second poorest country in the Western Hemisphere. In the words of Carl Greenidge:

> "Comrade Speaker, if I might summarise the essence of the economic problem elaborated so far, I would do it in the following manner: The Government's long-standing inability to garner enough revenues to finance its important activities has resulted over the years

> in the rapid expansion of credit. Concomitant with those developments has been almost uncontrollable increases in the State's domestic borrowing. The burden of the interest payments currently weighs very heavily on the state's revenues, and one of the consequences of the rapid credit creation has been an equally precipitous decline in our foreign exchange reserves." – National Assembly (1986, 39).

The social sectors were also contending with some of the worst systems of water and sanitation, healthcare, and education in the Caribbean. In 1990, the percentage of students reaching Grade 6 fell from 84.1 per cent in 1987 to 8 per cent in 1989. Similarly, the *per capita* supply of calories, as a percentage of total requirement, also fell from 101.1 in 1985 to 77 in 1989. The country's physical infrastructure was similarly deteriorated, with roads, bridges, stellings, and airports in a state of severe disrepair, placing Guyana among the lowest-ranked nations in the Western Hemisphere in terms of infrastructural quality.

Being classified as a Highly Indebted Poor Country (HIPC), the new PPP/C Government had an uphill task in fixing the country's broken economy, social sectors (health, education, water and sanitation, and housing), and physical infrastructure. Under the theme "Reconstruction for Human Development," the new government began the process of rebuilding the country for the benefit of every Guyanese.

Re-energising the productive sectors

The first national budget introduced by the newly elected PPP/C government sought to chart a new way forward amid the weak economic foundations inherited from the PNC. Due to decades of gross economic mismanagement, the economy had suffered a significant blow, with all major exporting sectors – such as sugar, bauxite, and rice – experiencing sharp declines in productivity and export earnings. In fact, between 1987 and 1989, net foreign earnings for sugar declined from US$90.4 million to US$70.5 million, primarily due to a sharp contraction in production from 220,995 tons in 1987 to 154,100 tons in 1989. In the bauxite industry, the situation was even worse – export earnings fell from US$86.2 million to US$73.4 million due to a sharp drop in bauxite production. Due to the increased strain on the national economy, the government eventually issued fiscal transfers to help clear the increase in bank overdrafts. In the year that followed, the poor economic performance continued, with the bauxite industry recording 15 per cent less than its projected target and 22 per cent less of its forecasted revenue. In the sugar industry, output also fell to an all-time low of 130,000 tons, representing only 75 per cent of the targeted amount. In the rice industry, output contracted by more than 40 per cent, and 34 per cent below the output achieved in 1989, an all-time low in fourteen years. Other sectors, such as livestock, also experienced a significant decline in their output of almost 30 per cent. To help reboot the economy and counter the forces of a stalled economy, the government decided to increase circulation by another 48 per cent, leading to higher prices and a greater loss in purchasing power.

In 1990, due to the lacklustre performance of key sectors, the gross domestic product (GDP) contracted by approximately 3.5 per cent, further compounding the existing pressure on domestic savings and real income. At the Bank of Guyana, net domestic credit – that reflects the government's indebtedness to the bank – increased to \$3.5 billion, almost \$250 million more than projected. Domestic debt services also increased to 38.5 per cent or \$4.2 billion of central government expenditure. To exacerbate the situation, the Guyanese dollar underwent significant devaluation, from \$19.5 to \$101.75 per US dollar between 1987 and 1991 (Eugome-Bossogo, 2000). This rapid depreciation in the purchasing power of the local currency, coupled with limited fiscal space, meant the government was able to allocate only 7 per cent of its revenue to social services. The crisis was compounded by a narrow tax base and a chronic shortage of skilled personnel across both the public and private sectors, hindering the effective execution of government policies.

It was clear that the task ahead was analogous to a man climbing a mountain with both his hands and feet tied while carrying a heavy haversack. To bootstrap the country out of its marred financial situation and improve the quality of life for its people, when the PPP government took office in 1992, it immediately increased budgetary allocations towards the social sectors and provided liveable wages to public servants. The government also implemented a series of institutional reforms aimed at enhancing accountability and transparency, including strengthening the legal and regulatory framework to guide public spending. Due to improved fiscal management, budgetary allocation increased as a result of targeted efforts to reduce waste and extravagance among government ministries and other state entities.

After nearly two decades of economic decay, the country recorded strong growth in real GDP during the first PPP/C term in office, spanning 1992 to 1997 (see Figure 3.2). The average economic growth during the first term was approximately 7.3 per cent, compared with an average growth rate of -2.8 per cent during the 1980s (see Figure 3.2). Leading the economic recovery were the sugar, rice, bauxite, and gold sectors.

Sugar production expanded by 70.1 per cent, from 162,484 tonnes in 1991 to 276,349 tonnes by 1997, because of improvements in field operations, capital equipment, and management of the sugar corporation (see Figure 3.3). During the corresponding period, rice production grew more than two-fold, from 150,794 tonnes in 1991 to 340,699 tonnes by 1997 (see Figure 3.3). The improved performance of the rice sector was due to increased cultivation stimulated by a liberalisation of the sector and greater investment in drainage and irrigation by the Government. Between 1991 and 1997, bauxite production increased almost three-fold due to the reorganisation of the industry, which contributed to changes in the output mix (see Figure 3.3). Gold production expanded more than sevenfold from 59,254 troy ounces in 1992 to 467,832 troy ounces by 1997. The revival of all the key productive sectors reflected the successful efforts of the PPP/C government to diversify the country's economic base.

Figure 3.2: Real GDP growth rate (%), 1992-2014

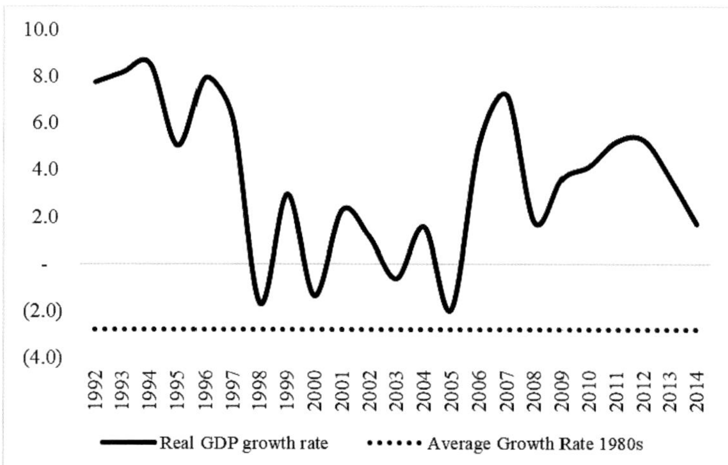

Source: World Bank and the author's calculation

Figure 3.3: Output of key commodities, 1992-2014

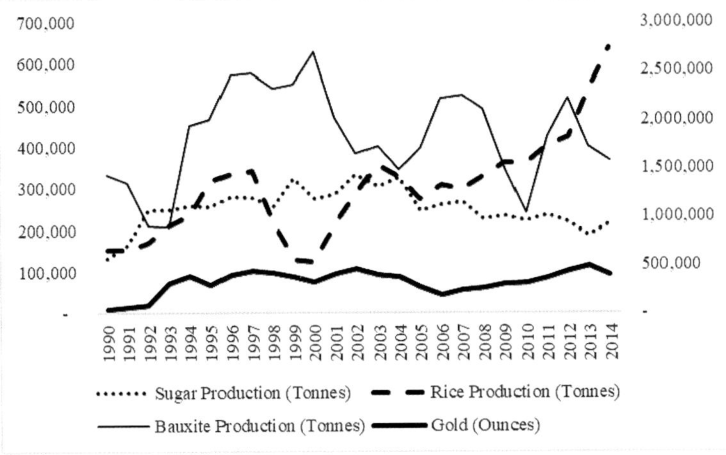

Bank of Guyana Annual Reports (various years)

Unfortunately, the economy slowed due to a wave of violent PNC protests during the period 1998-2001. The protests began in 1998 after the opposition PNC refused to accept the results of the 1997 elections, arguing that the elections had been rigged. To end the violence, the PPP/C brokered a peace accord (called the Herdmanston Accord) with the PNC. This political treaty paved the way for constitutional reform and fresh elections in 2001, thereby reducing the PPP/C's term in office by two years. The violence did not end but continued with a 56-day strike instigated by the Guyana Public Service Union (GPSU). This strike further crippled the economy.

Like the 1997 elections, the PNC refused to accept the results of the 2002 elections. There was another wave of politically motivated violence when five high-profile criminals escaped from the Camp Street Prison on February 23, 2003. Due to the unstable business and economic environment, the economy registered suboptimal growth between 2001 and 2005. Other exogenous factors that conspired to disrupt productive activities in the key sectors since 1997 included extreme El Niño, flooding, deterioration in commodity prices, and loss of preferential markets for rice and sugar (IDB, 2008). However, political instability was a significant contributing factor to the sub-optimal performance of the economy between 1998 and 2005 (Pasha, 2024; Staritz, Atoyan, and Gold, 2007).

Fresh elections were called in 2006, which the PPP/C won. There was no political violence after these elections. Consequently, the economy recorded steady growth between 2006 and 2011. Rice production and gold declarations by small and medium-scale miners reached unprecedented levels. The construction and services sector also contributed to Guyana's economic growth despite the global financial and economic crises that led to negative economic growth in most countries worldwide. This remarkable performance was not accidental but rather due to improved governance, sound macroeconomic management, and favourable commodity prices (Grenade and Pasha, 2012), all of which provided the ideal conditions for greater local and foreign investment in our country. The sterling performance of the various sectors was also due to the successful efforts of the PPP/C to diversify the economy. The rapid expansion in the key economic sectors, coupled with the 'all-inclusive' nature of the PPP/C's policies, resulted in more employment opportunities, improved disposable income, and general improvement in the well-being of citizens across the country (rural, urban, hinterland).

In 2011, the PPP/C government won its fourth term. However, this time, the PPP/C did not gain a majority of seats in parliament. The PNC, which formed an alliance with the AFC, took advantage of its one-seat majority in parliament to stymie the PPP/C government. The APNU-AFC used its one-seat majority in parliament to cut the budget and a no-confidence motion, which prematurely curtailed the PPP/C's term in office by two years. The PNC also instigated several protests to destabilise the economy. The first major demonstration took place in Linden and culminated in the blockade of the Mackenzie-Wismar Bridge. The aim was to paralyse the mining sector, as the Wismar-McKenzie Bridge is a critical logistical artery for the interior region. The unrest in Linden subsequently ignited further disturbances in Agricola, aimed at spreading fear and terror on the East Bank of Demerara (EBD).

Practicing Fiscal Prudence

The PPP/C government embraced prudent fiscal policy throughout the twenty-three years spanning 1992 to 2014. This was manifestly evident in its success in controlling the fiscal deficit, maintaining sustainable debt levels, and minimising expenditure through reforms aimed at improving efficiency in the public sector while promoting sustainable economic growth and macroeconomic stability. During the 1980s, the average fiscal deficit as a percentage of GDP was 31.3 per cent. However, within its first term in office (1992–1997), the PPP/C government succeeded in reducing the overall fiscal deficit to 0.68 per cent of GDP – a significant turnaround from the unsustainable levels inherited from the previous administration. Fiscal discipline also remained consistent within the period, well below 10 per cent, until 2015, when the government was replaced in the disputed election (see Figure 3.4).

Additionally, the average tax revenue as a percentage of GDP, which averaged 39 per cent during the 1980s, declined to 17.1 per cent by 2014, suggesting a decline in tax burden by almost 50 per cent. A similar trajectory was observed in recurrent expenditure, which declined from 54.5 per cent of GDP in 1992 to 15.7 per cent in 2014 (see Figure 3.4). These trends serve as a testament to the significant improvement in fiscal prudence under the PPP/C government, underscoring the government's commitment to macroeconomic stability and the creation of a more efficient and sustainable public sector framework.

Unlike the PNC, the PPP/C government invested significantly in the economic infrastructure and social sectors to stimulate the productive sectors

Figure 3.4: Fiscal deficit, current revenue and current expenditure as a percentage of GDP, 1992-2014

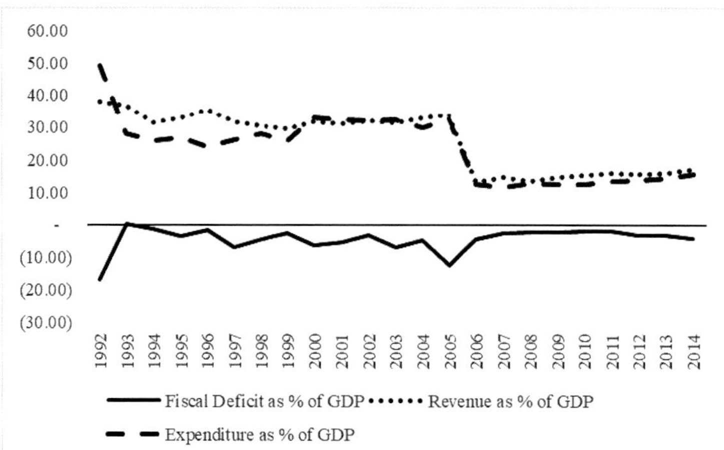

Source: Ministry of Finance and author's calculation

Figure 3.5: Relative share of capital investment in the social sectors and economic infrastructure, 1992-2014

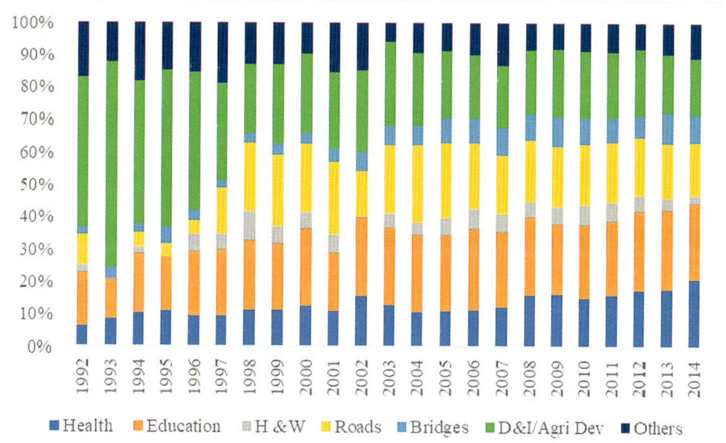

Source: Ministry of Finance

and reduce poverty. The government's capital expenditure trended upward from $4.4 billion in 1992 to $51.0 billion in 2014, representing an increase of more than eleven-fold. Figure 3.5 shows the relative share of capital investment in the social sectors (health, education, housing, water and sanitation) and economic infrastructure (roads, bridges, drainage and irrigation, and agricultural development) at the regional level. Notably, between 1992 and 1996, the capital allocations for D&I exceeded 40 per cent. Since then, capital allocations for the social sectors have increased significantly, averaging more than 40 per cent annually between 1994 and 2014. This pattern of expenditure underscores the PPP/C's commitment to human development, reducing inequality and poverty through infrastructural development and human capital investments.

One of the daunting tasks the PPP/C Government had to undertake was restoring the country's creditworthiness, which was deemed bankrupt under the PNC in 1982. Through skilful negotiations, the PPP/C Government secured significant external debt relief. The stock of external debt, which stood at US$2,116.4 million in 1992, declined to US$1,058.9 million by 2007. Consequently, the country's debt-to-GDP ratio trended downward from 570.6 per cent in 1992 to 39 per cent by 2007. By 2014, one year prior to exiting office, the debt-to-GDP ratio declined further to 38.7 per cent (see Figure 3.6).

Figure 3.6: Debt-to-GDP ratios, 1992-2014

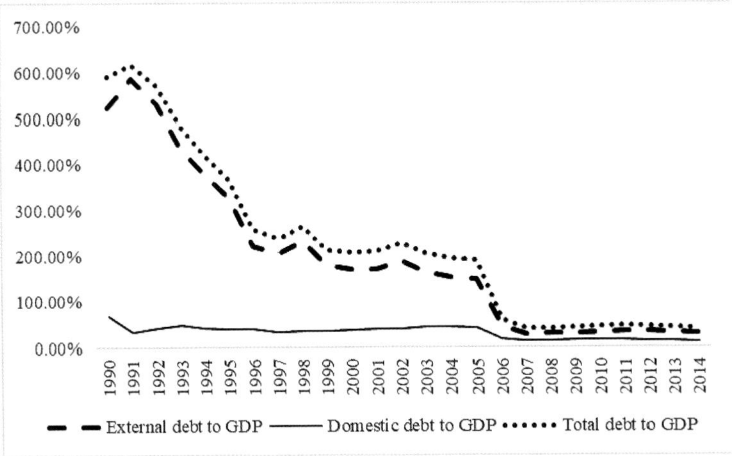

Source: Ministry of Finance

With the reduction in the country's public debt, the actual debt service as a percentage of the government's current revenue fell to 12.4 per cent in 2008 from approximately 90 per cent in 1992 (see Figure 3.7) and remained relatively stable through 2014, just one year prior to demitting office. Similarly, total debt service as a proportion of GDP and exports displayed a similar trend (see Figure 3.7). Specifically, the total debt service as a percentage of GDP decreased from 34.1 per cent in 1992 to 4.2 per cent in 2014, while debt service as a percentage of exports contracted from 21 per cent in 1992 to 12 per cent in 2014, an indication of reduced vulnerability, especially to external shocks (see Figure 3.7).

The improvement in the country's macroeconomic framework was largely due to strong fiscal discipline, macroeconomic reforms, and the effectiveness of the PPP/C administration in addressing the debt burden. One such initiative was the debt write-off and cancellation under the Multilateral Debt Relief Initiative (MDRI) and the Enhanced Heavily Indebted Poor Countries (HIPC) Initiative. These efforts restored international confidence in Guyana's economy and helped boost spending in key social sectors, which directly targeted human development and poverty alleviation.

The success enjoyed by the government in restoring its creditworthiness is by no means trivial. Considering Guyana's state in 1992, this achievement was commendable. For instance, the stock of outstanding debt in 1964 increased

Figure 3.7: Total Public Debt Service to GDP and Total External Debt Service to Exports, 1992-2014

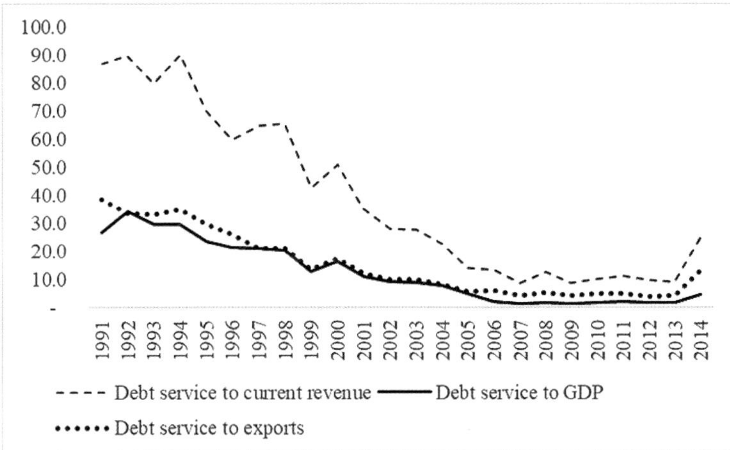

Source: Ministry of Finance

from US$60.8 million, or US$89 per capita, to US$1.5 billion by 1985, and then further to US$2.1 billion in 1992 (or US$2,785 per capita). Total domestic debt also followed a similar pattern, having increased from $53 million in 1981 to $4.2 billion in 1991. As a share of domestic production, external debt increased from 31.3 per cent in 1964 to 729.7 per cent in 1991. The sharp increase was linked to the rise in nationalisation loans, government loans to public enterprises, and an increased dependence on bilateral loans to meet the government's domestic consumption needs. The overall deterioration of the local economy significantly impacted the government's ability to service its debt obligations. For instance, as a share of exports, debt services increased from 4.1 per cent between 1960 and 1964 to 71.5 per cent by the end of 1991. As a share of total revenue, debt services increased from 14.9 per cent in 1964 to more than 90 per cent by the end of 1992. This led to almost every dollar of revenue generated by the government being used to finance external debts.

Meanwhile, the net international reserve, which was - US$102 million in 1990, increased continuously to US$652.2 million by 2014 (see Figure 3.8). Prior to 1991, there were severe shortages of foreign currency, leading to an unbridled parallel market. A key reason is the gross mismanagement of the economy and deterioration in the country's productive and service sectors. The

Figure 3.8: Net International Reserves (US$ millions) and Debt-to-GDP (%), 1990-2014

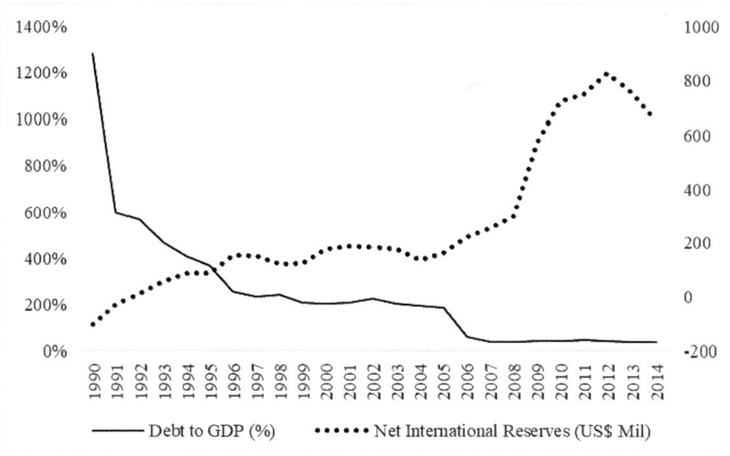

Source: Bank of Guyana and Ministry of Finance

shortage of foreign currency had placed significant restrictions on the importation of critical inputs necessary for the productive sector. These restrictions and constraining factors, in addition to inadequate budgetary allocations for basic operations and maintenance, led to the complete deterioration of the country's infrastructure network, including roads, irrigation, and drainage. The overall effect has led to the decline of the productive sector. At the level of the central government, the expansion of the public sector, coupled with economic stagnation, led to the accumulation of public debt in order to meet basic social needs.

Financial sector reforms and prudent monetary policy

With the installation of a democratically elected government and the liberalisation of the economy, credit to the private sector increased in both absolute and relative terms. At the end of 1997, private sector credit increased more than six-fold to $44,863.3 million from $6,672.4 million in 1992. Domestic credit to the private sector as a share of GDP also doubled during the corresponding period, from 17.1 per cent in 1991 to 42.1 per cent in 1997 (see Figure 3.9). Despite the unstable political environment created by the wave of

Figure 3.9: Domestic Credit to GDP (%), 1991-2014

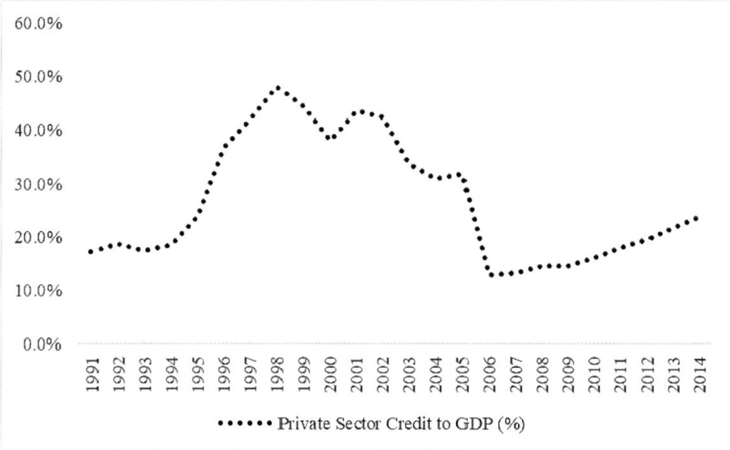

Source: Bank of Guyana and author's calculations

protests during the period 1998-2002, the share of private sector credit reached \$58,664.8 million (42.4 per cent) by 2002. However, the relentless effort by the PNC to make the country "ungovernable resulted in a sharp decline in private sector credit as a share of GDP, from 42.4 per cent in 2002 to 13 per cent by 2006. From 2007, the share of private sector credit rebounded continuously, reaching 23.7 per cent in 2014, due to the conducive business environment and the sound macroeconomic policies implemented by the PPP/C government.

The easy monetary policy pursued by the PPP/C government also contributed to the continuous decline in interest rates. One year before the assumption of office by the PPP/C government in 1992, the prime lending rate and the weighted average lending rate of commercial banks were 33.5 per cent and 35.22 per cent, respectively. The New Building Society's (NBS) Mortgage rate was 18 per cent at the end of 1991. When the PPP/C government left office in May 2015, the prime lending rate and weighted average lending rate of commercial banks were reduced to 12.83 per cent and 10.77 per cent, respectively. The monetary policy implemented by the PPP/C government was designed to maintain macroeconomic stability while encouraging credit expansion in productive sectors of the economy. The mortgage rate at the NBS was also at an all-time low of 6.45 per cent. This, of course, was in support of the PPP/C government housing programme to expand affordable homeownership. Collectively, these measures contributed to a housing boom that not only improved living standards but also stimulated growth in the construction and manufacturing sectors.

Bolstering disposable income to improve the standard of living

During the twenty-three years in office, the prudent monetary policy implemented by the PPP/C contained inflation at low single-digit levels, except for 1994 and 2007. The introduction of VAT and El Niño were mainly responsible for the high inflation in 2007. This policy dividend from the government's monetary policy was significant, as the average inflation rate in Guyana during the 1980s was 28.4 per cent (Greenidge and DaCosta, 2009), more than twice the highest inflation rate recorded under the PPP/C government between 1992 and 2015 (see Figure 3.10). By containing inflation, the PPP/C government helped sustain the purchasing power of the people.

Another positive outcome of the Government's monetary policy was the relatively stable exchange rate. The principal exchange rate (Guyana dollar (G$) to the United States dollar (US$), which suffered the sharpest deterioration between 1988 and 1991, was stabilised during the period 1992-2015 (see Figure

Figure 3.10: Annual inflation rate (%), 1992-2014

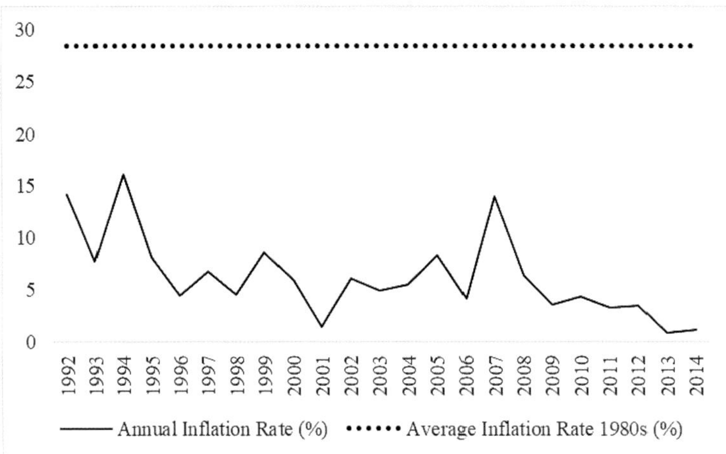

Source: Bureau of Statistics and Greenidge and DaCosta (2009)

Figure 3.11: Principal Exchange Rate and Volatility of the Principal Exchange Rate, 1988-2014

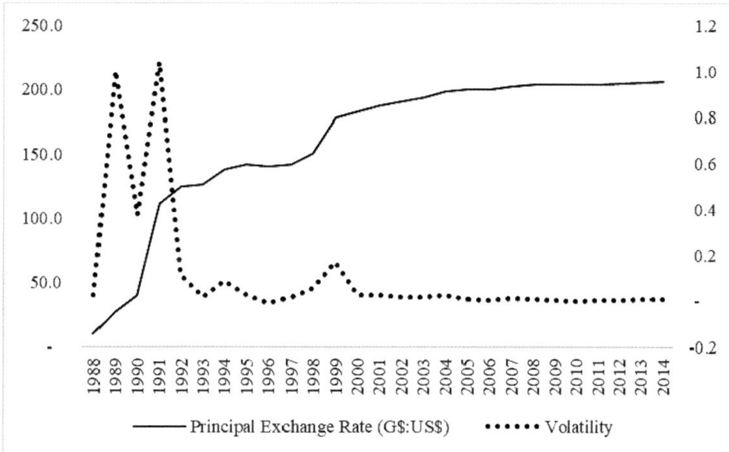

Source: Bank of Guyana and Author's calculation
Note: Volatility is measured by the standard deviation of the exchange rate

3.11). This, of course, helped create a conducive business environment that attracted both domestic and foreign investment. Given the country's dependence on imports of consumer goods, the stable exchange also preserved the real income of citizens.

Upon assuming office in 1992, the Government immediately implemented a series of policy measures aimed at reversing the socioeconomic decline inherited from the preceding PNC regime and improving the standard of living for all Guyanese. One of these was the increase in the minimum wage and salary of public servants. Between 1992 and 1997, the public sector minimum wage more than doubled, from $3,137 per month in 1992 to $8,804 per month by 1997. This upward trajectory continued into the early 2000s, marking the period as one of the most aggressive phases of wage recovery. Specifically, the most significant annual increase in the minimum wage occurred during the first nine years of the PPP/C governance. The increases in the minimum wage were as follows: 23.2 per cent (1992), 37.5 per cent (1993), 27.5 per cent (1994), 16.0 per cent (1995), 15 per cent (1996), 20 per cent (1997), 30 per cent (1998), 31.1 per cent (1999) and 26.7 per cent (2000) (see Figure 3.12).

From 1992 to 2015, the public sector's wage bill increased exponentially. Specifically, in 1992, the total employment cost of the public sector was $2.3

Figure 3.12: Public Sector Minimum Wage ($) and percentage change in public sector minimum wage (%), 1992-2014

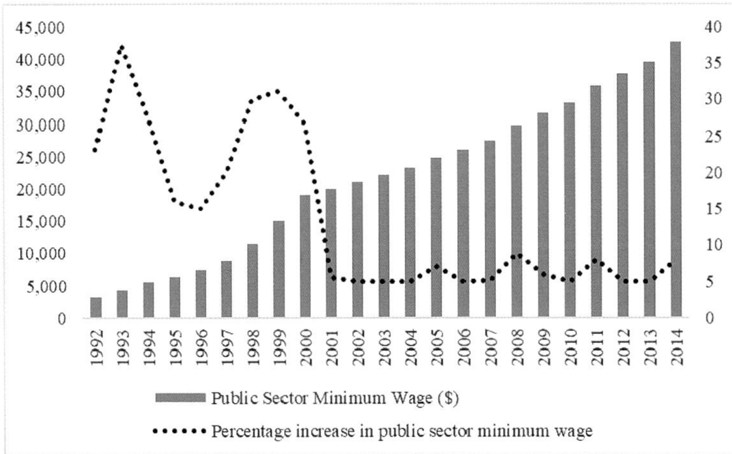

Source: Ministry of Finance

Figure 3.13: Public Sector Wage Bill ($ million) and percentage increase in Public Sector Wage Bill, 1992-2014

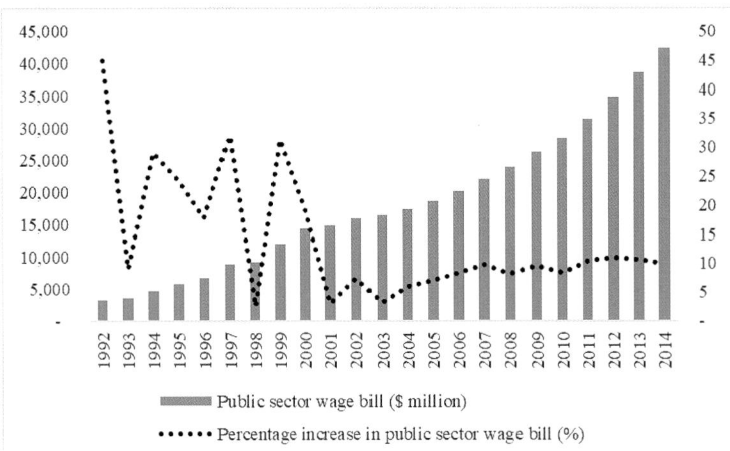

Source: Ministry of Finance

billion. By 2014, this figure had grown to $42.3 billion, an eighteen-fold increase over the period (see Figure 3.13). The increase in the public sector wage bill was due to the annual increases in public sector salaries and the increase in the minimum wage (see Figure 3.12). This was part of the government's broader commitment to improving living standards and restoring dignity to public servants. As shown in Figures 3.12 and 3.13, the early years of the PPP/C administration represent a phase of significant fiscal prioritisation of human capital, driven by the belief that a well-compensated and motivated public workforce is essential to delivering effective governance and sustaining economic recovery.

Rebuilding the Social Sectors

As noted elsewhere, the water and sanitation, health care, and education systems inherited by the PPP/C Government in 1992 were among the worst in the Caribbean. At that time, the country was also the second poorest in the Western Hemisphere, characterised by widespread poverty, deteriorating infrastructure, and depleted human capital. The new administration had the daunting task of rebuilding essential social services in an environment characterised by extremely limited fiscal space. To fulfil its pledge, the PPP/C administration implemented an ambitious strategy to rebuild the social sectors, ensuring that every Guyanese has access to high-quality healthcare, education, housing, water, and sanitation. The PPP/C Government has consistently allocated a sizable portion of its budget to these sectors.

Health Sector and Education

In 1991, public expenditure on health as a percentage of the national budget was 2.9 per cent. From the time the PPP/C assumed office in 1992, it progressively increased the share of the national budget allocated to the health sector, reaching 7.3 per cent in 1997 and 9.9 per cent by 2014 (see Figure 3.14). During the twenty-three years in office, the national budget allocated to the health sector averaged 8.1 per cent, nearly three times the level in 1991. Public spending on health as a percentage of GDP, which was 1.8 per cent in 1991, increased during the PPP/C tenure in office, averaging 3.02 per cent in the 1990s and 3.72 per cent in the 2000s (see Figure 3.14). By 2014, public health spending as a per cent of GDP was 3.95 per cent (see Figure 3.9). Total public

Figure 3.14: Allocation of the Health and Education Sectors, relative to the National Budget, 1992-2014

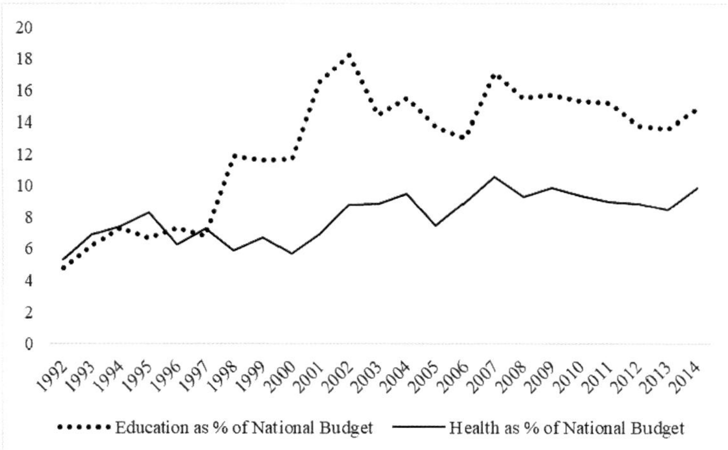

Source: Ministry of Finance

health expenditure per capita also trended upward from US$6 (or $700) in 1992 to US$137 ($27,750) by 2014.

The increased spending in the health sector by the PPP/C government was aimed, among other things, at expanding and upgrading health facilities, building human resources within the sector, and ensuring adequate supplies of drugs throughout the country. As discussed in Chapter 2, most of the health facilities outside the capital city lacked basic equipment in 1992. Indeed, patients bypassed the regional health facilities and went to those in Georgetown. During the twenty-three years in office, the PPP/C Government dedicated a significant portion of its budget to upgrading and expanding the existing network of health facilities. The total number of health facilities increased from 216 in 1992 to 370 by 2010, an increase of 154 new facilities across the country (see Table 3.1). Consequently, the number of beds per 10,000 population increased fivefold from 5 in 1990 to 25.4.

The PPP/C government also inherited a health sector that was significantly understaffed. The vacancy rates in this sector ranged from 25 per cent to 50 per cent. Almost 70 per cent of the doctors were based in Georgetown, and more than 90 per cent of the specialist medical staff in the public healthcare system were expatriates (PAHO, 2001). There was an immediate need to build human

Table 3.1: Types of Public Health Facilities, 1992-2010

Facility Types	1992	1999	2002	2010
Health Post	110	166	182	212
Health Centre	84	112	112	127
District Hospital	16	18	18	20
Regional Hospital	4	4	4	7
Referral Hospitals	2	2	2	3
National Laboratory	0	0	0	1
Total	**216**	**302**	**318**	**370**

Source: Ministry of Health

Figure 3.15: Health Facilities by Regions, 2000 and 2015

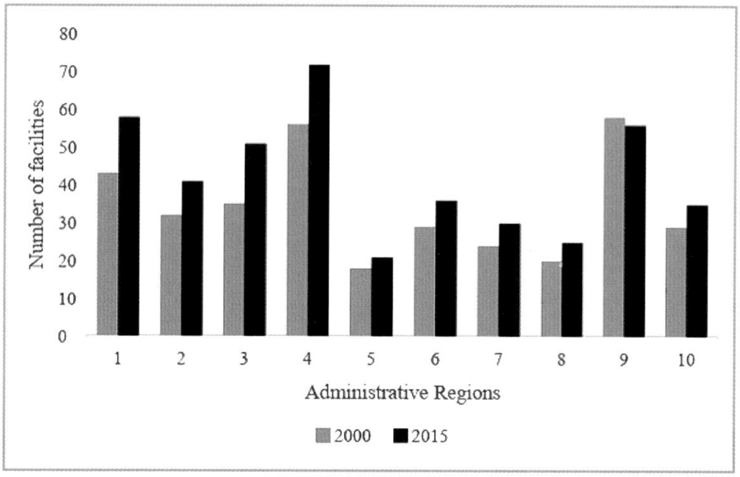

Source: Ministry of Health

capital in the public healthcare system by training nurses, doctors, and other specialists. During its twenty-three years in office, the PPP/C government trained and recruited medical doctors to increase the number of physicians and nurses in the public healthcare system. The number of physicians per 10,000 population and nurses per 10,000 population increased from 2 and 5.9 in 1992 to 13.3 and 30.5, respectively, in 2014 (see Figure 3.16).

Improvements were also noted in key health indicators, including immunisation coverage, life expectancy, infant mortality, and average daily per capita caloric and protein intake. Between 1992 and 2015, the life expectancy rate increased from 62.8 years in 1992 to 67.3 years in 2014, while the crude death rate per 1,000 and infant mortality rate per 1,000 decreased from 8.3 and 50.2 in 1992 to 7.8 and 31.2 in 2014 (see Figure 3.17). The per capita daily protein intake and daily per capita calorie intake also improved from 64.4 grams and 2,327 kilocalories in 1992 to 93.1 grams and 2,816 kilocalories, respectively, by 2014. It is worth noting that the per capita expenditure in the health sector in Regions 1, 4, 7, 8, 9, and 10 was consistently above the national average per capita health expenditure.

Apart from the government's investments in healthcare, Gafar (2005) argues that the GDP growth contributed to improved health outcomes. Specifically, Gafar (2005) found evidence that per capita GDP was strongly associated with improvement in children's healthcare, crude death rate, infant mortality rate, and average daily per capita caloric intake. Using annual data from 1992 to 2014 and OLS models similar to Gafar (2005), we found that a 1 per cent increase in *per capita* GDP is associated with a 35.43 per cent improvement in life expectancy, 12.27 per cent reduction in crude death rate, 5.43 per cent decrease in infant mortality, 11.83 per cent increase in daily per capita caloric intake and 6.65 per cent increase in per capita in protein intake (see Table 3.2).

Like the health sector, the education sector was neglected by the PNC government during the twenty-eight years they managed our country. Given the state of the education sector, the PPP/C Government increased the education budget in absolute and relative terms during the period 1992-2014. The budget allocated to the education sector increased progressively to $23.229 billion (or 12 per cent of GDP) in 2015, up from $1.7 billion (or 6 per cent of GDP) in 1992. The larger education budgets were aimed at achieving the strategic goals set out in the education plans formulated by the PPP/C Government (1995-2000, 2003-2007, and 2008-2013 plans). These included, increasing literacy and numeracy rates across all levels

Figure 3.16: Number of physicians and nurses per thousand population, 1992-2014

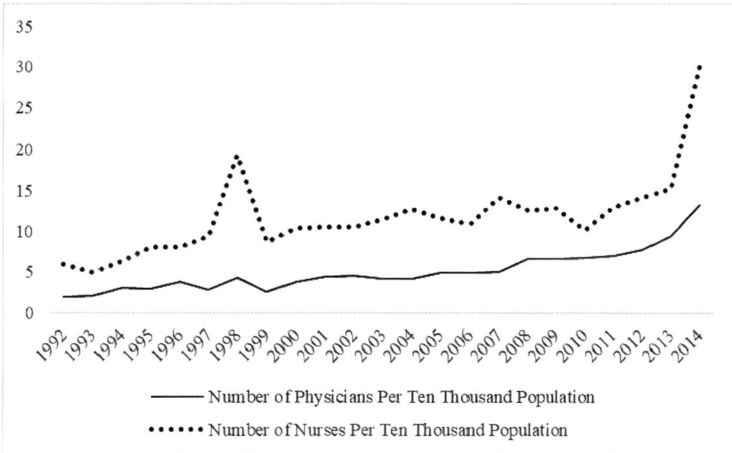

Source: Ministry of Health

Figure 3.17: Life expectancy (years), infant mortality (per 1,000), crude death rate (per 1,000) and daily per capita protein intake (grams)

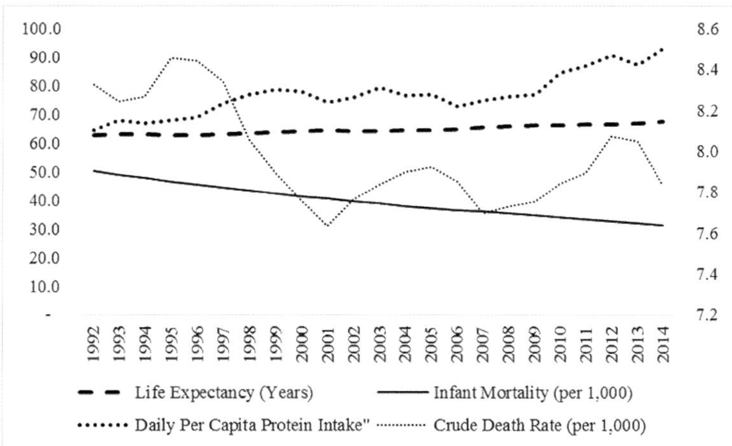

Source: World Bank and Our World Data

Table 3.2: Health Indicators and per Capita GDP (1992-2014)

Independence variables	Constant	Log GDP per capita	R^2
Life expectancy	-140.28 (-11.86)*	35.43 (12.48)*	0.88
Crude death rate	32.89 (2.96)*	-12.27 (-2.29)**	0.20
Infant mortality rate	27.29 (14.42)*	-5.43 (-10.51)*	0.84
Daily per capita caloric intake	-85.69 (-3.83)*	11.83 (4.16)*	0.45
Daily per capita protein intake	-21.44 (-3.96)*	6.65 (5.33)*	0.57

*Note: *, ** and *** denotes statistically significant at the 1%, 5% and 10% levels of significance respectively*

of education with emphasis on early childhood, primary and secondary school, reducing disparities in education outcomes by addressing the needs of vulnerable groups, including children in remote hinterland regions, those with disabilities and from low-income families, improving teacher training, recruitment and retention, expanding technical and vocational education and training to better prepare youths for the labour market, and introducing and promoting better monitoring and evaluation to ensure data-driven decision-making in the education sector.

In every administrative region, better-equipped and better-maintained educational facilities have been established as a result of the increased budgetary allocations to the education sector. The enhanced budgetary allocations also facilitated the construction of new technical institutes in Region 3 and 5 and the establishment of a campus of the University of Guyana at Tain, Berbice. Between 1992 and 2014, the government hired and trained more instructors. At every level and administrative zone, the trained teacher-to-student ratio improved as a result. Access to education, as reflected by the gross enrolment at the primary, secondary, and tertiary levels, has also improved since 1992. School enrolment at the primary level increased from 93.38 per cent in 1992 to 97.81 per cent by 2012. At the secondary level, school enrolment improved from 77.24 per cent in 1987 to 97.3 per cent by 2011. School enrolment at the tertiary level doubled, from 5.46 per cent in 1990 to 11.62 per cent by 2012. Initiatives to boost student attendance and performance were also introduced, such as (i) one laptop per family initiative, (ii) a school feeding programme, (iii) free textbooks, and (iv) school uniforms and the *Because We Care Cash Grant*.

Housing sector

The country was plagued with the scourge of squatting when the PPP/C took office because of the failed housing programmes of the PNC. According to the UN (1999), in 1995, an estimated 108,000 persons lived in squatter settlements. Unfortunately, most of these squatters' settlements were unfit for habitation, lacking basic amenities such as sanitary facilities, potable water, and any kind of infrastructure.

To address the housing problem, the PPP/C pursued a strategy to distribute land to eligible citizens, regularise squatter settlements, and facilitate access to finance for Low-income households. The government also encouraged community participation in sustainable settlement development. Between 1993 and 2015, the PPP/C government distributed over 115,000 house lots across the ten administrative regions (see Table 3.3). The largest share of house lots was distributed in Region 4 (32.6 per cent), followed by Region 3 (27.4 per cent) and Region 6 (9.7 per cent), with the most significant housing deficits (see Table 3.3). Additionally, more than 17,000 house lots were allocated through the regularisation of squatter settlements (see Table 3.3). These positive outcomes of the government's housing programme significantly improved the lives of countless households by laying the foundation for secure and stable housing conditions.

Low-income households were the most significant beneficiaries, as the PPP/C government's housing programme targeted these households. All of the house lots distributed were also highly subsidised. According to the Housing Policy and Implementation Strategy (2012), the subsidy represented 75 per cent of the market value of the house lots distributed to low-income beneficiaries. In this regard, the housing program of the PPP/C government not only enhanced the housing and living conditions of beneficiaries but also contributed to a significant wealth transfer to low and middle-income households.

To make housing affordable for every Guyanese, the PPP/C government amended the New Building Society Act and Income Tax Act to encourage

Table 3.3: Number of houselots distributed by Administrative Regions, 1993-2015

Period	1	2	3	4	5	6	7	8	9	10	SS	Total
1993	-	-	-	359	-	-	-	-	-	-	-	359
1994	-	73	-	1,055	-	48	-	-	-	-	-	1,176
1995	-	597	137	2,080	413	-	-	-	-	1,500	-	4,727
1996	-	227	1,203	2,064	-	-	-	-	-	1,000	-	4,494
1997	-	-	459	-	-	545	126	-	-	1,934	-	3,064
1998	-	269	2,585	3,340	384	1,106	-	-	-	50	-	7,734
1999	-	-	1,271	3,498	200	743	457	-	-	375	-	6,544
2000	96	1,067	8,562	7,953	608	3,588	265	57	111	92	-	22,399
2001	-	-	43	532	-	400	-	-	-	-	-	975
2002	14	343	359	1,507	474	-	-	-	-	116	1,382	4,195
2003	-	568	1,384	1,225	-	807	13	-	-	18	724	4,739
2004	-	208	505	1,551	-	557	59	-	26	314	1,783	5,003
2005	-	109	932	883	-	516	35	-	-	174	2,391	5,040
2006	-	9	708	1,394	128	69	-	-	-	812	1,294	4,414
2007	-	1	503	190	6	38	-	-	95	19	705	1,557
2008	-	1	1,812	282	13	136	10	-	178	6	521	2,959
2009	-	53	2,187	374	146	303	2	-	19	387	906	4,377
2010	-	385	2,677	885	32	686	2	16	18	6	1,675	6,382
2011	-	96	2,921	2,228	30	511	-	17	65	1,054	2,073	8,995
2012	-	-	705	2,256	347	412	264	5	1	142	1,737	5,869
2013	-	166	1,796	1,965	23	243	49	-	11	164	613	5,030
2014	-	1	605	1,282	44	470	3	-	120	32	889	3,446
2015	-	99	286	754	9	73	1	-	-	-	711	1,933
Total	**110**	**4272**	**31640**	**37657**	**2857**	**11251**	**1286**	**95**	**644**	**8195**	**17404**	**115411**

Source: Ministry of Housing, Central Housing and Planning Authority

financial institutions to offer loans at lower interest rates and longer repayment periods to low-income borrowers. These initiatives led to a decline in the interest rate for mortgages offered by the New Building Society, from 18 per cent in 1992 to 6.45 per cent by 2015 (see Table 3.4). Meanwhile, loans extended by the New Building Society (NBS) increased more than 158-fold, from 236.3 million in 1992 to 37,446.4 million by 2015 (see Table 3.4).

The various initiatives implemented by the PPP/C contributed significantly to the notable increase in the country's housing stock. The number of housing units expanded by 42 per cent, from 154,153 in 1991 to 219,509 by 2012 (see Table 3.5). This outturn may be attributed to the largest increase in housing stock, which occurred in Region 4 (22,745 units), followed by Region 3 (14,072 units), and Region 6 (6,017 units). Together, these regions accounted for 65.5 per cent of the increase in housing units between 1991 and 2012. In relative terms, the hinterland regions recorded the highest increases in housing stock: Region 1 (74 per cent), Region 7 (71 per cent), Region 8 (159 per cent), and Region 9 (128 per cent). Based on the 2012 Census, approximately 63.7 per cent of the housing units in the country were constructed between 1990 and 2012.

The number of households residing in their own dwellings increased by 44 per cent, from 97,414 in 1991 to 140,002 by 2012, while the number of households occupying private rentals decreased by 3,709 (or 12 per cent) during the corresponding period (see Table 3.6). Together, these statistics highlight the success of the PPP/C government in promoting home ownership over rental.

Access to water and sanitation also improved due to significant investment in water and sanitation by the PPP/C government. According to the census reports, access to improved sanitation increased from 31 per cent in 1991 to 63.5 per cent by 2012. The proportion of households with access to safe drinking water also increased from 50.1 per cent in 1990 to 74.2 per cent by 2012. Based on the PPP/C government's investments in the social sectors, extreme and moderate poverty have been reduced continuously since 1992. Extreme poverty, which stood at 28.7 per cent of the country's population, declined to 18.6 per cent by 2006, while moderate poverty was reduced from 43.2 per cent in 1992 to 36.1 per cent by 2006.

A comparison of the Multidimensional Poverty Index (MPI) for Guyana between 2009 and 2014 also underscores the country's progress in reducing poverty. Only 3.4 per cent of the population was multidimensionally poor in 2014,

Table 3.4: Interest Rate and Mortgage Portfolio by Non-Bank Institutions, 1992-2015

	New Building Society		Total	Trust Companies	Finance Companies	Insurance Companies	Pension Schemes
Period	Interest Rate (%)	($ Mn.)	($ Mn.)	($ Mn.)	($ Mn.)	($ Mn.)	($ Mn.)
1992	18.00	236.3	1,372.8	615.0	615.0	142.7	-
1993	16.00	744.5	1,539.2	740.3	740.3	58.6	-
1994	14.00	1,096.4	1,858.9	908.6	908.6	41.7	-
1995	14.00	1,861.4	2,348.1	1,150.7	1,150.7	46.7	-
1996	14.00	2,653.8	3,523.8	1,727.5	1,727.5	68.8	-
1997	12.00	3,602.6	4,739.7	2,298.5	2,298.5	142.7	-
1998	11.00	4,921.3	2,888.6	2,677.1	-	211.5	-
1999	11.00	6,088.8	3,134.1	2,907.1	1.3	225.7	-
2000	11.00	7,281.8	3,385.0	3,110.9	1.5	272.6	-
2001	8.00	8,305.7	3,630.9	3,309.7	3.1	308.1	10.0
2002	9.95	9,776.5	3,329.5	3,122.3	4.9	118.7	83.5
2003	9.95	10,868.8	3,475.6	2,825.8	7.5	592.3	50.0
2004	8.95	12,412.8	3,051.0	2,318.0	12.4	670.6	50.0
2005	8.95	13,896.6	1,985.8	1,449.2	299.9	210.3	26.4
2006	7.50	15,600.2	2,718.6	1,956.6	440.9	103.8	217.3
2007	7.50	16,991.6	5,642.2	1,380.3	2,446.0	1,736.9	79.0
2008	7.50	19,046.0	4,060.4	889.7	1,667.0	1,166.4	337.4
2009	8.45	20,965.0	3,205.0	913.6	1,683.1	255.9	352.3
2010	7.35	21,624.9	3,149.9	1,006.6	1,520.0	236.8	386.4
2011	6.85	23,571.6	3,238.6	1,223.4	1,297.1	206.1	512.0
2012	6.85	27,790.7	3,773.8	1,925.6	902.2	194.0	752.0
2013	6.45	32,976.6	2,313.9	2,012.8	300.2	200.3	750.2
2014	6.45	37,053.0	2,768.7	2,440.9	326.5	303.6	1,051.1
2015	6.45	37,446.4	2,926.5	2,553.0	372.8	312.3	375.2

Source: Statistical Abstract (various years)

Table 3.5: Housing Stock, 1991-2012

Region	1991	2012	Increase (1991-2012)	
	No.	No.	No.	%
1	3,271	5,701	2,430	74
2	9,199	14,248	5,049	55
3	21,416	35,488	14,072	66
4	63,765	86,510	22,745	36
5	11,255	15,869	4,614	41
6	29,770	35,787	6,017	20
7	3,250	5,548	2,298	71
8	921	2,382	1,461	159
9	2,703	6,171	3,468	128
10	8,603	11,805	3,202	37
Total	**154,153**	**219,509**	**65,356**	**42**

Source: Bureau of Statistics

Table 3.6: Owned Dwelling, 1991-2012

Region	1991	2012	Increase (1991-2012)	
	No.	No.	No.	%
1	2,627	4,003	1,376	52
2	7,037	10,205	3,168	45
3	14,691	22,019	7,328	50
4	33,604	55,153	21,549	64
5	8,407	10,775	2,368	28
6	21,107	21,997	890	4
7	1,752	3,367	1,615	92
8	788	1,922	1,134	144
9	2,427	4,352	1,925	79
10	4,973	6,940	1,967	40
Total	**97,414**	**140,733**	43,319	44

Source: Bureau of Statistics

compared with 5.4 per cent in 2009. The proportion of the population experiencing deprivation in the key indicators (health, education, and living standard) declined between 2009 and 2014 (see Table 3.7). This suggests that the investments in the social sectors by the PPP/C government yielded positive results.

Equally remarkable was the continuous improvement in Guyana's Human Development Index (HDI) from 0.538 in 1990 to 0.651 in 2015, representing a 21 per cent increase (see Table 3.8). This may be attributed partly to the increase in life expectancy at birth, expected years of schooling, mean year of schooling, and Gross National Income (GNI) per capita. Life expectancy at birth increased from 62.5 years in 1990 to 68.1 years by 2015 (see Table 3.8). During the same period, the expected years of schooling and mean years of schooling increased from 8.6 years and 5.3 years in 1990 to 12.6 years and 8.1 years, respectively, in 2015 (see Table 3.8). Additionally, the GNI per capita (2021 PPP$) increased by more than 553 per cent, from 1,766 in 1990 to 11,539 by 2015 (see Table 3.8).

The improvement in the HDI resonated throughout all corners of Guyana. Between 1990 and 2015, every region in Guyana, from the hinterland regions

Table 3.7: Multidimensional Poverty Indicators, 2009 and 2014

	Year of Survey	
Indicators	2009D	2014M
Nutrition	3.52	2.08
Child Mortality	0.72	0.60
Years of schooling	1.53	0.58
School attendance	1.25	1.10
Cooking fuel	3.12	2.20
Sanitation	2.61	2.00
Drinking water	2.28	1.60
Electricity	4.56	2.77
Housing	3.54	2.20
Assets	3.75	1.89

Source: UNDP Reports

Table 3.8: Guyana's HDI, 1990-2015

Period	HDI	Life expectancy at birth	Expected years of schooling	Mean years of schooling	GNI per capita (2021 $)
1990	0.491	62.5	8.6	5.3	1,766
1995	0.536	62.7	9.3	5.6	3,256
2000	0.567	64.1	10.2	6.0	3,947
2005	0.610	64.4	11.2	6.6	6,424
2010	0.647	66.2	11.4	7.3	9,032
2015	0.690	68.1	12.6	8.1	11,539

Source: UNDP Reports

Figure 3.18: HDI by Regions, 1990-2015

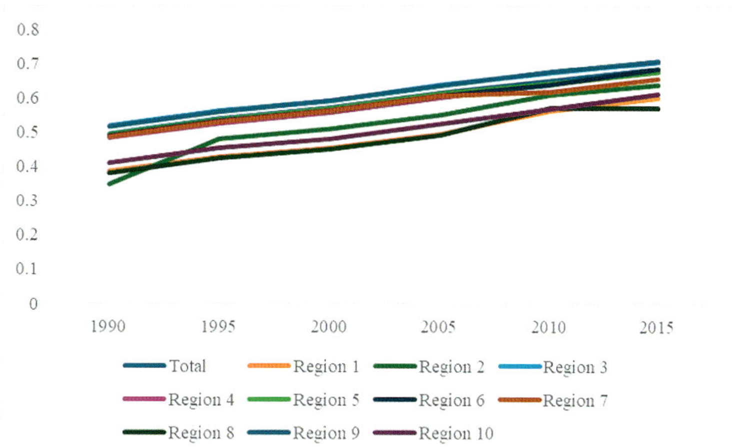

Source: Global Data Lab, GDL Area Profiles, 1990-2015

Table 3.9: Gini coefficient wealth inequality, 1990-2015

Period	Total	R1	R2	R3	R4	R5	R6	R7	R8	R9	R10
2006	0.20	0.25	0.33	0.14	0.17	0.18	0.17	0.24	0.39	0.18	0.39
2009	0.17	0.27	0.30	0.13	0.13	0.16	0.15	0.20	0.35	0.14	0.37
2014	0.13	0.16	0.24	0.09	0.12	0.10	0.13	0.16	0.33	0.12	0.26

Source: Global Data Lab, GDL Area Profiles, 1990-2015

(Regions 1, 7, 8, 9, and 10) to the coastal regions (2, 3, 4, 5, and 6), experienced notable improvements in HDI (see Figure 3.18). The widespread progress can be attributed to the investments made by the PPP/C in education, healthcare, and economic development, and reflects the government's commitment to balanced and inclusive development. Importantly, the gap in the HDI between the hinterland and coastal regions narrowed from 1990 to 2015, a key indicator that prosperity is being shared more evenly across Guyana.

The reduction in the Gini Index (GI), which measures inequality, also provides clear evidence that prosperity is being shared more equitably across Guyana. Table 3.9 shows that the overall Gini index trended downward for the entire country and every region between 1990 and 2014. Given the growth in GNI *per capita* and the reduction in the Gini coefficient, it means that the PPP/C government has not only been able to grow the economic pie but also ensure it is shared equitably, thereby improving the well-being of every citizen throughout the country.

Conclusion

Notwithstanding the state of the economy at the time the PPP/C was voted into office in 1992 and the PNC's relentless attempt to destabilise the government, the country made significant progress between 1992 and 2015. The PPP/C government implemented measures to establish and maintain well-functioning democratic structures. As a result, the country underwent a transformation from an authoritarian state to a strong democracy between 1992 and 2014.

The country registered positive economic growth every year since 1992, except for four years (1998, 2000, 2003, and 2005) due to political instability and other external shocks (IDB, 2008). Economic expansion may be attributed to sound macroeconomic management, improvements in governance, a favourable external environment (Grenade and Pasha, 2012), and a stable political environment. Indeed, Pasha (2024) demonstrated that violence and anti-government demonstrations orchestrated by the PNC to undermine the PPP/C government have consistently hindered the country's economic growth since the 1960s.

Coupled with the PPP/C's investment in the social sectors, the robust economic performance from 1992 to 2014 led to a notable reduction in poverty and an improvement in the well-being of citizens throughout Guyana, as reflected by a steady improvement in the HDI during this period due to enhanced longevity, education, and income across the country.

REFERENCES

Eugome-Bossogo, P. (2000). Money Demand in Guyana. IMF Working Paper No. 00/119, Available at SSRN: https://ssrn.com/abstract=879867.

Inter-American Development Bank (2008), "IDB Country Strategy with Guyana", http://www.iadb.org/?lang=en.

Gafar, J. (2005a). The Impact of Economic Reforms on Health Indicators in Guyana, Caribbean Studies, 33(1), 149-176.

Gafar, J. (2005b). Gafar, J. (2005). Do the poor benefit from public spending? A look at the evidence. *The Pakistan Development Review*, 81-104.

Greenidge, K. & DaCosta, D. (2009). Determinants of Inflation in Selected Caribbean Countries. *Business, Finance & Economics in Emerging Economies*, 4(2), 371-397.

Grenade, K. & Pasha, S. (2012). Accelerating Guyana's Growth Momentum. *Journal of Developing Country Studies*, 2(9), 1-11.

Government of Guyana (2000). Poverty Reduction Strategy Paper (PRSP).

Ishmael, O. (2012). From Autocracy to Democracy in Guyana.

Ministry of Finance (1993). Budget Speech 1993.

National Assembly. (1986). Budget Speech 1987, Towards Economic Balance and Reconstruction. https://www.parliament.gov.gy/documents/documents-laid/9467-budget_speech_1987.pdf

PAHO (2001). Health Systems and Services Profile of Guyana. https://www3.paho.org/hq/dmdocuments/2010/Health_System_Profile-Guyana_2001.pdf

Pasha, S. (2024). The Impact of Political Instability on Economic Growth: The Case of Guyana. In: DaSilva-Glasgow, D., Khemraj, T., Thomas, D. (eds) *Economic Challenges in Early 21st Century Guyana*. Palgrave Macmillan, Cham. https://doi.org/10.1007/978-3-031-75019-9_3

Stabroek News (2019, April 1). What President Carter Said about October 5th, 1992. https://www.stabroeknews.com/2019/04/01/opinion/letters/what-president-carter-said-about-october-5th-1992/

Staritz, R., Atoyan, R. & Gold, J. (2007), "Guyana: Why has Growth Stopped? An Empirical Study on the Stagnation of Economic Growth", IMF Working Paper 07/86, International Monetary Fund.

Human Development Report (1999). Chromeextension://efaidnbmnnnibpcajpcglclefindmkaj/https://hdr.undp.org/system/files/documents/hdr1999ennostats.pdf .UNDP.

Worrel, D. (2024). Development Performance and Economic Policy in Guyana, 1990–2021. In: DaSilva-Glasgow, D., Khemraj, T., Thomas, D. (eds) Economic Challenges in Early 21st Century Guyana. Palgrave Macmillan, Cham.

4

Two Decades of Political Manoeuvres to Destabilise the PPP/C

They have lived for these many years by putting on certain masks, by trying to fool the outside world - and even some Guyanese who live right here, with the mask of democratic government because they have a joke institution called a parliament [...] It is just a matter of time - they take when they want to take, they give when they want to give until the time when the people intervene. Unmask them and show them that power belongs to the people. DR WALTER RODNEY, People's Power, No Dictator, 1979

Following its electoral defeat in 1992, the PNC actively employed a combination of parliamentary and extra-parliamentary manoeuvres to destabilise the PPP/C government between 1992 and 2015. These tactics included violent street protests and politically inspired strikes in the late 90s. Some of the radical members of the party even went so far as to support prison escapees who wreaked havoc in the country openly. The PNC also collaborated with the AFC to prevent the PPP/C from passing important laws and its national budget. These manoeuvres harmed the economy and lacerated the country's social fabric.

This chapter discusses the campaign of the PNC to destabilise the PPP/C government since 1992. It also critically examines the economic management of the PNC in its new incarnation, the APNU-AFC coalition, during the period from 2015 to 2020. Through this examination, this chapter distils the implications of the PNC's strategy to divide and rule on the social and political stability as well as the economic and social progress of our country.

A new era of political instability

Dissatisfied with the outcome of the 1992 elections and unable to appeal to the electorate given its disastrous track record in government for twenty-eight years, the PNC launched a campaign to sow fear by alleging that the PPP/C government would engage in discriminatory practices and marginalise its supporters. This campaign gained momentum prior to the death of the late President Cheddi Jagan when he came under attack for his remarks about the treatment of blacks in the United States during a speech in Toronto on October 30, 1996.

The PNC propagandists promptly distorted the former President's remarks, levelling allegations of divisiveness and racism against him. Despite his best efforts to clarify his comments, the PNC propagandists spared no effort to brand President Jagan a racist and divisive leader. A few months later, the President died, and Prime Minister Samuel Hinds became the Head of State. Janet Jagan was sworn in as the Prime Minister and First Vice President on March 17, 1997 (OAS, 1998). She was subsequently nominated as the presidential candidate of the PPP/C on August 31, 1997, for the elections scheduled for December 15, 1997. Throughout the election campaign, her ethnicity and age were the focus of the PNC, led by Hugh Desmond Hoyte (OAS, 1998). Despite the racialised vitriol directed at her, she led the PPP/C to victory, with the party securing more than 55 per cent of the votes and winning 29 of the 53 seats.

Upset with another electoral defeat, the PNC demanded a recount of the votes, alleging that the elections were rigged by the PPP/C. The PNC also attempted to prevent Janet Jagan from being sworn in and started a campaign of '*kith and kin*' to sow division in the country. However, they failed, and on December 19, 1997, Janet Jagan was sworn in as President, making her the first democratically elected female President in South America. This triggered a wave of street protests by the PNC starting on December 19, 1997, that warranted the deployment of riot police officers to disperse the protestors and maintain law and order. The daily protests, the hurling of racial attacks against Janet Jagan, and the beating and burning of white dolls were a standard feature that continued into the new year. These demonstrations led to arson, looting of stores, and violent attacks on innocent citizens as the PNC created an atmosphere of unrest with their rhetoric of 'slow fire,' 'more fire,' and 'making the country ungovernable.'

The protest reached a boiling point on January 12, 1998, after the court refused to grant an injunction to prevent Janet Jagan from assuming the Office of the President. The so-called peaceful demonstration by the PNC in Georgetown turned into a riot where innocent Guyanese were beaten and robbed. To end the protests and restore order, CARICOM brokered a peace accord (known as the Herdmanston Accord) with the opposition leader, Hugh Desmond Hoyte, on January 17, 1998 (CARICOM 1998, July 2).

The Herdmanston Accord included provisions for an election audit, constitutional reform, and new elections following the presentation of the report on constitutional reform (CARICOM, 1998, July 2). While Janet Jagan adhered to the provisions of the Herdmanston Accord in good faith, Hugh Desmond Hoyte failed to reciprocate. In fact, he refused to attend the initial and subsequent sittings of the National Assembly and deliberately abstained from participating in the constitutional reform process that had been mutually agreed upon as part of the accord. As is customary, Janet Jagan, in her role as President, addressed the National Assembly at the ceremonial opening of the Seventh Parliament. A hostile crowd, visibly supporters of the PNC, was assembled outside the parliament buildings to disrupt the ceremony. The crowd heckled her during her presentation and hurled stones at the presidential escort as it exited parliament.

Notwithstanding the peace accord, the PNC filed an election petition to remove the PPP/C government from office. Meanwhile, the Guyana Public Service Union (GPSU) took to the streets on April 29, 1999, to demand a 40 per cent increase in salaries for 1999 and a 50 per cent increase for 2000. However, due to IMF conditionalities in place to enhance debt sustainability, the government could only offer a 3 per cent salary increase over ten years. As the government and GPSU could not agree on the salary increase, a 57-day strike ensued, bringing the economy to a standstill. The strike ended after both parties agreed to arbitration, and the public servants were awarded increases of 31.6 per cent and 26.6 per cent for 1999 and 2000, respectively (SN, 11/02/2010). Later that year, when the election audit confirmed that the results declared by the Chief Election Officer reflected the will of the people and that there was 'no electoral fraud'. Despite the audit's findings, unrest continued to destabilise the political environment. A resolution was eventually reached on July 2, 1998, when President Janet Jagan and Opposition Leader Hugh Desmond Hoyte signed the St Lucia Statement, under which the PNC agreed to take its seat in the National Assembly and bring an end to the protests (GC, June 6, 2020). In an interview with Ira Mathur, former President Janet Jagan stated (TG, 21/11/1998):

> The St Lucia accord brought us back from the brink of disaster. If we had not held back our supporters this country may have returned to the Sixties, when we had racial fighting and villages were bombed and burned.

She went on to explain that "… National Unity is a political goal we'll achieve if the racists just stay out of it. Guyanese people don't want violence. They live and work together." The PNC took its seat in the parliament on July 15, 1998, following the St Lucia Statement. The Constitutional Reform Commission, chaired by Ralph Ramkarran, was sworn in on January 22, 1999. A few months later, Janet Jagan fell ill and resigned from office on August 8, 1999, paving the way for Minister of Finance Bharrat Jagdeo to be sworn in as Head of State on August 11, 1999. The Constitutional Reform Commission submitted a series of proposals that were enacted in 2000 and 2001. These included the introduction of several Parliamentary Sectoral Committees and the Constitutional Commission, as well as amendments to limit the presidential term. Increased parliamentary oversight, promoting participatory governance, and fostering improved ethnic harmony were the primary objectives of these changes.

On January 16, 2001, Justice Claudette Singh declared the 1997 elections null and void because eligible voters were required to produce voter ID cards to participate in those elections. However, Justice Singh found that the so-called 'irregularities' claimed by the PNC did not affect the election results. Due to the court's decision, elections were scheduled before the constitutional date. These elections were held in March 2001, and the PPP/C emerged victorious, with Bharrat Jagdeo as the President. Once again, the PNC, which was renamed PNC-R, initiated another round of violent protests, disputing the results despite international observers declaring that the elections were free and fair. The demonstrations culminated in the attack on the Office of the President (OP) on July 3, 2002. Two protestors who invaded the OP were killed, and five were injured. The officer in charge of the Presidential Guards at OP was severely beaten and sustained head injuries while several staff members and work-study students were held at knifepoint in the compound (SN, 04/07/2002). Later that day, several business establishments situated between Camp and Wellington Streets were destroyed by fire amid the escalating unrest. As firefighters struggled to contain the blaze, there were simultaneous attempts to set fire to the Strand Cinema, situated near the affected commercial area. The wave of arson attacks continued throughout the week, culminating in the destruction of the Guyana Refrigerators Ltd. (GRL) building – an incident widely believed to have been the result of deliberate sabotage.

In an official statement, the former Chairman of the Caribbean Community (CARICOM) and Prime Minister of Barbados, Owen Arthur, fully endorsed the findings of the CARICOM Electoral Observer Mission, which concluded that the elections were conducted in a free and fair manner. He further emphasised that the Heads of Government collectively recognised the legitimacy of the elected administration and called upon all political actors to respect the will of the electorate and abide by the election results.

To quell the unrest, President Jagdeo, like his predecessor, engaged in dialogue with the opposition leader, Hugh Desmond Hoyte. However, the talks were abruptly disrupted in March 2002 when the PNC-R staged a walkout during the 2002 Budget Debate. The breakdown in dialogue led to renewed public tension and incidents of unrest across several communities. Although the impasse persisted for several months, by late August 2002, the country experienced a brief period of calm when the opposition returned to parliament. This easing of tensions paved the way for a renewed engagement, this time between President Jagdeo and the new Leader of the Opposition, Robert Corbin. Their dialogue marked a return to a more conciliatory political climate, offering cautious optimism for future bipartisan cooperation.

On February 23, 2002, the country entered a dark period marked by unprecedented violence and national insecurity when five high-profile criminals escaped from the Camp Street Prison. The jailbreak triggered a sustained wave of criminal activity that proved detrimental to the country. Although the escaped individuals were linked to the murder of 55 citizens (Pasha, 2024), elements within the opposition, most notably the PNC, were accused of portraying them as political dissidents or "freedom fighters," a characterisation that further inflamed public sentiment and deepened divisions. In the months that followed, parts of the village of Buxton became associated with the harbouring and support of the fugitives, widely referred to as the "Buxton Gang" or "Buxton Army." While some residents provided shelter and other forms of aid to the criminal elements, the vast majority of Buxton's population suffered deeply, becoming victims of the very violence unleashed by the gang operating in their midst. This period also saw a series of politically charged attacks, including attempts to disrupt the PPP Congress in Port Mourant and arson targeting gas stations at Eccles and Camp and New Market streets in Georgetown. The crime spree, coupled with the parliamentary boycott, created an atmosphere of instability and fear unparalleled in Guyana's modern history.

In 2006, the PPP/C and the PNC agreed to another phase of constitutional reform and subsequently held fresh elections. The PPP/C emerged victorious, and the elections were relatively peaceful. Under the visionary stewardship of President Bharrat Jagdeo, Guyana experienced a period of sustained economic growth between 2006 and 2011, despite the global financial and economic crises of 2007–2008 that adversely affected much of the developing world. Jagdeo eventually served his full term in office until 2011, when fresh elections were held. Former General Secretary of the PPP, Donald Ramotar, led the PPP/C, while a former army officer, Brigadier, led the PNC, albeit renamed A Partnership for National Unity (APNU). The PPP/C emerged with 32 seats, while the APNU and AFC won 26 seats and seven seats, respectively. The combined opposition, therefore, had one seat more than the PPP/C. Since the PPP/C won the plurality of the votes, Donald Ramotar was sworn in as president. The APNU&AFC, with a one-seat majority in the National Assembly, took control of the legislative branch of government. Soon after Donald Ramotar was declared president, he called the opposition to a meeting to determine the date for reconvening the 10th Parliament and to select the Speaker of the National Assembly. The combined opposition, however, was determined not to work constructively with the newly elected government. This was evident from the opposition's decision to select Raphael Trotman of the AFC as Speaker of the National Assembly without consulting the government (GC, 08/02/2012).

In the interest of the country's development and its people, President Ramotar continued to engage with the opposition on every important matter. However, armed with its one-seat majority in parliament, the combined opposition conspired to prevent the government from passing important legislation and cut the government's budgets. The amendment to the Anti-Money

Laundering and Countering the Financing of Terrorism (Amendment) (AML/CFT) Act, which was necessary to avoid sanctions by the Caribbean Financial Action Task Force and the Financial Action Task Force, was blocked by the combined opposition. Meanwhile, the APNU and AFC conspired to slash the 2012 Budget by $20.8 billion (SN, 27/04/2012). The opposition targeted the Amaila Falls Project, the Amerindian land titling project, the Amerindian Development Fund, small and micro enterprises, and the Cunha Canal (SN, 27/04/2012). However, Anil Nandlall, the Attorney General, moved to the courts and obtained an interim ruling from Acting Chief Justice Ian Chang that the budget cut was unconstitutional (SN, 08/04/2013). Despite the interim court ruling, the APNU and AFC proposed to cut the 2013 budget by $38 billion. This time, the combined opposition targeted the proposed budgetary allocations for the Cheddi Jagan International Airport, ICT development under the Office of the President, the Sport and Art Development Fund, the Board of Industrial Training, the ERC, and two government news agencies (DW, 17/04/2013). The following year, the combined opposition threatened even deeper cuts to the 2014 Budget (GC, 17/04/2014).

To destabilise the government, the APNU instigated a protest in Linden after agreeing with the government to gradually remove the electricity subsidy given to residents in the mining community (Sutherland, 2012, July 21). During the protest, the Mackenzie-Wismar Bridge was blocked, and several buildings and vehicles were destroyed. Four persons were killed when the police attempted to remove the protestors from the bridge. On October 11, 2012, there was another orchestrated protest at Agricola where many commuters who were traversing the East Bank Highway and the Georgetown Ferry Stelling were robbed, and vehicles were toppled and burnt (SN, 13/10/2012). According to former President Donald Ramotar (SN, 13/10/2010):

> The protestors, many of whom were criminals, robbed scores of people and many of them were attacked and beaten in that vicinity and at the Georgetown Ferry Stelling, where many people had to go to use the boats to get across the river,

Determined to disrupt the Government's business and divide our country, the AFC also threatened to move a no-confidence motion against the government.

In a letter to former President Ramotar, the AFC made its intention clear by stating (KN, 19/07/2014):

> Our Party sees no other alternative than to proceed with this constitutional mechanism for removal of an unpopular Government that has ceased to enjoy the confidence of the National Assembly and who by its actions has demonstrated an unlawful and contemptuous disregard for the Supreme Law of the Country

The leader of the APNU, David Granger, subsequently signalled his intention to support the AFC's no-confidence motion (SN, 05/11/2014). In response, former President Ramotar prorogued Parliament to facilitate dialogue with the Opposition (SN, 09/11/2015b). In a televised address to the nation, President Ramotar urged the combined opposition to return to the table and engage constructively on several critical matters that were pending before the National Assembly. He was concerned that proceeding with the no-confidence motion against his party would derail important legislative and developmental matters. Unfortunately, the president's calls fell on deaf ears, and he was forced to dissolve parliament and set the date for new elections. The term of the PPP/C government was again shortened by the machinations of the PNC and its new partner, the AFC. The leader of the AFC publicly expressed satisfaction following the announcement of the dissolution of Parliament, viewing it as a strategic victory (SN, 05/11/2014).

On May 11, 2015, the country held elections. For these elections, the PNC, the People's National Congress (PNC), and several minor political parties, including the Alliance for Change (AFC), coalesced to establish the APNU (A Party of National Unity). The elections were tainted by controversy due to allegations of electoral malpractice attributed to the APNU&AFC coalition. The PPP/C had sufficient evidence to show that the elections were rigged and requested a recount of some of the ballot boxes (Thomas, 2015, May 16). However, the Guyana Elections Commission refused to facilitate the request for the recount. David Granger was subsequently sworn in as president, while Moses Nagamootoo, leader of the AFC, was appointed prime minister. The PPP/C nonetheless took its seat in parliament and filed an election petition after receiving clearance from Acting Chief Justice Ian Chang to do so. The petition is yet to be heard by the High Court.

During the election campaign, the APNU-AFC coalition pledged to govern with transparency, accountability, and responsiveness. They assured the electorate that public resources would be allocated equitably, contract awards would reflect national development priorities, and state assets would not be misappropriated or diverted for private enrichment. In addressing the economic well-being of the populace, the APNU&AFC coalition government emphasised prioritising job creation and resolving challenges faced by rice farmers and sugar workers. However, none of this happened. Instead, the administration's tenure was marked by a visible lack of capacity to govern effectively, with widespread evidence of corruption and policy inconsistency that undermined public confidence and national progress.

By the end of 2019, the economy had experienced notable contractions in all the key sectors. The net international reserves declined from US$594 million in 2015 to US$575 million by 2019 (see Table 4.1). For contextualisation, the net international reserves stood at US$652 million in 2014, the year preceding the APNU&AFC's assumption of office, representing a nearly US$77 million or 11.8 per cent decrease compared to 2019. The decline observed under the APNU&AFC reflected the underperformance of traditional sectors, including rice and sugar.

Ironically, while foreign reserves decreased, the total debt surged. Specifically, between 2015 and 2019, the total debt increased by over $14.7

Table 4.1: Selected Indicators, 2014-2019

Indicators	2014	2015	2016	2017	2018	2019
Net International Reserve (US$ Millions)	652	594	596	584	528	575
Total Public and Publicly Guaranteed Debt (PPG) ($ Millions)	78,437	81,693	90,571	88,816	98,151	96,321
Current revenue as a share of GDP (%)	17	18	19	20	22	22
BoG Surplus ($ Millions)	5092	3513	3376	3751	3332	1881
Government Deposits at BoG ($ Millions)	21,417	- 2,339	- 21,307	- 26,417	- 55,183	70,688

Source: Various Budget Estimates

billion, representing an 18 per cent rise. Taxes also skyrocketed due to the imposition of over 200 new taxes. Revenue as a proportion of GDP increased from 18 per cent in 2015 to 22 per cent by 2019. This signified that citizens were remitting nearly 4 cents more on every dollar in supplementary taxes to the government by the end of 2019 compared to 2015. Even more alarming was the sudden and sharp expansion in the government's overdraft. Between 2015 and 2019, the Bank of Guyana's overdraft increased from $2.3 billion to $70.6 billion. It is as if the government were bent on eviscerating the public purse at any cost.

Broken promises and the collapse of productive sectors

Under the APNU&AFC government, the citizens of Guyana endured significant socioeconomic and political hardships. From victimisation to ethnic cleansing in the public sector, Guyanese of all walks of life felt the wrath of a government that was bent on corruption, cronyism, nepotism, and divisive politics. The state apparatus was also weaponised and selectively applied to target members and supporters of the PPP/C. These actions not only undermined institutional integrity but also set the stage for electoral manipulation, as the administration sought to entrench itself in power through undemocratic means.

It was clear from the beginning that the APNU&AFC government had little intention of honouring the promises outlined in its campaign manifesto. Among the commitments made for execution within the first 100 days of taking office were the establishment of a Constitutional Reform Committee, the liberalisation of the telecommunications and ICT sectors, the announcement of a date for long-overdue local government elections, the development and implementation of a comprehensive national crime prevention strategy, the operationalisation of a Public Procurement Commission, the adoption of a long-term sustainable development plan, and the enforcement of amendments to the Anti-Money Laundering and Countering the Financing of Terrorism (AML/CFT) Act.

Rather than establishing the Constitutional Reform Committee with the mandate to draft amendments and present them to the National Assembly within nine months, the APNU&AFC opted instead to set up a Steering Committee on Constitutional Reform. This committee was tasked with defining the scope and direction of the constitutional reform process. A report by the Steering Committee was submitted in April 2016, and the government subsequently announced that constitutional reform would commence within that same year. However, the commencement date for the reform process was deferred to 2017. In his November 2018 budget speech, the Minister of Finance reiterated his promise to establish the Commission. In his final budget speech, he announced that funds would be allocated. After serving its full term, the Constitutional Reform Commission did not materialise, even after the coalition government completed its full term in office.

The coalition government also failed to deliver on its commitment to liberalise the telecommunication and ICT sectors. Although the Telecommunication Act 2016 was tabled and passed by the APNU-AFC government, it was never enacted into law. As a result, these sectors remained non-liberalised throughout the entire tenure of the coalition government. Likewise, the commitment to develop and implement a comprehensive Public Security Plan within the first 100 days was never fulfilled. In fact, the plan was never presented to the people or laid in the National Assembly for public consumption. While the coalition eventually established the Public Procurement Commission, it did so only after more than 500 days in office, significantly exceeding the promised timeline. The long-term sustainable development plan promised within 100 days was also never completed; instead, a task force was established to address the issue.

These are but a few examples of the coalition's chronic inability to fulfil its manifesto promises, not only those it pledged to deliver within the initial 100 days. There are numerous examples of broken promises. Below is a brief review of the deviation by the coalition government from the fourteen points, which they clumsily referred to as the foundations for development. In practice, however, it became a catalogue of unfulfilled ambitions. What follows is a concise examination of these promises, juxtaposed against the coalition's actual performance – a review that confirms the disconnect between the coalition's rhetoric and reality.

BROKEN PROMISE 1: Make Guyana the Singapore of the Americas through development driven by the private sector, the state, and cooperatives. During its tenure, however, the coalition government viciously attacked all the productive sectors, resulting in a sharp contraction in output levels and key commodity exports.

On the campaign trail, a promise was also made to set up a Commission of Inquiry (COI) to "... investigate and remedy the problems plaguing GUYSUCO". In fact, the party vowed to keep all the estates open and pay sugar workers better. However, assuming office, these assurances were swiftly abandoned. The COI's recommendation to diversify GUYSUCO's operations was disregarded, leading to the dismantling of four estates (Wales, Skeldon, Enmore, and Rose Hall), which placed over 7,000 sugar workers on the breadline. These layoffs started during the Christmas season. Families and communities that depended on the sector were devastated. Thousands of families were plunged into poverty, with many parents struggling to keep their children in school. According to an ILO study, the livelihoods of the fired sugar workers were also severely harmed, leading to increased instances of suicide, alcohol consumption, and crime.

The decision to close the estates led to a decline in sugar production, from 216,186 metric tons in 2015 to 88,890 metric tons, a 59 per cent decrease by 2020. The export revenue from sugar also contracted by 72.6 per cent, from US$88 million in 2015 to US$24.1 million in 2020. The value of sugar cane produced (measured in real terms) declined from $13,303.9 million in 2014 to $5,468.9 million in 2020. Using 2014 as the base year, the cumulative decline between 2015 and 2020 amounted to $28.3 billion in real terms. Export revenue from sugar contracted continuously from $18.1 billion in 2014 to $5.6 billion by 2020.

The APNU-AFC administration also launched a direct assault on the rice industry through steep increases in Drainage and Irrigation (D&I) fees and land rental charges, by 220 per cent and 600 per cent, respectively. These increases translated into $1.4 billion in additional expenditure for farmers annually. Compounding the problem, the government neglected critical maintenance of the Drainage and Irrigation infrastructure. Like the sugar workers, rice farmers were misled into believing they would receive better paddy prices and have expanded access to international markets. When the rice farmers reminded the government of its promise, they were bluntly told that rice is a 'private business'.

The government's heavy-handed economic approach continued in the mining and forestry sectors, where punitive taxes and duties were levied on mining equipment. These measures led to higher costs of capitalising operations, thereby discouraging investment. From 2014 to 2020, log production declined by 37.2 per cent to 255,139 cubic meters. The export revenue from timber products also decreased by 48.1 per cent to reach US$27.7 million. Due to the collapse of the sector, direct and indirect employment dropped by 10,500. Revenue of the Guyana Forestry Commission (GFC) also declined by $250 million annually. By 2020, under the stewardship of the APNU-AFC government, the once-viable Guyana Forestry Commission (GFC) had been rendered financially insolvent – unable to meet its basic obligations, including the payment of staff salaries and utility bills. To further exacerbate the sector's decline, five concessions held by Baishanlin International Forest Development Inc. (BIFDI) were repossessed, while Barama Company Limited, one of the country's largest forestry operators, ceased its concession operations altogether. The latter came to Guyana in the 1990s, and after investing over $45 billion and operating for 25 years in Guyana, the company closed its operation because "it became unviable to operate in our country." During the APNU-AFC tenure, there was no new investment to compensate for the exit of these large investors from the sector.

In the bauxite industry, government mismanagement also led to the closure of RUSAL operations, resulting in a sharp decline of 61.9 per cent in bauxite production, from 1,563,563 tonnes in 2014 to 595,943 tonnes by 2020. The export revenue from bauxite declined by 41.2 per cent to reach US$73.3 million in 2020, from US$124.7 million in 2014. The workforce in the sector also declined by 50 per cent between 2015 and 2020.

BROKEN PROMISE 2: Confront serious crimes through innovative strategies and by engaging international partners such as the Federal Bureau of Investigation (FBI), Scotland Yard, and the Royal Canadian Mounted Police. It also pledged to increase the salaries of all law enforcement officers by 20 per cent in the first year. These commitments were never honoured by the coalition government. Instead, sixty prisoners were pardoned.

As part of their innovative strategies, rather than implementing comprehensive institutional reforms, as promised in their manifesto, such as the establishing a Ministry of Justice and National Security, fully executing the recommendations of the Disciplined Forces Commission, permitting the United States Drug Enforcement Administration (DEA) to set up operations in Guyana, creating the Drug Enforcement and Control Agency (DECA), founding a Law Enforcement Academy, and operationalising a Police Air Unit at the Ogle International Airport, among others, the government resorted to superficial measures including the procurement of horses and dogs.

Unable to control the crime spree, the government implemented a 2:00 A.M. curfew, which was met with public outrage. Apart from failing to control crime across the country, the APNU&AFC regime presided over the worst prison riots in our history. Under their watch, the Camp Street Prison was destroyed entirely on July 9, 2017, where seventeen prisoners lost their lives.

BROKEN PROMISE 3: Equal political, economic, and social opportunities for all. A promise was even made to reform the Ethnic Relations Commission (ERC) and issue Ethnic Impact Statements to the Cabinet whenever necessary. However, the complete opposite manifested under their watch. Citizens who were not considered supporters were openly discriminated against. Evidence of this is seen in the dismissal of the 2,000 CSOs and 7,000 Sugar workers. Even if there were doubts that the coalition government was practising discrimination, those doubts were dispelled after an infamous statement by the Public Health Minister and Chairperson, Volda Lawrence of the PNC, at a conference in Region Four held on November 25, 2018. At that meeting, she screamed (SN, 30/11/2018b):

> Well I got news for you: The only friends I got is PNC, so the only people I could give work to is PNC. And, right now, I looking for a doctor who can talk Spanish or Portuguese and ah want one that is PNC.

Another glaring example of the government's divisive politics was the accusation by Minister Keith Scott that Amerindians were *avaricious* simply because they requested security of tenure for the lands they occupied. When Minister Scott was confronted about his statement by the Indigenous leaders, he said (SN, 26/08/2017):

> I am not going to utter an apology for that. If I say something wrong by first virtue, I will say that I have done something wrong because I have done so before in Parliament... I did not insult you but I saw the political side of what you said and I also saw the comments you made about the commission of inquiry... I had pointed out that 14 per cent of Guyana was given to Amerindians, but all these years Blacks who have done so much for this country, from slavery to now, have gotten nothing... I am certain too that many of us didn't

> know that there were moves to get an additional 10 per cent of Guyana, I brought that out... We are not saying that we are taking away anyone land but you need to look at the entire speech and let us look the contents and then we can have discussions...

In his letter to the editor dated June 11, 2019, David Hinds called for a Commission of Inquiry (CoI) into the public service to expose the PPP moles (GC, 11/06/2019), providing yet another example of the divisive orientation of the APNU&AFC government. His request amounted to a call for the systematic exclusion of individuals from the public sector on the basis of their ethnic identity.

BROKEN PROMISE 4: Constitutional Reform to promote democracy and freedom of speech and reduce the powers of the president. As noted earlier, the government not only failed to deliver on its promise of constitutional reform but also flagrantly trampled upon the constitution during its tenure. Some of the infamous examples of constitutional breaches, as affirmed by the Judiciary, exemplified the coalition government's disregard for the rule of law and democratic norms. These included the instruction from former Minister Simona Broomes to the Public Service Commission to suspend all promotions. Equally troubling was the unlawful seizure of transported and titled core homes from citizens, as well as the revocation of leases for rice farmers in Region 5, which undermined property rights and due process. The administration also attempted to seize the Red House, a national heritage site, and persistently refused to constitute the Judicial Service Commission, thereby stalling key judicial appointments. Other actions in stark violation of the Constitution include the unilateral appointment of the Chairman of GECOM.

Additionally, Joseph Harmon (Minister of State) directed the Police Service Commission to halt the promotion of officers in the Guyana Police Force (GPF) – another unconstitutional interference in the functioning of an independent constitutional body. Perhaps most consequentially, the government's refusal to accept the No-Confidence Motion persisted even after its validity was upheld by the Caribbean Court of Justice (CCJ). This defiance was then followed by the blatant and internationally condemned attempt to rig the 2020 elections, marking one of the most serious assaults on Guyana's democratic framework in modern times.

However, these actions were nothing strange. The hardline indoctrination of the PNC has always been one that espouses undemocratic governance. This was exemplified by David Granger during his early tenure as president of Guyana. In an address to the North American Region of the PNC at its 5th Biennial Conference, a forum dedicated to analysing past strategies and planning future mechanisms for political retention, Granger emphatically reaffirmed his commitment to upholding the ideologies of the founding leader of the party, Forbes Burnham –a figure that is synonymous with authoritarian rule. At that meeting, he said (Chabrol 2017, November 5):

> Whatever you will choose to discuss today and the weeks and months to come, I think there are several questions that you have to ask yourself as you look to the future. You have to ask yourself 'how did the PNC gain office in 1964?' Ask yourself 'how did the PNC remain in office?' and 'what did it do during that period? Ask yourself 'how the PNC regained office in 2015?' and ask yourself 'how would the PNC retain office after 2020?

Given the overwhelming evidence that the PNC gained power with the support of the USA and remained in government for twenty-eight years by rigging elections, the answer to these rhetorical questions was obvious. The unilateral appointment of Justice James Patterson as Chairman of GECOM was not accidental but rather aimed at ensuring control over the Commission. This was certainly in keeping with the Burnham tradition. Similarly, the establishment of the Ministry of Citizenship to deal directly with the registration of births and deaths was intended to pad the voters' list – another Burnham-type gambit.

BROKEN PROMISE 5: Developed a youth policy that focuses on the active involvement of young people in the nation's decision-making process. The policy also promised increased access to educational and economic opportunities, including scholarships, vocational training, and targeted subsidies. Non-financial support was also part of the plan to facilitate youth participation in the arts, music, and cultural activities alongside initiatives to enhance health and nutritional awareness, particularly through the Regional Youth Conference. Plans were also afoot to offer sector-specific interventions, including the provision of special scholarships for youths in engineering, agro-technology, medicine, business, and information technology. Free lunch and transportation for children were part of the vision.

However, while the vision appeared ambitious and well-articulated, it ultimately remained aspirational. None of the key initiatives materialised in any substantive form. On the contrary, the government increased tuition fees at the University of Guyana, imposed a Value-Added Tax on educational services, and discontinued the "Because We Care" cash grant, which denied our children billions of dollars annually. The relegation of the Ministry of Youth Sports and Culture to a department within the Ministry of Education also reflected the minimal importance the coalition government assigned to our youth.

BROKEN PROMISE 6: Introduce policies that encourage the rebuilding of Guyana's family structure and enhance democracy to develop peaceful communities, eradicate poverty, and combat violence against women. Like other promises, however, the government did not fulfil any of the commitments. Instead, during their tenure, they implemented a barrage of policies that eroded the well-being of citizens, such as the introduction of 200 new taxes, the discontinuation of transfers to vulnerable groups, including electricity and water subsidies for older people, and the *Because We Care Cash Grant*. The dismissal of the sugar workers and CSOs also led to many being placed on the breadline.

Apart from their failure to introduce policies that enhance democracy, the government directly assaulted the very fabric of our democracy, which was meant to be strengthened, by disregarding the results of the 2018 No Confidence Motion, unilaterally appointing Justice Patterson as the Chairman of GECOM, and attempting to rig the elections blatantly.

BROKEN PROMISE 7: Create Free Trade Economic Zones in Linden, Bartica, Madhia, and Lethem, and immediately commence negotiations with the State and Federal Governments of Brazil to construct the Linden to Lethem Road and the Madhia to Bartica Road. Furthermore, they promised to ensure that the Indigenous culture, land rights, and the environment remain protected. However, the Free Trade Economic Zones in the three areas never materialised, nor did they build the Linden to Lethem and Madhia to Bartica roads. Instead of protecting the culture and land rights of the Indigenous people, the coalition government trampled upon them and stopped the land titling program. To add insult to injury, a sitting minister of the coalition government labelled the Indigenous people *avaricious* when they reminded the government of its promise to protect their land rights.

BROKEN PROMISE 8: Establish Diaspora Desk offices at Embassies and High Commissions in New York, Toronto, London, and the Caribbean. This promise was also never honoured.

BROKEN PROMISE 9: Raise social assistance and pensions, create more residential homes, and improve educational opportunities for citizens with special needs. However, while pensions and social assistance marginally increased, the government discontinued the water and electricity subsidies previously provided to pensioners by the PPP/C. Additionally, it did not follow through on its promises to establish more residential homes and enhance educational opportunities for citizens with special needs.

BROKEN PROMISES 10: Rebuild a skilled and highly educated workforce by implementing public policies aligned with the Millennium Development Goals (MDGs). A commitment was also made to meet the nutritional and transportation needs of primary and secondary school students as well as to reduce unemployment among young people. Despite the rhetorical ambition of these promises, none of them actually came to fruition. A limited number of buses, boats, and bicycles were procured and distributed to a handful of communities, many of which were strongholds of the APNU&AFC government.

BROKEN PROMISES 11: Professionalise the public service and support the development of the private sector and market systems. This, however, never materialised. Rather than instituting reforms targeting meritocracy, the administration compelled many contracted employees in the public sector to transition to the pensionable establishment, thereby reducing their emoluments by at least 22.5 per cent. At the same time, more than 3,000 persons were fired – which many believed was part of an ethnic cleansing undertaking – and replaced with thousands of contract workers, many of whom were hired at significantly higher salaries than their predecessors. This was made possible by the establishment of a Public Service Commission (PSC), over which the coalition government was able to exercise control. In October 2016, President Granger suspended the Chairman of the PSC and appointed Patrick Yarde in May 2017 to act as Chairman of the Commission. The appointment sparked widespread controversy among many, including trade unionist Jermain Hermanstyne, leader of the GPSU, who argued that it was inappropriate for Patrick Yarde to also serve as Chairman of PSC, given his roles and affiliations.

The dismissive and demoralising attitude of the coalition government was also meted out to Public Servants. For instance, when asked about the increase promised to them on the campaign trail, the government was quick to point out, conveniently, that compensation would be based on performance. President Granger, while receiving the Commission of Inquiry (COI) Report, remarked that lazy people will receive lazy pay. He went on to vent that (GT, 14/05/2016):

> Many people expect that there is going to be some bonanza. I hope they will discover that the bonanza will come from their own efforts. The bonanza will come when they work hard and do better than the next person. If they work hard they will be rewarded for their hard work. This is what people in every area of endeavour must learn, that actual output is related to input.

Meanwhile, Minister of Finance, Winston Jordan, publicly stated (SN, 21/03/2016):

> As an economist and the Minister of Finance, I can only say that I agree with the IMF on this particular front and from (the) time I came in, I have been advising caution as it relates to wage increases and meeting exaggerated demands for wage increases. Even in good times, paying exaggerated salaries have serious short and long term impacts.

Ironically, while the government made excuses about not having sufficient resources to grant public servants the increase promised to them on the campaign trail, it controversially awarded itself a 50 per cent salary increase for Ministers and Members of Parliament (MPs). In the end, public servants received a mere 5 per cent increase in wages, plus $5,000 per month. This was in addition to the removal of the one-month tax-free bonus from members of the Disciplined Services.

BROKEN PROMISE 12: Macroeconomic stability. The gross mismanagement and lack of fiscal prudence were evident at all levels of the government. For instance, there was a sharp decline in the Bank of Guyana reserves. According to the various statistical abstracts of the Bank of Guyana, the Gold Reserve fell from $25 billion in 2014 to $635 million in 2019. This represents a decline of nearly 97 per cent.

Additionally, according to the Bank of Guyana's Statistical Abstract, the government's overdraft in 2019 was $92 billion, representing a 430 per cent increase from the 2014 level. The central government's overall deficit also increased quite significantly. For instance, between 2015 and 2019, the central government deficit increased from $9.3 billion to $30 billion, representing a nearly 222 per cent increase. A similar pattern was also recorded by state agencies. Public enterprises, for instance, moved from having a surplus of $8 billion in 2015 to a deficit of $9.3 billion by the end of 2019. This represents an increase of almost $17 billion, or 216 per cent.

The key traditional sectors have also witnessed a sharp decline in output levels. For instance, in the sugar industry, total production contracted by almost $21.2 billion between 2014 and 2019, while forestry and bauxite production contracted by $31.3 billion and $9.5 billion, respectively (see Table 4.2). This represents 8 per cent of the 2019 GDP at 2012 prices. At the aggregate level, the decline in exports had surpassed US$283 million during the same period.

At the macroeconomic level, it was evident that the APNU&AFC administration failed to manage the economy effectively, resulting in a significant

Table 4.2 Production Level: Base Year 2014 ($ billions)

SECTOR	2015	2016	2017	2018	2019	TOTAL LOSS (Adjusted for Inflation)
Sugar	$ 1.00	$ (2.20)	$ (4.80)	$ (6.80)	$ (7.60)	$ (21.28)
Forestry	$ (2.40)	$ (7.40)	$ (6.40)	$ (6.40)	$ (7.40)	$ (31.30)
Bauxite	$ (2.50)	$ (2.30)	$ (2.30)	$ (1.70)	$ (0.30)	$ (9.49)
Total						**$ (61.5)**

Source: Budget Estimates (various years) and author's calculation

increase in the tax burden on citizens. The introduction of over 200 new tax measures has led to a staggering 66 per cent increase in tax revenue, from $136 billion in 2014 to $226 billion in 2019, with VAT alone increasing by 43 per cent. The effective tax rate increased from 15 per cent to 22 per cent, meaning people are now paying $0.22 in taxes for every dollar earned, compared to $0.15 in 2014. This resulted in a drastic decrease in private consumption, which fell by over $77 billion from 2014 to 2019.

The government's increased borrowing had damaged the prospects of the business community, as domestic credit to the central government rose from $28 billion in 2014 to $128 billion in 2019, while credit available to the private sector increased only slightly. This has led to a decline in credit available to critical industries, such as agriculture, manufacturing, and construction, with each sector experiencing a decrease in credit of billions of dollars. This decline has been reflected in the banking sector, with the return on equity for the six major commercial banks dropping from an average of 22.3 per cent in 2014 to a paltry 2.5 per cent by March 2020 (see Table 4.3). Additionally, non-performing loans (NPLs) increased by 91.9 per cent, from $5.5 billion at the end of December 2014 to $10.6 billion at the end of December 2019, with the housing sector being the most affected. In the business enterprises industry, NPL increased to $19.5 billion at the end of December 2019, up from $12.7 billion at the end of December 2014, representing a 52.9 per cent increase. The increase in default payments was linked to the persistent economic hardship that had gripped the nation since 2015.

Table 4.3 Profitability Ratios of Commercial Banks, March 2014 and March 2020

Commercial Banks		RBL	GBTI	BNS	DBL	CB	BoB
Return on Equity	2014	22.0%	19.9%	22.1%	33.8%	17.5%	18.6%
	March 2020	3.7%	1.8%	5.24%	2.4%	2%	0.74%
Non-Performing Loan/Gross Loan	2014	3.6%	14.5%	8.9%	1.5%	8.8%	0.45%
	March 2020	4.19%	32.3%	9.18%	3.7%	10.0%	28.7%

Source: Bank of Guyana

Compounding these shortcomings was a sharp increase in unemployment across several key sectors of the economy. In the forestry sector, for instance, an estimated 5,171 jobs were lost between 2014 and 2018, representing a 26 per cent reduction in employment, from approximately 24,848 to 19,640 – according to the 2014-2018 Forest Sector Information Annual Report. This was primarily attributed to the withdrawal of the two most prominent investors in the sector and the imposition of taxes on machinery and equipment, which impacted capital investment and operational sustainability.

In the sugar industry, the situation was equally dire. The closure of the four estates resulted in the dismissal of 7,000 workers, severely impacting communities that were heavily reliant on the industry for employment and income stability. In the hinterland regions, another 2,000 Community Service Officers (CSOs) were fired, affecting the livelihood of Indigenous communities. The situation was further compounded by the closure of RUSAL, which led to a dramatic downturn in the bauxite industry, resulting in the loss of almost 50 per cent of the sector's workforce.

BROKEN PROMISE 13: Safeguard the rights, culture, and well-being of Indigenous peoples. However, upon assuming office in 2015, the administration's actions were in stark contradiction to this commitment. Rather than advancing the protection and empowerment of Guyana's First Peoples, the land titling and demarcation process was considered flawed, which, ironically, was funded with proceeds from the PPP/C-initiated LCDS. This, of course, left Indigenous communities exposed to economic exploitation by external actors such as those engaged in logging and mining, affecting the overall well-being and livelihood of residents. According to the 2020 Freedom of the World Report, an internationally recognised publication:

> ... the land rights of indigenous communities are impaired by flawed consultation and demarcation procedures, as well as by unauthorized exploitation of titled indigenous lands." Concerning individuals enjoying equal opportunity and freedom from economic exploitation, the report indicated that "legal protections against exploitative working conditions are not enforced consistently. Those working in the informal sector and extractive industries in the country's interior are particularly vulnerable to abuses.

The blatant ostracisation and lack of empathy for Indigenous people by the APNU&AFC government further compounded these events. At the national level, the National Toshaos Council (NTC), an organisation representing the needs of all Amerindian villages, was allocated a mere $16 million in the 2018 budget, a direct attempt by the government to muzzle the organisation.

Neglected and broken infrastructure

Apart from destroying the productive sectors, the APNU&AFC government neglected the physical infrastructure and the electricity sector. During their five-year tenure, which ended in 2020, the government allocated more funds for refreshments, meals, local travel, subsidies, and personal security than it did to essential infrastructure maintenance, including roads, bridges, drainage, irrigation, and river defence combined. In fact, they had failed to complete a single transformative infrastructure project in office, even those inherited from the PPP/C. The CJIA project, which started under the PPP/C, was returned unfinished with a reduced scope and a higher price tag. Similarly, the East Coast Demerara Highway was returned to the PPP unfinished while abandoning the Ogle to Eccles by-pass road.

After five years in office, the only tangible outcome regarding the long-anticipated Linden-to-Lethem road was the completion of the design phase; no construction was initiated. In the case of the newly proposed Demerara River Bridge, the APNU&AFC managed to complete only a feasibility study, which was itself tainted by allegations of unlawful procurement practices. Meanwhile, the construction of a ferry to serve residents in Region 1 was stalled because the APNU&AFC insisted on awarding the contract to the highest bidder rather than the lowest, raising serious questions about the integrity of the procurement system and financial management in the public sector.

In the energy sector, the government's lacklustre performance also surfaced. Between 2015 and 2019, less than 14.2 megawatts of electricity were installed across the country. It was only after the December 2018 no-confidence motion that efforts were made to procure an additional 46.5 megawatts of generating capacity. However, this, too, never materialised due to a lack of finance. In the end, power outages continued to plague the nation. In retrospect, one of the most consequential decisions by the administration was the abandonment of the Amaila Falls Hydro Project, which would have added 165 MW of clean, renewable energy to the national grid. By abandoning this project, the coalition not only abandoned a long-term solution to energy security but also deprived citizens of access to a sustainable and affordable electricity supply.

Providing strong alternative leadership

Amidst the backdrop of the APNU&AFC's failed tenure in office, the PPP/C provided strong alternative leadership. Specifically, the PPP/C focused on uniting the people across ethnic and religious lines, building hope, winning trust, and dismantling the propaganda peddled by the government. The PPP/C used Parliament and every available avenue to champion the cause of citizens, especially the vulnerable, women, children, pensioners, the working class, and Amerindians. In 2017, the PPP/C submitted a motion to the National Assembly that called for the APNU-AFC government to implement various measures to stimulate the economy and alleviate the hardships experienced by citizens, especially the working class (NR, 10/10/2017). These included, among other things, the reversal of the onerous taxes imposed by the APNU&AFC government, increase in wages and salaries in the public service, restoration of the annual one-month tax-free bonus for all members of the Disciplined Services, restoration and increase in the *Because We Care Cash Grant* and school uniform vouchers, and among other measures, the reversal of the VAT on education goods and services. The motion, however, never gained traction or support from the government. On the ground, the increase in economic hardship fostered widespread resentment and social discord among the populace, reflecting growing frustration with the government's failure to alleviate the deteriorating living conditions. This was reflected in the results of the local government elections, where the PPP/C won 54,000 more votes compared to the APNU&AFC.

The government's disconnect from political reality was also evident in November 2018, when the former President and Leader of the PPP/C tabled a No-Confidence motion against the government. Prime Minister Moses Nagamootoo, in a press statement, confidently proclaimed that the motion had no reasonable prospect of success (SN, 24/11/2018a). He argued that for the motion to be successful, the opposition must have thirty-three members who are elected as members of the National Assembly.

On the night of December 21, 2018, when the motion was brought against the government, Chief Whip Amna Ally of the APNU-AFC government pompously taunted the opposition to "Bring it on! Bring it on!" However, when the motion went to a vote, and the APNU&AFC recognised that one of its members was prepared to support the No-Confidence motion, Raphael Trotman and Volda Lawrence asked for a 'time out.' However, Speaker of the National Assembly, Dr Barton Scotland, rejected the request and allowed the vote to continue (Kissoon, 2019, January 5). The voting process continued and culminated in the successful passage of the motion, with thirty-three members voting in favour and thirty-two against. Former AFC member Charrandas Persaud voted in favour of the Opposition-sponsored motion against the government.

Soon after, former Prime Minister Moses Nagamootoo, at an emergency press conference, declared that the outcome of the No-Confidence Motion would be respected, emphasising that the process had been "open and transparent". The following, President David Granger issued a statement that his government respected the motion and that he would "... do everything necessary to facilitate the smooth functioning of General and Regional Elections bearing in mind the need for normal governmental functions to continue uninterrupted" (SN, 13/10/2020).

However, in a dramatic turn of events, both Nagamootoo and Granger suddenly reneged on their earlier commitments to uphold the outcome of the No-Confidence Motion. Instead, they endorsed a new argument that an absolute majority – interpreted as thirty-four votes rather than thirty-three – is needed for it to be validly passed. A lengthy legal battle subsequently ensued, starting at the High Court, where the Chief Justice ruled that the motion was validly passed. Dissatisfied with the High Court's ruling, the APNU&AFC government appealed first to the Court of Appeal and then to the Caribbean Court of Justice (CCJ). On July 18, 2019, the CCJ delivered its definitive judgment that the No-Confidence motion was successfully passed. The Court upheld the principle that thirty-three votes constituted a majority in the 65-member National Assembly.

Between the passage of the No-Confidence motion and the holding of elections, the APNU-AFC continued to govern, completely ignoring the legal implications of the successful passage of the No-Confidence motion (Chabrol, 2018, December 22). In 2019, the government passed a budget of $300.7 billion, in clear violation of the constitution, and continued to spend billions more without the approval of the National Assembly in the following year.

Conclusion

Following its defeat at the polls in 1992, the PNC initiated a campaign to undermine the PPP/C government, which continued until it returned to office in 2015. In 1992, when it realised that it had lost the first free and fair elections, the PNC initiated violent protests in Georgetown. This campaign continued in 1997 when the party lost the elections once again. Unlike the 1992 protest, which lasted for a few days, these activities were sustained for several years until fresh elections were held in 2001.

The violence continued after these elections and gained momentum when a group of armed criminals terrorised the nation, creating an atmosphere of fear and insecurity. Instead of condemning the criminals, the PNC elevated them to the status of freedom fighters. To stir ethnic tensions and delegitimise the PPP/C government, the PNC accused the PPP/C of marginalising citizens and rigging elections since 1992. This campaign severely harmed the PPP/C's efforts to unify our people while in Government.

After a brief period of political stability from 2006 to 2011, the PNC, in its new incarnation under the banner of APNU, allied with the AFC, marking the beginning of a concerted effort to destabilise the PPP/C administration led by President Donald Ramotar. Using the one-seat majority the combined opposition slashed the government budget, refused to address important matters in the National Assembly and instigated violent protests. The combined opposition also moved a motion to shorten the PPP/C's term in office, thereby forcing President Ramotar to call early elections.

In the 2015 elections, the PNC joined forces with the AFC and successfully unseated the incumbent PPP/C government, though the results remained shrouded in controversy. However, rather than using the opportunity to uplift the nation, the PNC-led government immediately reverted to its old ways. With its new partner, the PNC-led government introduced over 200 taxes and fees, closed several sugar estates, raised land rental, and neglected the economic infrastructure that supports the agricultural sector. This, of course, led to the contraction of key traditional sectors, including sugar, which saw its output fall from 231,145 tonnes in 2015 to 88,890 tonnes by 2020, the lowest level since independence. The forestry industry also contracted, with output of sawn wood, roundwood, and total logs declining from 336,318 (cu. mt.) in 2015 to 255,139 (cu. mt.) by 2020 due to the downsizing of logging companies. Similarly, bauxite production also declined from 1,526,467 tonnes in 2015 to 608,168 tonnes by 2020, following the exit of a major producer in 2020. The poor performance of the key sectors contributed to slower economic growth between 2015 and 2019.

The PNC also trampled upon the Constitution and was in the process of establishing a machinery to rig elections to remain in office. The poor performance of the economy, coupled with numerous broken promises, scandals, and a total disregard for the rule of law, triggered a no-confidence motion by the PPP/C. Even though the motion was successfully passed on December 21, 2018, the PNC and its ally (AFC) refused to resign and hold elections within three months as required by the Constitution. Instead, the government held onto power, passed a budget in 2019 and exercised all the powers as an elected government rather than as a caretaker. It was only after the CCJ ruled that the No-Confidence motion was successfully passed that the PNC called elections in March 2020.

The PPP/C won those elections, but the APNU only conceded after a deluge of international pressure and threats of sanctions. Since returning to government in 2020, the economy has experienced robust growth and is now considered one of the fastest-growing economies in the world.

REFERENCES

Caribbean Community Secretariat (1998, July 2). *GUYANA: THE ST. LUCIA STATEMENT*. Caricom.org; CARICOM. https://caricom.org/guyana-the-st-lucia-statement/

Chabrol, D. (2017, November 5). *Gaining, retaining power "big questions" for PNCR - Granger*. https://demerarawaves.com/2017/11/05/gaining-retaining-power-big-questions-for-pncr-granger/

Chabrol, D. (2018, December 22). *PPP wins no confidence motion; AFC MP sides with opposition*. https://demerarawaves.com/2018/12/21/ppp-wins-no-confidence-motion-afc-mp-sides-with-opposition/

Guyana Chronicle (2012, February 8). *Government moving to fulfil campaign promises*. https://guyanachronicle.com/2012/02/08/government-moving-to-fulfil-campaign-promises/

Guyana Chronicle. (2019, June 11). *There is a distinction between whistleblowers and political spies and moles*. https://guyanachronicle.com/2019/06/11/there-is-a-distinction-between-whistleblowers-and-political-spies-and-moles/

Guyana Chronicle (2020, June 6). *A solution to the discontent* https://guyanachronicle.com/2020/06/06/a-solution-to-the-discontent/

Guyana Times (2016, May 14). Lazy public servants will get lazy person's salary – Granger. https://guyanatimesgy.com/lazy-public-servants-will-get-lazy-persons-salary-granger/

Kissoon, F. (2019, January 5). *Exactly 50 years ago, the government was illegal; it is now.* https://www.kaieteurnewsonline.com/2019/01/05/exactly-50-years-ago-the-government-was-illegal-it-is-now/

Pasha, S. (2024). The Impact of Political Instability on Economic Growth: The Case of Guyana. In: DaSilva-Glasgow, D., Khemraj, T., Thomas, D. (eds) *Economic Challenges in Early 21st Century Guyana.* Palgrave Macmillan, Cham. https://doi.org/10.1007/978-3-031-75019-9_3

Newsroom (2017, October 10). *PPP submits motion to reverse tax measures.* https://newsroom.gy/2017/10/10/ppp-submits-motion-to-reverse-tax-measures/

OAS (1998). *Electoral Observation in Guyana 1997.* https://www.oas.org/sap/publications/1997/moe/guyana/pbl_11_1997_eng.pdf

Stabroek News (2020, October 13). *Timeline of legal cases following the December 21, 2018 motion of no confidence.* https://www.stabroeknews.com/2020/10/13/news/guyana/timeline-of-legal-cases-following-the-december-21-2018-motion-of-no-confidence/

Stabroek News (2010, February 11). *Many 1999 strike issues still unresolved* https://www.stabroeknews.com/2010/02/11/news/guyana/many-1999-strike-issues-still-unresolved/

Stabroek News (2015, October 14). *Cabinet made giant blunder on 50% salary hike – Ram.* https://www.stabroeknews.com/2015/10/14/news/guyana/cabinet-made-giant-blunder-on-50-salary-hike-ram/

Stabroek News (2015, November 9). *Ramotar says doesn't regret proroguing Parliament.* https://www.stabroeknews.com/2015/11/09/news/guyana/ramotar-says-doesnt-regret-proroguing-parliament/

Stabroek News (2016, March 21). Same principle for Cabinet pay hike must apply to public servants -Lewis. https://www.stabroeknews.com/2016/03/21/news/guyana/principle-cabinet-pay-hike-must-apply-public-servants-lewis/

Stabroek News (2017, August 26). *Minister rejects toshaos' call for apology over "avarice" remark.* https://www.stabroeknews.com/2017/08/26/news/guyana/minister-rejects-toshaos-call-for-apology-over-avarice-remark/

Stabroek News (2018, November 24). *PM: No-confidence motion has no 'reasonable prospect' of success, will be debated in December.* https://www.stabroeknews.com/2018/11/23/news/guyana/pm-no-confidence-motion-has-no-reasonable-prospect-of-success-will-be-debated-in-december/

Stabroek News (2018, November 30). *"The only friends I got is PNC, so the only people I could give work to is PNC".* https://www.stabroeknews.com/2018/11/30/news/guyana/the-only-friends-i-got-is-pnc-so-the-only-people-i-could-give-work-to-is-pnc/

Stabroek News (2013, April 8). 35% of budget could be cut without affecting efficiency. https://www.stabroeknews.com/2013/04/08/news/guyana/35-of-budget-could-be-cut-without-affecting-efficiency/

Demerara Wave (2013, April 17). APNU proposes $33.7B in budget cuts. https://demerarawaves.com/2013/04/17/apnu-proposes-33-7b-in-budget-cuts/

Guyana Chronicle (2014, April 17). Gov't explores legal options over $37.4B budget cut. https://guyanachronicle.com/2014/04/17/govt-explores-legal-options-over-37-4b-budget-cut/

Kaieteur News (2014, July 7). AFC informs Govt of 'no confidence' motion. https://www.kaieteurnewsonline.com/2014/07/19/afc-informs-govt-of-no-confidence-motion/

Stabroek News (2014, November 5). Ramotar threatens early polls in face of no-confidence vote. https://www.stabroeknews.com/2014/11/05/news/guyana/ramotar-threatens-early-polls-face-confidence-vote/

Stabroek New (2014, November 5). Ramotar threatens early polls in face of no-confidence vote. https

Stabroek News (2012, April 27). Budget 2012 passed, Opposition slashes $20.8B, https://www.stabroeknews.com/2012/04/27/news/guyana/budget-2012-passed-0pposition-slashes-20-8b/

Stabroek News. (2002, July 4). *Presidential complex stormed*. https://www.stabroeknews.com/2002/07/03/news/guyana/presidential-complex-stormed/

Sutherland, G. (2012, July 21). *Terms for Linden probe to be set by Aug 2*. https://www.stabroeknews.com/2012/07/21/news/guyana/terms-for-linden-probe-to-be-set-by-aug-2/

Stabroek News (2012, October 13). Agricola unrest well-planned – President. https://www.stabroeknews.com/2012/10/13/news/guyana/agricola-unrest-well-planned-president/

The Guardian (1998, November 21). *Guyana's grande dame unsullied by political dirty tricks*. https://jagan.org/Janet%20Jagan/Images/JJ%20tribute%20-%20Ira%20Mathur%201997.pdf

Thomas, M. (2015, May 16). *Ramotar still not conceding polls*. https://www.stabroeknews.com/2015/05/16/news/guyana/ramotar-still-not-conceding-polls/

Stabroek News (2014, November 5). Ramotar threatens early polls in face of no-confidence vote. https://www.stabroeknews.com/2014/11/05/news/guyana/ramotar-threatens-early-polls-face-confidence-vote/

Stabroek News (2014, November 5). Ramotar threatens early polls in face of no-confidence vote. https://www.stabroeknews.com/2014/11/05/news/guyana/ramotar-threatens-early-polls-face-confidence-vote/

Stabroek News (2012, April 27). Budget 2012 passed, Opposition slashes $20.8B, https://www.stabroeknews.com/2012/04/27/news/guyana/budget-2012-passed-0pposition-slashes-20-8b/

5

A Test of Will: The NO-Confidence Motion and its Aftermath

The extensive electoral fraud was the result of a combination of padded voters' lists inside and outside Guyana, postal and proxy voting, and army seizure and tampering with ballot boxes. CHEDDI JAGAN, 1973

On December 21, 2018, in a momentous event in the National Assembly of Guyana, the People's Progressive Party/Civic (PPP/C) moved a no-confidence motion against the one-seat majority government of the A Partnership for National Unity/Alliance for Change (APNU-AFC) coalition.

The proceedings took an unexpected turn when Charrandas Persaud, a sitting member of parliament from the APNU&AFC, cast his vote in favour of the motion. What should have been a simple transition became one of the most significant tests of Guyana's democratic resilience. This development occurred almost two years before the government's constitutional term was set to expire, igniting a protracted political crisis.

The collapse of the APNU&AFC, a coalition of Indo-Guyanese and Afro-Guyanese politicians promising a new style of inclusive politics, was widely regarded as a surprise. Granger, the President, faced mounting challenges in controlling his fractious cabinet. His leadership was increasingly criticised as ineffectual due to his inability to develop the necessary regulatory and environmental framework to prepare Guyana for its first commercial oil production, which was shortly due. Of even greater concern was the lack of accountability and transparency that had ostensibly gripped the nation.

Under the APNU&AFC government, the country had witnessed some of the most outright and blatant skulduggery. For instance, the government initially lied to the nation, stating that it had never received any signing bonus from ExxonMobil following the signing of the contentious Production Sharing Agreement (PSA), a claim that eventually proved false when evidence was presented showing that US$18 million was paid out as a signing bonus. The

A section of D'urban Park

then Minister of Finance was aware of this transaction but continued to deny the accusation, even when questioned in the National Assembly. On a similar note, the government was unable to account for billions of dollars spent on the controversial $1.4 billion D'urban Park project due to missing financial records, a pattern that later became common and symbolic of the APNU-AFC government.

The no-confidence motion was led solely by Charrandas Persaud, a sitting member of parliament of the APNU&AFC government, in what was considered a "conscious vote" … "We are sitting in Parliament like 'yes-men' to APNU, and we are AFC ... And we have not blended with APNU" (GC, 24/12/2020). After Charrandas voted 'yes' and the government lost its majority, the eruption and threat that ensued in and out of Parliament led to Persaud being escorted through the back entrance of the Parliament building for security reasons. This marked the beginning of the end for the APNU&AFC government and the start of an arduous and uphill battle for the PPP/C. Ironically, the day after the no-confidence motion, the then President claimed that "the Government of Guyana will abide by the stipulations which have been imposed on it following the passing of the no-confidence motion last night in the National Assembly" (SN, 13/10/2020), a statement that turned out to be farfetched. In support of the President's claim, Moses Nagamootoo, the then Prime Minister, in his column "My Turn", a page in the state-run media dedicated to expressing his opinion on public matters, claimed that "[the] vote made history, as this is the first time that a government has to resign from office upon the approval of a no-confidence vote" (GC, 23/12/2018). In support of the outcome of the no-confidence motion and the democratic principles which he presumably proudly espouses, Mr Nagamootoo further posited that "...democracy could be a game of great uncertainty. However, the outcome must be accepted. It may come as a surprise to some, a shock to others; it may be welcomed by some, while others may rejoice over the results. But that is how democracy works" (GC, 23/12/2018). However, his claim would soon prove to be vacuous as the Granger-led government geared up to foil the no-confidence motion through a series of court battles and propaganda campaigns. In the words of Jason Calder, a representative of the Carter Center in Guyana, "the next several months will be a stress test for Guyana's democratic institutions and social cohesion" (NYT, 22/12/2018).

The first court battle occurred when a private citizen, Compton Herbert Reid, challenged the validity of Charrandas' appointment as a Member of Parliament on the grounds that he held Canadian citizenship at the time of his election – an alleged violation of Article 155 of the Constitution of Guyana, which prohibits dual citizens from serving in the National Assembly. Reid also requested that the court issue an order setting aside the Speaker's ruling on the no-confidence motion and to stay the enforcement of the motion (SN, 13/10/2020). In rendering her decision on the matter, Chief Justice Roxane George-Wiltshire dismissed the case, concluding that the vote was valid. This ruling was subsequently upheld by the Court of Appeal, which was a major setback to the Granger administration's attempt to reverse the no-confidence motion.

Not satisfied and steadfast in its attempt to frustrate the process, the APNU&AFC devised a new plan to delay the process further. This time, Attorney-at-Law Nigel Hughes came up with an argument that 34 of 65 votes in the National Assembly were needed for the successful passage of the no-confidence motion. His rationale was that the absolute majority of 65 is simply half of 65 plus 1. However, since half of 65 is 32.5, and there is no such thing as a 0.5 vote or individual, 32.5 must be rounded up to the nearest whole number. In this case, 33. Therefore, the absolute majority would be 33 plus 1, which is 34. The intention behind Mr Hughes' shameful claim was to persuade the court that the 33 votes gained by the PPP/C would be insufficient for the no-confidence motion to be validly passed.

The APNU&AFC took the matter to court based on Hughes' claim. In a historic ruling, Chief Justice Roxane George ruled that 33 is the majority required to carry a vote of no confidence in Parliament. The ruling was another setback for the APNU&AFC regime, which was desperately trying to invalidate the no-confidence motion. At the court hearing, the lawyers of the then government argued feverishly that the majority should be an absolute one plus the rounded-up 33 votes. The argument was widely criticised and even ridiculed by the Guyana Bar Association (DW, December 26, 2018). The Chief Justice also dismissed the request by the then Attorney General, Basil Williams, to preserve the *status quo ante* that the President and the Ministers shall remain in office pending the Court's final ruling on the validity of the No-Confidence Motion. The court's ruling paved the way for the holding of General and Regional Elections within 90 days, in accordance with Guyana's Constitution.

Not satisfied with the outcome of the ruling, the APNU&AFC appealed the decision at Guyana's Court of Appeal. In a surprising ruling, the court rejected the No-Confidence Motion on the grounds that the correct formula for determining the absolute majority was not applied. Of the three judges, Chancellor of the Judiciary (ag) Yonette Cummings-Edwards and appellate judge Dawn Gregory Barnes agreed that 34 votes were needed to guarantee the successful passage of the No-Confidence Motion, while the other judge, Rishi Persaud, dissented and supported the Chief Justice's ruling. In support of the ruling, the two learned judges conceded that what was required was an "absolute majority" and not a "simple majority." The former requires 34 votes, while the latter requires 33. Justice Persaud was the only judge who ruled against the argument that the "absolute majority" of the 65-member National Assembly is 34. He argued that the majority of 33 has always been used in the National Assembly without any complaint. Furthermore, the constitution of Guyana does not provide a mathematical formula for what constitutes a "majority." Therefore, in the absence of a prescribed formula in the constitution, the proposed notion of what constitutes a "majority," as argued by representatives of the government, not only has no application in the law but is illogical and nonsensical.

The ruling was another setback for the PPP/C, which had been mounting pressure for new General and Regional Elections within a three-month deadline, as stipulated in Guyana's constitution. Though distraught, the PPP/C respected the court's ruling and signalled its intention to appeal the matter through Guyana's final appellate court, the Caribbean Court of Justice (CCJ). Though momentarily, the APNU&AFC had managed to disentangle itself through conspiratorial means and delayed tactics from the clutches of the No-Confidence Motion. However, their reign was short-lived.

Almost three months after the Appeal Court's ruling, the Caribbean Court of Justice (CCJ) ruled on June 18, 2019, that the December 21, 2018, No-Confidence Motion was validly passed. In addition, the court affirmed that sitting MPs of the government can vote against their party lists, a ruling that went against the government's predisposition. The court also dismissed the arguments advanced in support of dual citizenship and the claim that an absolute majority of 34 votes was required to pass the No-Confidence Motion.

Following the CCJ's ruling on the No-Confidence Motion was the case involving the appointment of the Chairman of the Guyana General and Regional Elections Commission (GECOM). The case was first presented to the High Court of Guyana almost a year prior by the PPP/C Executive Secretary, Zulfikar Mustapha. According to the Constitution of Guyana, the president is bound to consult with the leader of the Opposition regarding the appointment of the Chairman of GECOM, the head of the country's election body. However, this was partially the case. The Leader of the PPP/C Opposition, Bharrat Jagdeo, submitted three lists to the president, all of which were rejected. In response, the President proceeded to unilaterally appoint the retired Justice James Patterson as Chairman of GECOM. In her court ruling, the Chief Justice contended that the president could reject the entire list submitted by the Leader of the Opposition and proceed to appoint the Chairman. The PPP viewed the ruling as a setback and argued that it was in violation of the spirit of the constitution, as it sought to "legitimize a unilateral appointment of a GECOM Chairman" (NR, 08/06/2018*)*. The matter was then presented to Guyana's Court of Appeal, where the decision was upheld once again. In a final bid to overturn the ruling, the matter was then brought before the Caribbean Court of Justice (CCJ). In its ruling, the CCJ states that the process was flawed due to the unilateralism and arbitrariness that characterised the appointment of Justice Patterson, as opposed to following an inclusive and consensual approach. The court further ruled that "the President and the Leader of the Opposition should, as soon as possible, embark upon and conclude the process of appointing a new GECOM Chairman" (SN, 13/10/2020). Having learnt of the judgement by the CCJ, Justice Patterson voluntarily resigned. The CCJ then advised the government that it should continue as caretaker for the country's affairs. However, it should not exercise legal authority, something the Government eventually failed to comply with.

Delayed Tactics: The House-To-House Registration and Voters List Manipulation

Not satisfied with the outcome of the CCJ's ruling, the Granger government resorted to a new strategy to delay the elections. This involved getting GECOM, a supposedly politically independent agency, to conduct House-to-House registration, which would further push the constitutionally required three-month timeline of holding General and Regional Elections to December of 2019, almost one year after the no-confidence motion was successfully passed. This would allow the Granger administration to create an APNU&AFC-friendly voters list illegally, thereby cementing the party's victory at the polls. Winston Felix, the Minister of Citizenship and a former commissioner of the Guyana Police Force, was also strategically appointed by the Granger administration to oversee the issuance of birth certificates, a key document that could be used to help add non-Guyanese voters to the electoral roll. The process was frustrated further when Deputy Chief General and Regional Elections Officer Roxanne Meyers posited that GECOM would need at least nine (9) months to conclude the House-to-House registration process (KN, 9/02/2019).

With time not on their side, the Granger administration used whatever means possible to forge ahead with the House-to-House registration process. At this point, GECOM was a mere puppet to the government, with its Head strictly complying with each request from the government.

Standing firm against this devious move by the Granger administration, supporters of the PPP/C staged a country-wide peaceful protest against the House-to-House registration process and called for action from GECOM to hold General and Regional Elections in September of 2019, three months after the final ruling of the CCJ that upheld the no-confidence motion. Across the country, many PPP/C supporters gathered at GECOM's offices, expressing strong dissatisfaction with the registration process and vowing not to participate. However, the decision to boycott the registration would have resulted in a voter list being produced that favours Granger's government.

A small gathering of protesters outside the GECOM office in Georgetown, led by James Anthony-Bond, a member of the APNU, called on the agency to move ahead with the registration process to 'sanitize' the voters list. Supporters of the AFC also joined the 'support protest' calling for the registration exercise to conclude before the General and Regional Elections (NR, 22/06/2019). In August 2019, the legality of the House-to-House registration exercise was challenged in the High Court. Acting Chief Justice Roxane George-Wiltshire, in her ruling, posited that the House-to-House registration exercise is not unconstitutional. However, the onus is on GECOM to ensure that the registration process is in keeping with the law. Furthermore, it would be unconstitutional to remove names from the list if persons were not deceased (SN, 14/08/2019).

The decision to proceed, however, was subsequently aborted on August 31, 2019, by the new incoming GECOM Commissioner, Retired Justice Claudette Singh, following the High Court's ruling that alternative methods of verification could be used to create a new list of electors (NS, 26/11/2019). However, by this time, the House-to-House registration process had registered 370,000 people (GC, 03/09/2019). The data garnered from the exercise was then merged with the existing National Register of Registrants Database (NRRDB) (GC, 27/08/2019). However, many from the PPP/C caucus criticised the approach on the grounds that merging the data would contaminate the database.

While concerns were mounting, other delayed tactics were slowly taking hold. This time, by members of the commission representing the APNU&AFC government. These commissioners alleged, without substantiated evidence, that non-nationals were in possession of IDs without the relevant source documents. Therefore, new national identification cards (IDs) should be printed. These claims were reportedly based on unverified reports suggesting that the fake documents were provided by Region Nine's Freedom House. It was clear that these tactics were clearly designed to frustrate the election process.

To filter out duplicates among the 370,000 registrants, the data was sent overseas to Gemalto, an international digital security company, for cross-matching with the National Register of Registrants Database (NRRDB). The company found that some 37,300 of the registrants were new registrants, meaning they were above the age of 18. However, GECOM did its own assessment and found that of the new registrants, 17,000 were already on the voter's list. The process was vehemently criticised by the Opposition because it had not been verified by all political stakeholders. To have the remaining 20,000 added to the voters' list, the Government-nominated Commissioners suggested conducting a sample survey of 10 per cent of the 20,000, which would be used to determine the validity of the remaining number of registrants. The exercise was viewed as retrograde by the PPP/C Opposition, as it impinged on the integrity of the Official List of Electors (OLE), and by extension, the upcoming General and Regional Elections scheduled for March 2020 (IN, 14/12/2019). Under pressure from the PPP/C-elected Commissioners, GECOM then decided to embark on a field exercise to verify the 20,000 names, as 4,000 were found to be duplicates, while the remaining 16,000 couldn't be accounted for (GT, 20/12/2019). GECOM subsequently published the list of registrants, even though it had yet to decide on the purpose of the data generated from the controversial House-to-House registration exercise. The PPP/C called for its immediate withdrawal, as they greatly suspected the APNU&AFC's intent to rig the upcoming General and Regional Elections.

The Revised List of Electors (RLE) that was subsequently published attracted even more criticism. For instance, GECOM contended that some of the information gathered during the House-to-House registration was inconsistent with information from its database, as the addresses and other details of some individuals had been updated. The PPP/C contended that this data was never subject to the legal requirement of a *Claim and Objections* process, thereby rendering its inclusion illegal. In another statement, the PPP labelled the changes as 'tampering', [and] "unlawful" and argued that it is "intended to cause chaos and confusion on General and Regional Elections day by facilitating duplicate voting, permitting unqualified persons to vote and preventing qualified persons from voting ..." "[I]f a person's name or address is changed on the NRR, it is that change that will appear in the Official List of Electors (OLE), which in turn will require the voter to vote at a different location from where he/she is residing or being prevented from voting altogether." (SN, 09/01/2020).

The Attorney General, Basil Williams, who was another agent determined to manipulate the electoral process, moved to the Court of Appeal to reverse the decision of the Chief Justice, who had initially ruled against the arbitral removal of persons from the list of registrants, particularly those residing overseas. The Court, however, upheld the ruling by the Chief Justice that residency is not a requirement for voting in Guyana, arguing that every citizen has an inherent right to vote, which cannot be taken away except by means of disqualifications, as set out in the Constitution. The ruling was seen as a safeguard against the potential disenfranchisement of eligible voters.

As the legal labyrinth gained momentum, it became evident that it was being used to frustrate the process. The APNU&AFC government seized the opportunity to indulge in massive spending. At this point, it was clear that the APNU&AFC government had deliberately and knowingly led the entire country down a rabbit hole to satisfy its agenda of remaining in office, irrespective of the cost. It also became apparent that the Granger government was about to execute an almost-perfectly rigged election plan had it not been for the No-Confidence Motion. During this period, the style of governance underwent a drastic shift for the worse. Institutions collapsed due to the repeated violations of the constitution, public financial management deteriorated, and there was a direct attack on the public treasury. State assets were also disposed of, often in a clandestine manner, to friends and families without adherence to the necessary regulatory framework. Contracts were also awarded unlawfully to the APNU&AFC party comrades and supporters. Overall, litigation expenses alone cost taxpayers over $100 million.

To ensure little or no parliamentary oversight or scrutiny, the sittings of the National Assembly were effectively suspended. Throughout 2019, the legislature convened on no more than three occasions. Notably, by May 2019, the government sought supplementary financing from the National Assembly totalling $7.9 billion. For the remainder of the year, their behaviours continued unabated. In 2020, the situation became worse. Though parliament was dissolved in December 2019, the Minister of Finance continued to authorise spending, including new capital projects. Even after the March 2 elections, the abuse of power continued for another five months. Since the passage of the no-confidence motion up until August 2, 2020, when the PPP/C took office, almost $419 billion was expended.

While the Constitution permits a caretaker government to incur expenditure for the provision of essential public services, the APNU&AFC abused this prerogative and engaged in discretionary and non-essential spending, thereby violating the law. Sections 36 (2) and (3) of the Fiscal Management and Accountability Act state that:

> Drawing rights issued pursuant to subsection (1) shall, for each month in respect of each budget agency, be subject to a drawing limit of one-twelfth of the amount that was expended by that budget

> agency in the immediately preceding fiscal year; provided, however, that provision for a payment obligation under a multi-year contract referred to in subsection 55 (1) may be included in a drawing right:' "The Minister shall not issue a drawing right pursuant to subsection (1) in relation to a subject matter or for a purpose for which there was no appropriation in the immediately preceding fiscal year.

Notwithstanding, in June 2020, a contract valued at US$10.4 million, funded by the Islamic Development Bank, was executed. Additionally, another US$10.8 billion was withdrawn from the Consolidated Fund for Guyana Power and Light. During the same period, BK International, a known supporter of the Granger government, was awarded a $826.8 million contract for the construction of a school on the Soesdyke-Linden Highway. Furthermore, an additional $1.6 billion was allocated for civil work to upgrade the Infectious Disease Hospital, located at the privately owned Ocean View Hotel, for which the state reportedly paid a monthly rental fee of $13 million.

The APNU&AFC government also sought other means to access and withdraw funds through planned rollover projects. For instance, $20.1 billion in contracts were rolled over into 2020. However, on December 31, 2019, the bulk of the committed expenditure was signed by the government, knowing that the funds would automatically roll over into the following year. Not only was this an abuse of the financial laws and the constitution, but doing so without going through conventional parliamentary debate and consultation allowed for little or no assurance that the funds would be used to benefit the people of Guyana.

The Granger administration also took advantage of the lack of parliamentary oversight and the government-orchestrated chaos that ensued following the passage of the no-confidence motion. For instance, on January 3, 2019, the government illegally rushed through the passage of the Natural Resource Fund Bill in the absence of the PPP/C. This critical piece of legislation was intended to establish a robust institutional and management framework for Guyana's oil revenues, allowing for greater transparency and accountability. However, this was not the case. At the core of the concern was the unrestricted power vested in the Minister of Finance, coupled with the use of a complex formula to guide the withdrawal of funds, one that stood in stark contrast to established principles of sound resource management and governance. The deliberately opaque and overly complex formula was part of an orchestrated and nefarious scheme introduced by the government to obscure public understanding and serve as a tool for subjectively withdrawing funds through manipulative and unaccountable practices.

Ballots and Turmoil: The Fight for Guyana's Future

On March 2, 2020, the people of Guyana went to the polls to cast their votes in the General and Regional Elections – a pivotal moment in the nation's democratic trajectory. The elections were seen as a crucial test of the resilience of Guyana's electoral system and democratic institutions. The discovery of oil in recent years also elevated the stakes, creating a unique opportunity for the incoming government to uplift and transform the country.

Guyana's electoral system is based on proportional representation, where seats in the National Assembly and the Regional Democratic Councils (RDCs) are distributed using the largest remainder method, known as the "Hare quota" method. As a result, there is a ballot for the national election and one for the RDCs. Of the 65 members of parliament in the National Assembly, 40 are elected from a national "top-up" list, while the remaining members are elected from district lists representing the country's 10 administrative regions. Before participating in the General and Regional Elections, each party must submit a national "top-up" list and at least six geographical lists. The president is elected during the general election.

As has been customary since the restoration of democratic elections in 1992, several international observers were present to monitor the electoral process and safeguard the integrity of the vote. Among them was the Carter Center, which deployed more than 40 observers who conducted 220 observations across the ten administrative regions of Guyana (Carter Center, 2020). On election day, the voting procedures observed across the polling stations were deemed satisfactory. Law enforcement personnel were present at the various polling stations and performed their duties professionally and impartially. Overall, the voter identification process was deemed credible, and the polling staff provided clear instructions to voters.

The people of Guyana received praise from the British High Commissioner and the Ambassador of the United States for a successful and peaceful election day. The two high-ranking diplomats also commended the GECOM Officials, the Guyana Police Force, and representatives of all political parties for maintaining an orderly process. They also called on GECOM to conclude the tabulation process swiftly. Two days later, GECOM began releasing preliminary results. However, on the third day after the elections, the country was stuck in a political deadlock as the two main parties, the APNU&AFC and the PPP/C, declared victory at the polls (BBC, 05/03/2020). President Granger claimed a narrow victory against Dr Irfaan Ali of the Opposition PPP/C party.

While tension mounts, credible allegations have surfaced suggesting that the tabulation process might have been compromised, and plans are afoot to rig the elections in favour of the incumbent APNU&AFC government. In response, the US and other countries expressed grave concern over the integrity of the tabulation process, leading to a strong condemnation from the US Bureau of Western Hemisphere Affairs, which declared that no candidate should declare victory or be sworn in "while serious questions remain" (BBC, 06/03/2020). In a joint statement by the US, British, Canadian, and EU officials, calls were made on Granger to "avoid a transition of government which we believe would be unconstitutional as it would be based on a vote tabulation process that lacked credibility and transparency" (BBC, 06/03/2020). This unequivocal declaration confirms the strong international support for the preservation of democracy and serves as a sober reminder to those complacent in undermining democratic norms that democracy is alive and well.

In a swift move, the PPP/C secured a High Court injunction restraining officials of GECOM from declaring the 2020 General and Regional Elections results without first going through the prescribed process as per the constitution (KN, 06/03/2020). In a consequential ruling, Acting Chief Justice Roxane George-Wiltshire found that the Returning Officer for Region 4, Clairmont Mingo, failed to comply with the constitution in the purported declaration of results for Region 4, and therefore, the results are null, void, and vacated. The Acting Chief Justice further ruled that GECOM cannot declare any results until the declaration process complies with the law.

GECOM nonetheless released unverified results for Region 4, which purported that the APNU&AFC had won the most votes in clear violation of the court injunction. The declaration drew criticisms from international observers and key members of the diplomatic corps, who argued that the process was unconstitutional and lacked transparency. The country's private sector organisations also expressed grave concern, accusing the Granger-led administration of condoning electoral fraud.

Across the country, chaos ensued, sending Guyana deeper into the abyss of a political crisis. Supporters of the main Opposition party blocked roads, burned tyres, and clashed with the police in the countryside of Guyana as they vehemently rejected attempts by the Granger administration to steal the elections. In Georgetown, the government stronghold area, many businesses remained shut, and the streets were desolate. The unrest that ensued engendered one of the worst waves of ethnic violence the country has seen in more than a decade. The electoral predicament placed Granger in a dilemma: either declare himself the winner and risk international sanctions or agree to a recount that would likely have cost him a defeat. However, the way forward was already decided. Just one week after the March 2 elections, the head of Guyana's Supreme Court, Judge Roxane George-Wiltshire, ordered a partial recount of votes and ruled that GECOM should not declare a winner until the recount is finished. The ruling of the Court coincided with the arrival of a delegation of several Caribbean Prime Ministers who visited the country to help resolve the election impasse (BBC, 12/03/2020).

However, in clear defiance and contempt of the Court's order, Clairmont Mingo, the Returning Officer of Region 4, made a quick dash to declare APNU&AFC as the winner of the 2020 General and Regional Elections. Region Four was regarded as the most crucial region, as any declaration of votes would have inevitably led to a winner. The entire ordeal was well orchestrated, or so it was thought to have been. On the evening of the planned announcement, members of the media were invited to witness the declaration. However, upon arrival, several reporters were denied entry, physically assaulted, and chased away by a group of APNU-AFC supporters that was strategically positioned in front of the location, presumably to facilitate the rigging of the process.

Shortly after the ordeal, Mingo made a declaration and was quickly escorted with the aid of police officers to a waiting vehicle. The announcement was followed by loud cheering outside the GECOM office, and photos were immediately circulated to media houses in an apparent attempt to lend legitimacy to the process. According to the released figures, the APNU&AFC gained 136,057 votes in Region 4, while the PPP/C received 77,231 votes, resulting in a difference of 58,826 votes, which allowed the APNU&AFC to close the nearly 52,000-vote gap held by the PPP/C in the other nine regions (SN, 14/03/2020). Such a margin would have meant that the APNU&AFC won the General and Regional Elections had the results been deemed credible.

Sase Gunraj, one of the Opposition-nominated GECOM Commissioners, noted that "there were visible alterations…figures changed, numbers scratched out and replaced" (SN, 14/03/2020). In response to these irregularities, the four Western diplomats that were present at the GECOM counting centre – the United States Ambassador, Sarah-Ann Lynch; British High Commissioner, Greg Quinn; Canadian High Commissioner, Lilian Chatterjee; and European Union Ambassador, Fernando Ponz-Canto – walked out of the centre less than an hour after the tallying process commenced, insisting that "it was clear that a transparent and credible process was not put in place by the responsible officials" (SN, 14/03/2020). The diplomats expressed concern about the intimidation tactics used by supporters of the APNU&AFC against those seeking to ensure the process was credible and transparent. A member of the Guyana Bar Association Observer Group received threats from APNU&AFC Counting Agent Carol Joseph. Later that day, the Observer Mission from the Organization of American States (OAS) announced that it was withdrawing completely from Guyana.

In a separate statement, the Commonwealth Observer Group, one of the independent observer groups to the March 2 elections, stated that the tabulations of Region Four by Returning Officer Clairmont Mingo were not credible nor transparent, citing "blatant instances of disregard for the rule of law and electoral ethics, despite its vested authority to independently ensure credible General and Regional Elections" (SN, 18/03/2020c). The observer mission was headed by Owen Arthur. On March 15, 2020, the group formally departed from Guyana.

Realising that one of the greatest election frauds in modern times was on the verge of materialising, the PPP/C launched their counterattack. Anil Nandlall, an executive member of the party, formally urged the GECOM Chair to direct Clairmont Mingo to refrain from declaring the votes cast or communicating them to the Chief General and Regional Elections Officer, Keith Lowenfield. Furthermore, he insisted that she should refuse to accept any report from Lowenfield purporting to declare final election results on the grounds that such a report is marred by illegality.

It was evident that some of the GECOM staff and certain high-ranking members of the APNU-AFC were complicit in committing electoral fraud on the Guyanese people and undermining the country's democracy.

Reluctant to be sworn in on disputed votes, Granger called the CARICOM Chair, Prime Minister of Barbados, Mia Mottley, and requested a high-level CARICOM team to supervise the recount of the cast votes (NR, 17/03/2020). Although initially sceptical of the proposal – given concerns over potential procedural manipulation – the PPP/C consented to have the recount as per Granger's request. The team was chaired by the former Attorney-General and Minister of Foreign Affairs of Dominica, Francine Baron. It also included former Minister of Finance of Grenada, Anthony Boatswain; Senior Lecturer in the Department of Government of UWI, Cynthia Barrow-Giles; Chief Electoral Officer of Barbados, Angela Taylor; and Chief General and Regional Elections Officer of Trinidad and Tobago, Fern Narcis-Scope. The recount was seen as a significant step in determining the will of the Guyanese people while also restoring confidence in the electoral process among domestic stakeholders and international bodies.

Before the recount started, both Granger and the Leader of the Opposition agreed to abide by the results. During this process, it was agreed that steps would be taken to secure the ballot boxes. Although the initial focus was on Region Four, the team subsequently agreed to recount all ten polling districts in full. The recount received mixed reactions from GECOM Commissioners, with the government-nominated Commissioners questioning the legality of the recount process. Nonetheless, the process received unequivocal support from the head of GECOM.

At the level of the APNU&AFC coalition, there were continued efforts by party agents to undermine the integrity and legitimacy of the recount process, from delays in the signing of the *aide memoire* outlining the terms of the recount to the filing of a legal injunction by Ulita Moore to block the recount process. Moore was an APNU&AFC candidate who participated in the Regional Election for Electoral District Four. In 2018, she also contested the Local Government Election as a candidate for the APNU (SN, 18/03/2020a).

In her ruling, High Court Judge Franklyn Holder granted the injunction restraining GECOM from allowing

> Any person or persons to any agreement between the President of Guyana and the leader of the Opposition and or any agreement between GECOM and the Caribbean Community or at all, to count or recount any ballots cast by electors at the March 2, 2020, General and Regional General and Regional Elections until the hearing and determination of the judicial review application (DW, 17/03/2020).

The interim decision also restrained the Chief General and Regional Elections Officer, Keith Lowenfield, from setting aside or replacing the declared results from the Returning Officers from the ten administrative districts with other documents or declarations until the conclusion of judicial review. In the PPP/C camp, the silence was deafening. They have realised that failure to secure an expeditious ruling from the High Court that repeals the order would inevitably lead to Lowenfield declaring the results on hand, paving the way for the swearing in of David Granger for a second term.

The injunction came two weeks after GECOM agreed to the recount exercise. In response, the Independent High-Level Team expressed its intention to withdraw from the recount exercise, thereby eroding the only opportunity available to restore credibility to the recount process. Mia Mottley, Chair of CARICOM, stated:

> It is clear that there are forces that do not want to see the votes recounted for whatever reason. Any Government which is sworn in without a credible and fully transparent vote count process would lack legitimacy (SN, 18/03/2020a).

The departure of the CARICOM mission left the Granger presidency without any credible pathway that would allow him to be sworn in. Sir Shridath Ramphal, a former Minister of Foreign Affairs of Guyana and former Secretary General of the Commonwealth, regarded the departure of CARICOM as utterly regrettable. The Roman Catholic bishops of the Antilles Episcopal Conference also joined the call to express their dissatisfaction with the current post-election crisis, deeming it a great disrespect to the people of Guyana (SN, 20/03/2020). A few days later, the Carter Center departed Guyana after carefully examining several factors, including the absence of an electoral process, restrictions on international travel due to COVID-19, and the deterioration of Guyana's security system in the wake of the impasse.

The APNU&AFC supporters were also on record harassing international observers by preventing them from doing their work. Threats were also made against members of the international community, further undermining the credibility of the electoral process. Across the country, the APNU&AFC coalition was busy organising and mobilising protesters, calling for Granger to be sworn in as president. At the international level, the General and Regional Elections ordeal in Guyana was quickly gaining more attention. During a news conference, the United States of America Secretary of State, Mike Pompeo, said that:

> The United States is closely monitoring the tabulation of votes in Guyana; the election took place on March 2. We join the OAS, Commonwealth, the EU, CARICOM and other democratic partners in calling for an accurate count. We commend CARICOM's role in seeking a swift democratic resolution. It is important to note that the individuals who seek to benefit from electoral fraud and to form illegitimate governments, regimes, will be subject to a variety of serious consequences from the United States (NR, 17/03/2020).

In an update to the nation, Granger claimed that the injunction granted by the High Court prevented GECOM and its agent from proceeding with the recount. His statement was widely perceived as duplicitous since he never mentioned that the person who filed the injunction was a member of the APNU&AFC, the party he leads. Instead, he went on at length, indicating that he would abide by the Constitution of the Co-operative Republic of Guyana, the decision of the Guyana Elections Commission (GECOM), and the ruling of the Supreme Court. His statement was in stark contrast to his prior commitment to have a supervised recount exercise in the presence of the high-profile CARICOM team.

Among civil society, the stalemate tactics employed by the APNU&AFC government created considerable discord and resentment. Among them was Major General (Ret'd) Joe Singh, a distinguished Guyanese military officer and public servant with a career spanning several decades. He called on Granger to call off the "dogs of war" and allow GECOM to complete its recount of all ballots. He contended that

> ... such a commendable initiative should be stillborn as a result of an Injunction originating from your own party, sends a worrying message that either you are being Machiavellian, or being manipulated, or you have simply lost control over the actions of members of your own inner circle (SN, 18/03/2020b)

Joining the call for the second time was US Secretary of State Mike Pompeo. In a statement congratulating the Organization of American States (OAS) Secretary General, Luis Almagro, Pompeo also called on Guyana to adhere to a free, fair, and credible electoral process. Dominic Gaskin, the son-in-law of President David Granger and an AFC executive, also called for a full investigation to determine whether any misconduct had occurred among officials within the Guyana Elections Commission (GECOM). Specifically, he called for an inquiry into the integrity of the Statement of Polls (SOPs) or the tabulation of the results of the General and Regional Elections (SN, 22/03/2020a). In another statement, Sir Shridath Ramphal called for democracy and the rule of law to prevail. He reminded Guyanese of the pledge made during the moment of independence, where we affirmed that "respect for the inherent dignity and the equal and inalienable rights of all persons are the foundations of freedom, justice and peace in society" (SN, 22/03/2020b).

Yesu Persaud, another Pioneering businessman, also called on President Granger to take steps to preserve democracy in Guyana. In an open letter to Granger, he warned that a declaration of unverified results could result in sanctions, affecting the well-being of citizens and the country (SN, 24/03/2020a). Persaud further related that there is still time for Granger to end the impasse by simply getting his party to withdraw the court challenge that sought to challenge the legality of the recount process. The US and other Western countries also further reiterated grave concerns over the electoral process in Guyana and suggested that if the election result is not fair, the OAS will be compelled to take action against Guyana (SN, 20/03/2020).

While pressure was mounting locally and internationally, ballot boxes were being relocated from the Arthur Chung Convention Centre (ACCC) to the GECOM office without notice. PPP/C agents on the ground, who were guarding the ballot boxes, objected to the surreptitious move, but to no avail. The move came one day after opposition political parties requested that GECOM secure

A container of Ballot Boxes in route from the ACCC to GECOM Office.
Photo: *Stabroek News*, 21/03/2020

all ballots cast on March 2, General and Regional elections. The joint statement arose from concerns that the Region 6 and Region 4 ballot boxes were not stored at the ACCC, where the remaining ballot boxes were kept (SN, 21/03/2020).

At GECOM headquarters, intimidation tactics re-emerged in an attempt to hijack the March 2; however, this time, they were perpetrated by elements within the Guyana Police Force. Robeson Benn, a PPP (Opposition) nominated commissioner of GECOM, was verbally abused upon his arrival at GECOM headquarters. In a letter to the Commissioner of Police detailing the ordeal, Benn explained that he arrived at the GECOM headquarters, where his office as a Commissioner of GECOM is located, around 3:40 am and was denied entry. He was there to check on the agents guarding the containers to ensure the security of the ballot boxes. At the gate, he was greeted by a female Special Constabulary Rank who told him that "… not any and everybody can come in here…that this was a serious place" (SN, 22/03/2020c). However, after a brief confrontation where he was verbally abused and threatened, the Rank allowed him to enter.

The week prior, Benn was in a similar situation at the Arthur Chung Conference Centre (ACCC). In the presence of other colleagues, including other

Opposition-nominated Commissioners, Benn was physically abused by members of the Tactical Services Unit of the Guyana Police Force. He recalled that:

> ... after 15 minutes or so of trying to cajole me to leave, they proceeded to brace me out of the position I was [in] on the ramp of the convention center. I refused to leave. I hopped around a bit and then they laid hands on me and tried to physically remove me...I held on to the rails and they dragged me along the ground to a point where I was lying on the ground. They said they were going to get a shield to put me on it and physically remove me. I kept refusing. I said I was a member of the GECOM and that they were here because of decisions made by the commission (SN, 24/03/2020).

The alteration was condemned by the Georgetown Chamber of Commerce and Industry (GCCI) in a public statement. In response, the Guyana Police Force claimed that the statement was "unfounded, biased, unmerited and highly fallacious" (SN, 24/03/2020).

Keeping watch to avoid tampering with the ballot boxes during the recount process was a group of youngsters, collectively referred to as the *Guardians of Democracy*, who mobilised as volunteer observers. Supporters of the movement were made up of the main Opposition party, the PPP/C, as well as smaller parties such as The Citizenship Initiative (TCI), A New and United Guyana (ANUG), the Liberty and Justice Party, The New Movement, and others. The gathering took place amidst the COVID-19 crisis, a period marked by widespread lockdowns, during which people were urged to stay indoors and avoid physical contact with the outside world. The movement began at the ACCC when the recount was announced and then shifted to GECOM headquarters after the storage containers had been transferred.

At the Office of the Leader of the Opposition, the PPP/C was busy mounting pressure on Granger to instruct Ulita Moore to withdraw her high court case, which sought to challenge the legality of a recount of ballots. They opined that since Moore was a member of the APNU and a candidate for the 2018 local government election, President Granger should be able to direct her actions. The move by the PPP/C was in response to Granger's claim that the total recount of votes cast at the March 2 General and Regional Elections, an agreement brokered by the CARICOM team, was stymied due to legal proceedings initiated by Ulita Moore. Granger's action was viewed as a façade and self-serving, one that was clearly and blatantly put together to mislead the public (SN, 23/03/2020).

Through the Court, Opposition Leader Bharrat Jagdeo made several appeals for the disclosure of Region Four SOPs, a request which was denied by Senior Counsel Niel Boston. Boston argued that such documents could only be produced within the framework of an election petition. Jagdeo's call stemmed from the findings, which revealed that the distribution of votes in Region Four, according to the Statements of Poll (SOPs) held by the opposition parties, varied substantially from the figures presented by Mingo, the Returning Officer for the Region. The intent of the request was for the SOPs to be disclosed so they could be thoroughly scrutinised against Mingo's figures in the interest of transparency. The request was submitted before Justice Franklyn Holder, the same judge who had previously ruled on the legality of the March 13 declaration of Region 4 General and Regional Elections results by Mingo. However, before addressing this issue, the Court was first required to rule on whether it had the jurisdiction to hear the lawsuit filed by Ulita Moore to halt the recount of ballots.

Ironically, in 2011, GECOM acquiesced to APNU's demand to release the SOPs after police injured several APNU protesters during a demonstration where calls were made for a verification of the documents. Following a meeting with the Private Sector Commission (PSC), GECOM agreed to hand over scanned copies of the SOPs to all parties that contested the election that year. The Public Relations Officer (PRO) of GECOM, Vishnu Persaud, agreed to share copies of the SOPs via DVDs with the respective parties for them to verify the tabulation of votes (SN, 26/03/2020a). The APNU's Vice Chairman, Rupert Roopnarine, commended GECOM for releasing the SOPs and even praised the PSC for "using its influence on the side of righteousness" (SN, 26/03/2020a). Khemraj Ramjattan, the Chairman of AFC and of the parties that coalesced with APNU, also supported GECOM's decision to give APNU copies of the SOPs, stating that GECOM had done the same for AFC in 2006 after the General and Regional Elections results were declared. However, five years later, neither the APNU nor the AFC could find it within themselves to release their SOPs to corroborate their claims of victory.

At the GECOM headquarters, pressure was mounting for the agency to swiftly conclude the electoral process in a manner that was both transparent and constitutionally compliant. However, the agency was reluctant to proceed without the Court's guidance. In a statement by GECOM, the agency claimed that

> … while the anxiety and frustration of the electorate is understandable, the Commission is cognizant that the matter is sub Judice and therefore awaits the outcome of the legal proceedings currently engaging the attention of the Court to inform its deliberations and next steps (SN, 26/03/2020b).

However, a few analysts argued that, given the power conferred upon GECOM by the constitution, the agency could take all necessary actions to resolve the election impasse, irrespective of the outcome of the court's ruling. Central to this position was the obligation of GECOM Chair Claudette Singh, who had given an undertaking to Chief Justice Roxane George that a recount of the ballots for Region Four would be done. Critics pointed out that she allowed Mingo to make two fraudulent declarations of results, the first was later found to be unlawful by Chief Justice George, while the second was the subject of a contempt hearing. Singh received sharp criticism for allowing the electoral process to descend into fraud and farce.

In the APNU&AFC camp, campaign co-chair Joseph Harmon expressed his unwavering support for the results declared by the Region Four Returning Officer, although they were widely described as rigged both in Guyana and abroad. The APNU&AFC party further called on GECOM to resolve the court matter so that Granger could be sworn in as President. The party held on to the belief that the Chief Election Officer, Lowenfield, had already prepared and submitted his report to the Commission for its consideration, as per the constitution. And notwithstanding that the process was interrupted by the filing of several court matters, once the matters were discharged, the Commission would declare the coalition the winner. What made the narrative even more plausible was that Lowenfield proceeded with the discredited results despite widespread and credible allegations of electoral fraud. Unperturbed by the mountain of allegations, Harmon, in a comment to the media, noted that the coalition was working to change the narrative of election fraud and rigging that had arisen both internationally and in Guyana in a bid to prevent the likelihood of any sanctions. However, the United States government maintained that should Granger be sworn in on disputed results, sanctions would follow.

In the Court, GECOM's Chair, Singh, withdrew an incorrect affidavit filed on her behalf in the *Ulita Moore* case, which sought to challenge the legality of the national recount of votes. Singh explained that her statement had to be retracted because it conflicted with a 'commitment' she had made to the Court on March 13, where she endeavoured to "facilitate a recount at the level of the Commission" should there be any discrepancies in the SOPs (SN, 27/03/2020). However, another inaccurate affidavit was filed on behalf of GECOM on March 24, asserting that the tabulation of Region Four votes was done in accordance with the law. The affidavit further contended that GECOM could not accede to any request for a recount based on a political agreement between the President and the Leader of the Opposition. While Singh did not comment on the content of the new affidavit, she did clarify that several contentious elements had been removed prior to its final submission. The filing of successive erroneous affidavits to the Courts that seemed to favour APNU&AFC's position fuelled speculations that forces within GECOM were aiding and abetting the attempt by the Granger administration to hijack the March 2, 2020, General and Regional Elections. At the level of the Commissioners, disparity also seemed to exist. The PPP/C commissioner, Sase Gunraj, in a Facebook post, explained that since March 17, "no discussions were had and certainly, no decisions were taken as a body in relation to the myriad of issues related to the General and Regional Elections, including the ongoing litigation" (SN, 27/03/2020).

In light of concerns following the March 2 elections, the Private Sector Commission (PSC) formally requested from the Chair copies of the Standard Operating Procedures (SOPs) for all electoral districts to validate the disclosure of the March 2 elections. The Chairperson, however, declined, claiming that the High Court's decision would guide her actions. In her response, she claimed that:

> ... while I understand your request is intended to contribute meaningfully to the process, you would be aware that this matter is currently engaging the attention of the court, and a decision will be forthcoming soon. In this regard, any further action on this subject would be dependent on the decision of the Court (SN, 28/03/2020).

A similar request was made to the High Court by the Leader of the Opposition, Bharrat Jagdeo, for the release of the SOPs. However, the request was likewise denied. The Court stated that the proper forum would be an election petition. Both GECOM and the High Court's decisions came at a time when the Opposition and other contending parties, besides the APNU&AFC, were accusing the GECOM of electoral fraud, favouring APNU&AFC.

In the much-anticipated court ruling, Justice Franklyn Holder ruled that the Court does have jurisdiction to hear the lawsuit filed by Ulita Moore, who moved to the Court for an injunction to halt the recount of ballots cast at the March 2nd elections, arguing that Jagdeo and Granger had no right to direct GECOM. However, Jagdeo, through his lawyer, Senior Counsel Douglas Mendes, argued that the Court does not have jurisdiction to hear the case. While the two parties were at loggerheads, the case took a new turn with the submission of an affidavit by Justice Claudette Singh, GECOM's Chair. In her submission to Justice Holder, Singh contended that GECOM has the legal authority to recount votes if needed. In a 21-page document, Singh argued that GECOM can exercise power over the electoral process, meaning the Commission can order a recount.

Being wary of what was unfolding in Guyana, the United States (U.S.) Assistant Secretary of State Michael Kozak summoned Guyana's Ambassador, Dr Riyad Insanally, to the United States to convey to the Government of Guyana "that any government sworn in based on flawed election results would not be legitimate" (SN, 29/03/2020a). Soon after, the Ministry of Foreign Affairs (MoFA) issued a public statement affirming that Guyana is a sovereign state governed by the rule of law, inferring that no country should meddle in its internal affairs. The statement further emphasised that the 2020 General and Regional Elections were conducted in accordance with the Constitution of Guyana and that the election process is managed by GECOM, an independent body with a constitutional mandate to conduct fair, free, and transparent General and Regional Elections and that "... the executive branch of Government has never tried to influence, interfere with or instruct GECOM in any way" (SN, 29/03/2020a). It was clear that the government was trying to reassure the international community that it had no involvement in the alleged electoral manipulation unfolding within GECOM, a narrative that was unravelling by the day.

As pressure increased for the recount of the votes, the Guyana Human Rights Association (GHRA) called on the chair of GECOM to 'act now' since the future of Guyana is 'in her hands', stating that "it is no longer a question of what she wants to do but what she must do – NOW!" (SN, 29/03/2020b). The Association also stressed that without GECOM's timely action, Guyanese will continue to suffer, stating that

> ... All they were asked to do, and did, was exercise their constitutional right to vote for the Party and leadership they wanted to entrust their livelihood over the next five years...In exchange what they are getting is the pain, the shame and the embarrassment of being a Guyanese and the promise of a future, not one gilded by the impact of their new found source of wealth, but one tarnished by the debilitating impact of international sanctions and a livelihood of unimaginable misery (SN, 29/03/2020b).

Similar calls were also made by other groups, including the Commonwealth Ministerial Action Group (CMAG). In a statement, the CMAG called on GECOM:

> ... to immediately fulfil its constitutional mandate and ensure the sovereign right of the people of Guyana to duly elect their Government is respected through a transparent and credible counting and tabulation process" and further warned that "any Government which is sworn in without a credible and fully transparent vote count and tabulation process would lack legitimacy (SN, 02/04/2020).

On March 31, 2020, the High Court discharged the injunctions granted by Justice Holder to Ulita Moore. Jagdeo, through his lawyers Senior Counsel Douglas Mendes and Attorney Anil Nandlall, argued that Justice Holder could not preside over the matter since Section 140 of the Representation of the People's Act prohibits the High Court from inquiring into the decision or acts by the GECOM and can only do so through an election petition. Nandlall was keen to point out that the provision was put in place by Parliament so that GECOM could complete the electoral process (SN, 31/03/2020a). The court ruling was handed down by Chief Justice (ag) Roxane George and Justice Naresh Harnanan, who said that the matter should have been brought to the Court by way of an election petition. The decision was widely regarded as a significant victory for democracy and the people of Guyana, bringing with it renewed hope that a full recount could be on the way. The ball was now in the GECOM's court. Moore's attorney signalled his intention to appeal the ruling and requested the Court to stay its decision. However, the Court denied his request.

On the sidelines, having realised that the effort to manipulate the electoral outcome was losing momentum, the AFC changed its narrative and instead issued a call for a government of national unity. This appeal emerged at a time when the governing coalition was facing a plethora of accusations, including allegations that it had lost the General and Regional Elections. Ironically, no such call was ever made prior to the General and Regional Elections or while the APNU was in government. As such, the party's sudden invocation of magnanimity and shared governance appeared self-serving rather than a genuine commitment to national unity. The party further stated:

> ... perceived anomalies in tabulations should not render an entire constitutional institution dysfunctional. There are available legal mechanisms for correcting these anomalies through fact and evidence-based proceedings. Any aggrieved party must utilize those proceedings in order to prevent a breakdown of law and order in our beloved country (SN, 31/03/2020b).

The comment by the AFC drew widespread public condemnation, as both domestic and international audiences were, by that time, witnessing on live television and social media one of the most egregious forms of electoral irregularities. Despite the unfolding crisis, neither the AFC nor the APNU took any action within their power to halt the compromised process. Nevertheless, the AFC remained confident that the APNU&AFC had won the March 2nd elections and was awaiting the final declaration.

In an effort to overturn the High Court ruling, almost a week after the ruling, the APNU&AFC candidate Ulita Moore, through her lawyers, approached the Court of Appeal. In a two-to-one decision, the Court ruled that while GECOM has the authority to recount the ballots, it cannot delegate its supervisory function to any other party. Shortly after the ruling, and following much deliberation at the Commission level, the Chairperson of GECOM, Justice Claudette Singh, decided that there would be a full recount of all the Regions, starting from Region 1 to Region 10. In a comment to the media, she posited that her decision is in accordance with Article 162 (1) (b) of the Constitution of Guyana, which mandates the Commission to "take such action as appears necessary or expedient to ensure impartiality, fairness, and compliance with the provisions of the Constitution" (SN, 03/04/2020). To kick-start the process, GECOM asked its CEO, Lowenfield, to provide a modality for the recount process. The recount of all the regions raised hopes of finally ending the impasse in the General and Regional Elections, which had then gripped the nation for more than a month. However, what appeared to be a step in the right direction turned out to be the unleashing of more delaying tactics to further frustrate the recount process. Former PNCR parliamentarian Jerome Khan was of the view that a "Burnhamite faction" had taken control of the PNC and had waged a "war of attrition" to safeguard their good life without fear or any repercussions, including sanctions (SN, 06/04/2020).

At GECOM, two days after the Chair gave the mandate, Lowenfield was yet to provide a framework that would facilitate the operationalisation of the recount exercise. This marked the beginning of a new wave of delay tactics. For instance, a scheduled meeting of the Commissioners to deliberate on the way forward in addressing the election impasse was abruptly postponed due to the need to "sanitise" the GECOM headquarters; no subsequent meeting was scheduled. There were also delays by the Government-nominated Commissioners in deciding the type of recount, specifically whether it would be a numerical recount or a recount of everything within the ballot box (SN, 04/04/2020). Speaking to the media, Vincent Alexander, one of the Government-nominated Commissioners, explained that GECOM must provide clear direction to the administration on the modalities of the recount. According to Alexander:

> The administration has made it clear that we have to give them clear directions about what we mean by a recount and how we proceed with the recount. That has not yet been done, that discussion has started...We have to decide whether the recount is

> merely a recount of the votes or whether all the materials in the box will be taken into consideration. That is the proxies, the people who voted without ID cards and all of that. (SN, 04/04/2020).

Alexander also stated that the result of the recount would not necessarily lead to the automatic declaration of the winner. Sase Gunraj, one of the PPP Opposition-nominated commissioners, had a different view. He asserted:

> the whole point of going to the recount is to establish the results of the General and Regional Elections because of the flawed procedure we have on our hands...the fact that we are moving to a recount the conjoined effect is that the previous declarations are set aside (SN, 04/04/2020).

Amid the growing suspicions about a possible delay tactics by GECOM, the Private Sector Commission (PSC) called on the Commission to recount the ballots only for Region Four, arguing that recounting all regions would be unnecessary. In a statement, the PSC contended that the tabulation was done fraudulently only in Region Four and, therefore, lacks credibility.

In another move to further stonewall the recount process, Lowenfield proposed a 156-day-long period for the recount of votes, a proposal that was deemed unacceptable, absurd, and unreasonable by most of the contesting parties, including the Opposition-nominated Commissioners at GECOM. When questioned about the practicality and reasons for such a lengthy period, the GECOM Secretariat quickly released a statement defending Lowenfield's proposal, citing the COVID-19 pandemic as a reason for the prolonged period. The proposed timeline was widely regarded as impractical and was seen more as a ploy to frustrate the recount exercise. In a statement, the GECOM Secretariat added that:

> ... in this regard, the Secretariat considered the request by the Commission for each ballot to be projected on screen, examination of the contents of the ballot box i.e. ascertaining the number of electors on the list, the number of electors who voted, counting votes cast for both General and Regional Election and validation of spoilt, questioned and rejected ballots. Against this backdrop, the

> estimated time for one ballot box to be counted was projected to be two hours, utilizing 3 workstations for 10 hours per day (9:00 - 19:00) at a central location to count 2339 boxes. Hence, the projected duration as indicated (SN, 09/04/2020).

The statement received widespread criticism from other political parties that contested the election, as well as supporters of the main opposition. It was clear that it was part of a ploy by Lowenfield to further delay and frustrate the recount of ballots. The PPP/C was also keen to point out that after the close of polls, the results are usually tabulated in two hours, and the constitution of Guyana allows for the declaration of results 15 days after the close of polls, inclusive of recounts. It was clear that Lowenfield was laying the groundwork to complicate the recounting process, as many components of the proposed procedure were wholly unnecessary. Having realised what was at play, the PPP/C urged Justice Claudette Singh to act swiftly and decisively in addressing Lowenfield's proposal and to ensure a transparent and legal framework is put in place to expedite the recount process.

At GECOM headquarters, PPP/C-nominated Commissioners were preparing to present a counterproposal that would see the process conclude within two weeks (SN, 09/04/2020). To many, the recount labyrinth was a brazen attempt to extend the life of the APNU&AFC in office while subverting the democratic principles of Guyana. Among the critics was Robert Badal, Head of Change Guyana, one of the parties contesting the elections. Badal sent a strong message to Lowenfield, urging him that his current actions would have lasting social and economic consequences on the country:

> The impact on our country moving forward is dependent on this. While they are paid to do a job, any sanction or delay in giving a credible result will affect the economy of this country and ultimately it is the poor of this country that will feel the brunt of those decisions. Credible results ensure that our democracy is upheld, which is a requisite for our participation among progressive countries. As the first world countries are already saying, the image of this country and its people will forever be tarnished if it fails to deliver credible results (SN, 09/04/2020).

Presidential Candidate of the Liberty and Justice Party was also candid in his dismissal of the proposed lengthy recount process, arguing that it is already an absurdity for Guyana to be waiting more than 35 days for a declaration of results, and to add another five months is insanity:

> It is absurd to say that you would need two hours per ballot box when the country has been waiting for 35 days. The fact that Mr Lowenfield worked for over a decade with the Commission and cannot come up with a plan today is beyond insanity. There is clearly an alternative agenda (SN, 09/04/2020).

The Citizenship Initiative, another new contestant, also ridiculed the proposal, labelling it as irrational and impractical. Ruel Johnson, its representative, said that if May 11, 2020, passes without a declaration, the country will fall into a constitutional crisis.

After considerable uproar over the proposed 156-day recount period, the Opposition-nominated Commissioners presented a counter-proposal that would see the number of days for the recount process reduced to 10. The new proposal involved using 20 workstations, each operating for 12 hours daily, with an average of one hour per ballot box. The Audit Office of Guyana, or an accredited audit firm, was suggested to be on-site throughout the process to ensure transparency. It was further proposed that the entire recount process be broadcast through television and online media platforms. The proposal was considered plausible and doable. While there were over 1,000 ballot boxes to be counted, many of them had less than 200 ballots. In fact, more than 200 boxes had less than 50 ballots. The proposal allowed for the simultaneous tabulation of all the regions. However, when the Commission met to review the report, the only consensus reached after almost eight hours of deliberation was that the Arthur Chung Convention Centre would continue to be the site for the recount. In addressing the other matters raised, Lowenfield indicated his willingness to have them reviewed, with a report to be presented at the subsequent meeting for further discussion. The meeting was then adjourned without confirming the date of the next meeting (SN, 10/04/2020).

As the other statutory electoral deadline approaches to discuss what was perceived to be a recount process of votes, GECOM again was yet to decide on the way forward, further stoking speculation of an ulterior motive by the head of GECOM. The speculation extends to include Government-elect Commissioners, raising widespread concerns about the impartiality and confidence in the recount process, especially when anti-democratic forces were still at the helm of the agency. Key among those that have raised concern was Bruce Golding, head of the OAS observer mission to the March 2, 2020, General and Regional Elections. Golding was particularly concerned about the delay in declaring credible and accurate results, suggesting that it remains crucial for Guyana to restore its internationally respected democracy. His comments underscored the prejudice that was already hovering over Guyana, serving as a sober reminder of the challenges that may lie ahead for the country. He also called for the exclusion of GECOM officials from the recount process who have openly demonstrated partisanship during the General and Regional Elections exercise. Calls were also made for Mingo to be excluded from the process because of his questionable behaviour. Golding's statement exerted a new wave of pressure on GECOM and the Granger administration not to stand in the way of finalising the election result.

Lending support to the call issued by the OAS was the Acting Assistant Secretary for the U.S. Department of State's Bureau of Western Hemisphere Affairs, Michael G Kozak. In a public statement issued via Twitter, Kozak unequivocally affirmed that the U.S. supports the OAS's call for GECOM to conduct a recount process without further delay. He further emphasised that any government sworn in on flawed General and Regional Election results would be considered illegitimate and, therefore, would not be recognised by the US government.

The Bar Council of the Guyana Bar Association (GBA) also added its voice to the growing chorus calling on GECOM to promptly facilitate the accurate declaration of the election result, emphasising that "time is of the essence" and the "constitutional clock is ticking" (SN, 17/04/2020). Their concern was that Article 69 of Guyana's constitution mandates the reconvening of Parliament within four months of its dissolution, thereby setting a constitutional deadline of April 30, 2020, for the next session. However, GECOM seemed ensnared in a haze of institutional inertia. The Bar warned of the creeping danger that could soon materialise due to the prolonged political limbo and urged that, without a declared government, the lack of parliamentary oversight of the country could undermine the rule of law and good governance. In another statement, the

Commonwealth observer group urged GECOM to undertake the recount of votes in full compliance with the law. The group expressed its desire for the process to be conducted in a timely and transparent manner, given that the people of Guyana have already suffered forty-five days of gruelling and unconscionable election turmoil.

With a recount start date yet to be announced, each passing day deepened the sense of national uncertainty and frustration. However, hope filled the air as the much-anticipated meeting between the Commissioners and the Head of GECOM was scheduled to take place. At the meeting, it was expected that Justice Claudette Singh would announce the start date of the recount and provide clarity on the way forward. However, this was far from what actually took place. Instead, a mere announcement was made for no more than 10 workstations to be used for recounting votes. The decision by the Chair was borne after careful consideration of all three proposals - the Opposition-nominated Commissioners, the CEO of GECOM, and the Government-nominated Commissioners – the circumstances surrounding the COVID-19 pandemic, and the need for social distancing. According to Singh, the decision to use 10 workstations was based on the availability of equipment and technology that would be used to display the ballots. Each workstation was expected to tabulate its own results for security reasons. All stations were to be located inside the ACCC. However, a timeline for the recount was yet to be provided.

In response, the PPP/C Opposition expressed its profound disappointment in Justice Singh's decision to "cede a large part of [her] responsibility to some anomalous Task Force" (SN, 19/04/2020). The criticism stemmed from Singh's announcement that she would seek guidance from the National COVID-19 Task Force via Prime Minister Moses Nagamootoo on working hours during the recount of ballots. The PPP/C's concern was that Nagamootoo was part of the cabal that was working to prevent the disclosure of credible results, and therefore, they viewed him as untrustworthy. It was also likely in Nagamootoo's interest to prolong the recount exercise, as this would allow him to spend a longer time in office.

The disappointment in Justice Singh's action was also echoed by other stakeholders, including Rondha-Ann Lam, the Head of The Citizenship Initiative (TCI). Lam was disappointed in the way Justice Singh dealt with the intervention. It was the expectation that, given the urgency of the matter due to international pressure and the level of frustration among our people, at least a definitive way forward should have been provided. That is, a clear plan of action with a time frame and assignment of each personnel. Instead, Singh's response was vague and open to several interpretations, including the possibility of allowing the recount process to last longer than the inconsiderate and ludicrous 156-day plan submitted by Lowenfield (SN, 19/04/2020). A New and United Guyana (ANUG), Change Guyana (CG), the Liberty and Justice Party (LJP), The New Movement (TNM), and the United Republic Party (URP) also shared similar views.

Nagamootoo, in his response to Justice Singh's request, was widely perceived as another instance of delaying tactics. In his response, Nagamootoo posited that the recount of votes must not extend into the COVID-19 curfew period, which runs from 6 pm to 6 am, and that a mandatory two-week quarantine period at a government-designated facility is required for observers entering the country for the recount process. Nagamootoo's disclosure was made via his column 'My Turn' in the state-owned *Guyana Chronicle*. His actions drew even more criticism for the manner in which the disclosure was made, given the urgency of the matter. The response also contained information that Singh had not disclosed to the public – that she had made a request for a 10-hour work schedule.

For the PPP/C, it was clear that Nagamootoo was intent on frustrating the process. In response, the PPP/C charged that:

> the direction that the exercise should end at 5:00 PM daily is simply nonsensical. Tens of thousands of persons throughout the country are permitted to work after 6:00 PM. This recount is arguably the most important exercise in this country and therefore, its speedy conclusion must be accorded every priority. There is simply no sensible reason why the exercise should not proceed beyond 5:00 PM daily. As regards persons coming into the country for the exercise, Nagamootoo's recommendation that they must be quarantined for two weeks, is even more preposterous. Once tested negative for COVID-19, there is absolutely no need for quarantine (SN, 20/04/2020)

The PPP/C also called on Singh to reject Nagamootoo's directives and proceed with the recount of votes. As the nation yearned for closure, GECOM slowly edged closer to unveiling the long-anticipated recount of the March 2, 2020, elections. In a low tone, standing before the press, Justice Singh lamented "not long from now" while expressing her reassurance that she was the first to speak about a recount and that she would ensure that it happens shortly. The 14-day quarantine period of CARICOM observers was also reversed following a barrage of criticism.

On April 22, 2020, more than seven weeks after the General and Regional Elections, the Commissioners were preparing to work on a draft Order, a document that would guide the recount of votes. The order was one of four documents that Justice Singh requested. The additional documents included a report from the Ministry of Health on the findings of the inspection conducted at the ACCC, a logistics plan from the Secretariat with a proposed timeline for the recount exercise, and other activities and resources required to operate a 10-station tabulation centre (SN, 22/04/2020). The following day, GECOM met and reviewed the draft orders. However, by the end of the day, a decision was still pending. It was as if GECOM had no intention of facilitating the recount of votes.

The procrastination and delay tactics took a new turn with every passing day. In a subsequent bombshell disclosure, Government-nominated Commissioner Vincent Alexander told reporters that the recount would take 25 days, subject to a review within the first week based on the progress of the work. And, while the recount exercise will be broadcasted, the request by the Opposition-nominated Commissioners to have live streaming has been denied. This request was part of several motions brought before the Commission by Sase Gunraj. Among the other motions rejected were calls for the public release of the Statement of Polls (SoPs) from Region Four, as well as the request for a local auditing body to be present during the recount.

Even more concerning was that Singh voted against the very motions that were expected to provide critical safeguards and ensure the recount process was credible and transparent. The PPP/C called her out for what appeared to be reneging on her commitment to ensure the recount of votes is done fairly, transparently, expeditiously, and lawfully. In a tweet, Michael Kozak further lambasted the government for the protracted delay in providing credible election results. Ralph Ramkarran, the presidential candidate for A New and United Guyana (ANUG), also expressed his concern about the great degree of partiality demonstrated by GECOM officials in favour of the APNU&AFC regime. The behaviour by GECOM further fuelled speculation that it may never conduct a fair, transparent, and credible recount –

> "By this time the entire GECOM must have been aware that under the Constitution the results are required to have been officially declared within fifteen days of the General and Regional Elections. The failure of GECOM to deliver the results in accordance with the Constitution, leading to its violation, is sufficient justification to assert that GECOM has failed in its constitutional responsibility and is adequate reason for GECOM to do the honourable thing" (SN, 27/04/2020).

The failures of GECOM gave rise to widespread anxiety and uncertainty among the population. Its pattern of behaviour led to further speculation that other ploys may be in the making that would see more false declarations or attempts to derail the recount completely. Despite these attempts by GECOM to frustrate the recount of votes, the US, Canada, and the United Nations publicly reaffirmed their support for the Carter Center's return as an observer of the recount exercise. After more than eight weeks following the March 2 elections, GECOM finally decided on May 6 as the start date of the vote recount. However, whether it would be live-streamed was yet to be determined, although the Chairperson had given a commitment to the High Court that such or similar systems would be in place to ensure the credibility, fairness, and impartiality of the process. In voicing his support for the live stream, Attorney-at-Law Anil Nandlall posited that the provisions of Section 22 of the Election Laws (Amendment) Act and Article 162 of the Constitution collectively empower GECOM to "issue such instructions and take such action as appear to it necessary or expedient to ensure impartiality and fairness." (Article 162(1)(b)). Notwithstanding these legal underpinnings, the GECOM Chairperson rejected the proposal for live streaming, citing Section 90 of the Representation of the People Act as the basis for her decision. In response, Nandlall expressed strong disapproval, contending that the Chairperson conveniently cherry-picked section 90 of the Representation of the People Act to support her decision (SN, 04/05/2020). He was further keen to highlight that –

> Section 90 of the Representation of the People Act has no relevance to a recount. It applies only to the counting of ballots at a polling station. It is intended to protect the identity of the voter before the declaration of the results. These results were not only declared but

> the Statements of Poll have already been posted at polling stations throughout the country. Live streaming, therefore, can only enhance integrity, boost public confidence and augment transparency and fairness, in the process (SN, 04/05/2020).

In a statement, Granger welcomed the announcement from GECOM that the national recount will soon commence. However, he remained silent on the denial of the Carter Center's return, despite the widespread criticism both locally and internationally for their decision. In a statement, the Carter Center said it had "deployed an observer to Miami who was prepared to travel to Georgetown, but unfortunately, his flight was denied approval to carry international election observers" (SN, 05/05/2020). As tension rose, a group of protesters gathered outside the home of the Prime Minister, Moses Nagamootoo, and the Ministry of Foreign Affairs, demanding that all accredited observers be present at the recount of votes exercises.

In a sudden twist of fate, and nine weeks after Guyanese went to the polls to cast their votes in the General and Regional Elections, GECOM was finally progressing toward the national recount of votes. An Order outlining the national recount procedure was finalised and published. The Order allowed for limited broadcasting of the counting process but prohibited the publication of photos or videos of the staff involved in counting ballots. According to the Order, each workstation shall be equipped with a system that exclusively captures and broadcasts (a) an image of the ballot box as delivered to the workstation and (b) an audio feed of the recount process. It also catered to an audio-visual facility established in the tabulation centre to broadcast the entire tabulation process live.

On May 6, 2020, the long-anticipated and long-awaited recount of ballots began. However, of the 2,339 ballot boxes to be counted, a mere twenty-five were completed on day one. This was largely due to a late start and some 'administrative' hiccups. Among the issues were a hole in one of the ballot boxes, missing poll books, and the random counting of the ballot boxes, with Region Four being overlooked. With much suspicion still lingering around the process, the results set the pace at which the remaining ballot boxes may be counted. While the initial period set aside for the recount was 25 days, the initial sluggishness was likely to push the timeline further. The day's proceedings were marked by tension and high activity as numerous officials, party agents,

Protesters outside the residence of the Prime Minister. Photo: *Stabroek News*, 2020

and observers convened at the Arthur Chung Conference Centre (ACCC) to oversee this critical phase to resolve the prolonged electoral impasse.

On day two, around noon, the tabulation process was yet to start. When questioned by the two observers of the PPP/C, Frank Anthony and Sasenarine Singh, about the commencement of the tabulation process, a GECOM supervisor indicated that he was awaiting instructions from the CEO. As the recount of votes continued, it became clear that the APNU&AFC representatives were attempting to cast doubt on the process in an effort to derail the tabulation. Intimidation and verbal confrontation were also part of the APNU&AFC's strategy.

The intimidation tactics did not spare the media personnel either – their tents were erected amid high grass, with no washroom facilities, furniture, or electricity. After a series of complaints by media operatives to GECOM regarding the need to improve accommodations outside the ACCC, GECOM spokesperson Yolanda Ward had the area weeded, lights and electrical outlets installed, along with a few chairs and tables provided. She also indicated that the washroom facility in the VIP room at the Aquatic Centre was available for use. However, when reporters attempted to use the facilities at the NAC, they were prevented from doing so by supporters of APNU&AFC. The request was later acceded to, and washroom facilities were placed outside the ACCC. By the end of the second day, GECOM had managed to recount votes cast in 65 of the 2,339 polling stations, representing a mere 3 per cent of the total polling stations. This development raised serious concerns about GECOM's ability to complete the recount within the designated 25-day period. Even more concerning was that if the recount process continued at the current snail's pace, the complete exercise would have taken around 75 to 100 days.

The delay in the recount process was attributed mainly to a barrage of objections and procedural queries raised by agents of the APNU-AFC coalition. During the reconciliation process, coalition agents alleged instances where individuals recorded as having voted were, in some cases, deceased, while others had emigrated and were not present in the country on the day of the election. They have also alleged the presence of a "clear and unmistakable pattern of irregularities, discrepancies, and worse have emerged" (SN, 11/05/2020). It was clear that these delayed tactics appeared to be deliberately engineered to derail the recount process of votes, thereby justifying the need for fresh elections. From their actions, it was clear that, subconsciously, APNU&AFC knew their faith was sealed.

Having tried twice to get Clairmont Mingo, Region Four Returning Officer, to make a false declaration and abusing the Courts to prevent the recount of votes, the APNU&AFC resorted to a change in plan: attack the credibility of the General and Regional Elections. The objective was to delegitimise the results in the hope of calling fresh General and Regional Elections or possibly striking a deal with the Opposition and likely winner, the PPP/C. Their plan to discredit the March 2nd General and Regional Elections gained traction when the GECOM Chair, Justice Claudette Singh, wrote the Chief Immigration Officer (CIO) on allegations made by APNU&AFC about illicit voting. It was evident that the APNU&AFC was on a quest to nullify the General and Regional Elections, with the GECOM's Chair being complacent. The allegations ranged from the names of a few deceased persons on the voters' list who voted at the March 2nd elections to individuals who were outside of Guyana and somehow voted. However, these allegations started to fall apart after facing scrutiny. For instance, one of the individuals identified as not being in Guyana on March 2, 2020, was found not only to be in Guyana but also to have worked as a local observer with the Guyana Bar Association on polling day. The claims were eventually rejected as nonsensical and farcical.

The APNU&AFC's plan to steal the General and Regional Elections was all too obvious, and those standing firm for democracy were not about to let that happen. Exposing their attempt to rig the General and Regional Elections, Bruce Golding, Head of the OAS observer mission to Guyana's March 2nd election, in a virtual meeting, reported that he "has never seen a more transparent effort to alter the results of an election" (SN, 14/05/2020). And the ongoing recount exercise has proven just that. For instance, for ballot box #4062, the Statement of Poll (SoP) recorded 182 votes for APNU&AFC and 43 votes for PPP/C. However, the Returning Officer's contentious spreadsheet presented altered figures, listing 292 votes for APNU&AFC and 33 votes for PPP/C. Following a recount of the said ballot box, the original results were consistent with the Statement of Recount (SoR), reaffirming the accuracy of the original SoP figures (SN, 14/05/2020).

In a letter to David Granger, U.S. Senator Marco Rubio and several of his colleagues urged them to allow more international observers to scrutinise the recount process in the interest of credibility. The call was supported by local protesters organised by the PPP/C outside the Ministry of Foreign Affairs, who were calling for the return of the Carter Center observers. However, the protest was quickly dispersed due to the 'emergency' ministerial order on the COVID-19 measures. Two protesters were later charged.

Weeks after expecting feedback, the Carter Center broke its silence, expressing great disappointment at not being able to return and observe the recount of votes. In a statement, the Center said it

> "... is disappointed that the government of Guyana chose not to demonstrate a genuine commitment to transparency by ensuring that all duly accredited organizations, including The Carter Center, be allowed to conduct their work" (SN, 22/05/2020)

Granger's claim that the Carter Center was denied entry due to COVID-19 travel restrictions was widely criticised for its duplicity, as the government had granted permission for hundreds of oil workers to enter Guyana, and the country was even preparing to receive flights of Guyanese stranded overseas.

After thirty-three days of the recount of votes for the March 2, 2020, General and Regional Elections, the emerging results indicated an unassailable lead for the PPP/C. According to the unofficial results, the PPP/C was poised to win the Presidency and 33 seats in parliament, with APNU&AFC securing 31 seats. The listed joining parties of LJP, ANUG, and TNM captured one seat. However, in their usual stance, the APNU&AFC claimed widespread fraud and reaffirmed its position that illegal votes cannot be used to produce a valid result. The narrative was in stark contrast to its initial claim of victory and calling for the swearing-in of David Granger, the incumbent President, due to massive electoral fraud.

As the nation awaited the declaration of the results, the coalition's campaign manager, Joseph Harmon, suggested that Keith Lowenfield could only submit a declaration report based on *valid* votes. His comments were in direct response to the Chairperson of GECOM's decision to have the CEO prepare a report based on the recount results. In a sudden twist of events, Lowenfield concluded that the election failed to satisfy the criteria of impartiality, fairness, and compliance as provided for under the Constitution. Instead, only 185,260 votes can be considered valid: 125,010 for the APNU&AFC and 56,628 for the PPP/C. His statement was met with much astonishment by the OAS and others. Unfazed by her request, the Chairperson further instructed Lowenfield to prepare a declaration using data from the National Recount. Ramjattan, leader of the AFC, was also on record saying that he believes certain legal peculiarities can be used to tip the electoral scale in the APNU&AFC's favour.

In complete defiance of the Chairperson of GECOM, Lowenfield did not submit the report. Furthermore, the meeting with the Commissioners was adjourned due to a lack of a quorum – two Government-nominated Commissioners did not attend the meeting. Coincidentally, and in what seemed to be a well-coordinated action, a court filing was made to prevent Lowenfield from submitting a report.

Back in his office, Prime Ministerial candidate Khemraj Ramjattan, who was also the Minister of Public Security, told members of his staff that he was prepared to accept the results of the national recount of votes, which showed the PPP/C as the winner. In a leaked audio, Ramjattan said that –

> I rather suspect that tomorrow there might be a declaration that the numbers were against us... I am prepared to accept and move on,

> and I wanted to not miss the opportunity because if it happens tomorrow say... I will be out, and I will not have said a word of thank you for provisioning of so many of your expertise and experiences that made me a better minister than when I came (SN, 20/06/2020)

At this point, it was clear that the Coalition had lost the General and Regional Elections. Dominic Gaskin, a former Minister under the APNU&AFC, in a Facebook post, accused the coalition of deliberately misleading and fooling its supporters with unsubstantiated claims of election fraud. He further urged the party to be honest and accept the defeat.

In response to the case that sought to stop the declaration of recount results, the GECOM Chair called for the dismissal of the case before the Guyana Court of Appeal. The case was seen as a last-ditch attempt by the APNU&AFC to prevent the declaration of the results that would inevitably lead to the PPP/C being declared the winner. In her affidavit, Singh argued that such a challenge cannot be entertained at this time since it's premature. Furthermore, any challenge to the validity of an election or claim of irregularities or illegalities can only be disputed through an election petition after the declaration of the election result.

Shortly after the filing of the court case, "the Court of Appeal by way of a majority decision issued an order that the word "more votes are cast" .... should be interpreted as "more valid votes are cast" (SN, 23/06/2020) However, the ruling was perceived of having little impact since GECOM had already decided what constituted valid votes - that is, votes tallied during the recount exercise. Lowenfield, in his usual defiance and gross insubordination, submitted a report to GECOM based on what he claimed to be "valid and credible votes". After single-handedly invalidating almost 115,000 votes, or 25 per cent of the votes cast at the March 2, 2020, General and Regional Elections, the report showed a victory for the incumbent APNU&AFC. The move by the CEO of GECOM received widespread condemnation from observers and international organisations. The PPP/C later appealed the decision to the Caribbean Court of Justice (CCJ), and an order was issued restraining GECOM from declaring the results of the March 2, 2020, polls. Amid the chaos, OAS continued to echo their call to end the 2020 General and Regional Elections saga using the results of the national recount. In a statement, the multilateral body declared that "there is a fine line between the right to redress and the use of the courts to stall the electoral process" (SN, 24/06/2020). Norway's Ambassador to Guyana, Nils Martin Gunneng, also joined the call for GECOM to use the national recount of votes for the declaration.

Determined to ensure that they remain in power, the APNU&AFC voiced their support for the report submitted by Keith Lowenfield. Some of the party's supporters took to the streets, despite the ongoing COVID-19 restrictions, chanting that only 'valid' votes should be counted to determine the winner. The leader of the APNU&AFC, David Granger, also expressed these sentiments. In an interview on Benschop Radio, the caretaker president insisted that the election results should not be decided solely on the quantity of votes cast but on the quality. The latter refers exclusively to the 'valid' votes. According to Granger –

> it is unacceptable for the CEO to present a report that doesn't take into account the fact that these irregularities have occurred and have affected the validity of the votes...this is the reason why the Court of Appeal ruled votes must mean valid votes, if votes are fraudulent or if votes exceed the number of persons on a list, they cannot be valid votes (SN, 30/06/2020).

His statement came moments after APNU General Secretary Joseph Harmon stated that Granger would not concede, and any right-thinking person would agree that conceding must be one of the most "ridiculous and nonsensical propositions" (SN, 30/06/2020).

After several hours of deliberation, the Caribbean Court of Justice (CCJ) delivered its judgment, overturning the Court of Appeal's decision to insert the word 'valid' into the vote tabulation process for the election of a president. President of the Court, Adrian Saunders, ruled that the decision of the Court of Appeal was null and void and of no effect. The Court also ruled that the decision by the Chief Election Officer (CEO) Keith Lowenfield to remove 115,787 votes is invalid and of no effect. The ruling by the CCJ paved the way for the GECOM Chair to declare the recount results, which showed the PPP/C as the winner of the elections and the new party to ascend to government.

In a statement, the new CARICOM Chair, Ralph Gonsalves, urged all stakeholders to respect the ruling of the CCJ and reiterated his call for an early declaration by GECOM. The United Nations Secretary-General, Antonio

Guterres, also called for announcing the final results as soon as possible in light of the CCJ's rulings. Similar calls were also made by Baroness Sugg, Britain's Parliamentary Under-Secretary of State for the Overseas Territories and Sustainable Development. The delay in announcing the results, despite the clear ruling by the CCJ, along with the lack of confidence in Chief Election Officer Keith Lowenfield, prompted me to join the call for his dismissal due to insubordination. It was clear that his actions were an assault on democracy, the rule of law, and the will of the people.

In yet another bizarre and audacious move, Lowenfield, for the sixth time, presented figures to GECOM showing a victory for the APNU&AFC in apparent defiance of the instruction by Claudette Singh to use the recount figures. His fictitious declaration was accompanied by another court challenge. This time, a Tucville resident, Misenga Jones, was blocking Claudette Singh from declaring the winner of the March 2nd General and Regional Elections using the results from the recount process. Jones contended that Singh can only declare a winner based on the report submitted by Lowenfield, and neither Singh nor the Commission can dictate to Lowenfield what the report should contain. Jones petitioned the Court to instruct Lowenfield to use the June 11, 2020, report, which was based on the declarations made up to March 13. This report included the manipulated results for Region Four, falsely indicating that APNU&AFC was the winner.

With his back against the wall, the *de facto* President David Granger gradually changed his tone about what it would take for him to concede. In a statement, Granger declared that he would abide by any declaration by the Chairman if it were in keeping with the laws of Guyana. His position changed slightly compared to a few months prior, when he told reporters that he would accept any declaration from the Commission. Coincidentally, the new caveat of "in keeping with the laws of Guyana" was added the same day a fresh court matter was filed to block the declaration from the Commission.

As the election fiasco continued, the international community made fresh calls for GECOM to utilise the recount results. Democrat Congressmen Albio Sires and Gregory Meeks, Chairman and Vice Chair, respectively, of the U.S. House Foreign Affairs Subcommittee on the Western Hemisphere, Civilian Security, and Trade, issued a stern warning condemning all efforts to undermine the credibility of the March 2nd General and Regional Elections including the action by Lowenfield to manipulate the vote count and disenfranchise thousands of voters. The United States government also called on the APNU&AFC to step aside in recognition of the March 2nd election results. And for the first time, visa restrictions were announced for persons and their family members who were complicit in undermining democracy.

In what seemed as a major defeat to the APNU&AFC as they made their last-ditch attempt to prevent GECOM from using the national recount results to declare a winner of the March 2nd General and Regional Elections, Acting Chief Justice Roxane George-Wiltshire ruled that only the result from the national recount exercise can be used to make a final declaration. With a legitimate defeat looming over the horizon, the APNU&AFC pulled another bunny out of the hat. This time, three private criminal charges were filed against the GECOM Chair. Keith Ondaan of Amelia's Ward, Linden, alleged that Singh recklessly and unlawfully disregarded the advice by the Commission's legal officer and Chief Parliamentary Counsel that the recount was unlawful, leading to the facilitation of the recount. Another misconduct challenge alleged that Singh acted recklessly and unlawfully by breaching the recount order gazetted on May 4th and the amended order of May 29th. Misconduct charges were even filed against Singh for her refusal to accept Lowenfield's report. Clearly, the sole intent behind these charges was retaliatory in nature and meant to intimidate the GECOM Chair. It also served as a testament to the lengths to which the PANU&AFC was willing to go to derail the electoral process. The allegation, however, was short-lived. A few days later, the Director of Public Prosecutions (DPP), Shalimar Ali-Hack, discontinued all criminal charges of misconduct filed against Justice Claudette Singh.

In another landmark victory for the people, the Appeal Court unanimously dismissed the appeal filed by Misenga Jones against the Chief Justice's decision to use the recount votes to declare the result of the March 2nd General and Regional Elections. The Court also upheld the Chief Justice's decision that Lowenfield is under the direction and control of the Commission, and therefore, he is mandated to comply with its instructions (SN, 13/10/2020).

On the fateful day of August 2, 2020, under the watchful gaze of the GECOM assembly, the PPP was declared the winner. By the end of that day, I stood as the nation's 10th President, my oath freshly sworn, and a chapter of uncertainty closed behind our country. A future filled with hopes of prosperity and success had begun.

REFERENCES

Newsroom (2018, June 8). PPP says High Court decision on GECOM chair could mean more unilateral appointments. https://newsroom.gy/2018/06/08/ppp-says-high-court-decision-on-gecom-chair-could-mean-more-unilateral-appointments/

Guyana Chronicle (2018, December 23). Historic no-confidence vote. https://guyanachronicle.com/2018/12/23/historic-no-confidence-vote/

Demerara Waves (2018, December 26). Guyana Bar Association rejects unofficial calculation of no-confidence vote, calls for elections by March. https://demerarawaves.com/2018/12/26/guyana-bar-association-rejects-unofficial-calculation-of-no-confidence-vote-calls-for-elections-by-march/

Guyana Chronicle (2020, December 24). Charrandas enters Parliament in full confidence, sees no Coalition MP in seat. https://guyanachronicle.com/2020/12/24/charrandas-enters-parliament-in-full-confidence-sees-no-coalition-mp-in-seat/

Kaieteur News (2019, February 9). 9 months required for House-to House registration – GECOM. https://www.kaieteurnewsonline.com/2019/02/09/9-months-required-for-house-to-house-registration-gecom/

Newsroom (2019, June 22). Court action, more protest if house to house registration blocked-APNU. https://newsroom.gy/2019/06/22/court-action-more-protest-if-house-to-house-registration-blocked-apnu/

News Room (2020, March 17). Granger 'deeply disappointed' at withdrawal of CARICOM recount team. https://newsroom.gy/2020/03/17/granger-deeply-disappointed-at-withdrawal-of-caricom-recount-team/

Stabroek News (2019, August 14). Current house-to-house registration not illegal – CJ. https://www.stabroeknews.com/2019/08/14/news/guyana/current-house-to-house-registration-not-illegal-cj/

The New York Times (2018, December 22). Guyana's Government Falls in No-Confidence Vote. https://www.nytimes.com/2018/12/22/world/americas/guyana-government-falls.html

Guyana Chronicle (2019, August 27). GECOM sets new timeline for house to house registration. https://guyanachronicle.com/2019/08/27/house-to-house-registration-to-halt-from-august-31/

Guyana Chronicle (2019, September 3). 370,000, final count for H2H. https://guyanachronicle.com/2019/09/03/370000-final-count-for-h2h/

Newsroom (2019, November 26). GECOM grapples with unmatched fingerprints from House-to-House data. https://newsroom.gy/2019/11/26/gecom-grapples-with-unmatched-fingerprints-from-house-to-house-data/

INews (2019, December 14). GECOM places onus on PPP to check 20,000 unverified registrants. https://www.inewsguyana.com/gecom-places-onus-on-ppp-to-check-20000-unverified-registrants/

Guyana Times (2019, December 20).

GECOM to verify 'new registrants'. https://www.guyanatimesinternational.com/gecom-to-verify-new-registrants/

Stabroek News (2020, January 9). GECOM updating voters' list with house to house data. https://www.stabroeknews.com/2020/01/09/news/guyana/gecom-updating-voters-list-with-house-to-house-data/

Carter Center (2020, March 4). Guyana General Election Preliminary Statement. https://www.cartercenter.org/resources/pdfs/news/peace_publications/election_reports/guyana-preliminary-statement-021420.pdf

BBC (2020, March 5). Guyana election: Two main parties declare victory as tensions rise. https://www.bbc.com/news/world-latin-america-51763283

BBC (2020, March 6). Guyana election: US concerned over 'electoral fraud'. https://www.bbc.com/news/world-latin-america-51775111

Kaieteur News (2020, March 6). Injunction granted to stop declaration of unverified election results. https://www.kaieteurnewsonline.com/2020/03/06/injunction-granted-to-stop-declaration-of-unverified-results/

BBC (2020, March 12). Guyana election: Top court orders partial recount of votes. https://www.bbc.com/news/world-latin-america-51851620

Stabroek News (2020, March 14). Region Four vote count completed after suspect process. https://www.stabroeknews.com/2020/03/14/news/guyana/region-four-vote-count-completed-after-suspect-process/

Demerara Waves (2020, March 17). High Court blocks CARICOM-supervised recount of Guyana's general election votes. https://demerarawaves.com/2020/03/17/high-court-blocks-caricom-supervised-recount-of-guyanas-general-election-votes/

Stabroek News (2020, March 18a). Mottley says 'it is clear there are forces that do not want to see the votes recounted'. https://www.stabroeknews.com/2020/03/18/news/guyana/mottley-says-it-is-clear-there-are-forces-that-do-not-want-to-see-the-votes-recounted/

Stabroek News (2020, March 18b). Joe Singh calls on President to call off 'Dogs of War', let vote recount proceed. https://www.stabroeknews.com/2020/03/18/news/guyana/joe-singh-calls-on-president-to-call-off-dogs-of-war-let-vote-recount-proceed/

Stabroek News (2020, March 18c). Tabulations by Mingo were not credible – Commonwealth observer group. https://www.stabroeknews.com/2020/03/18/news/guyana/tabulations-by-mingo-were-not-credible-commonwealth-observer-group/

Stabroek News (2020, March 20). Pompeo cites Guyana's electoral process as a challenge for OAS. https://www.stabroeknews.com/2020/03/20/news/guyana/pompeo-cites-guyanas-electoral-process-as-a-challenge-for-oas/

Stabroek News (2020, March 21). Ballot boxes moved without notice from Arthur Chung centre to GECOM HQ. https://www.stabroeknews.com/2020/03/21/news/guyana/ballot-boxes-moved-without-notice-from-arthur-chung-centre-to-gecom-hq/

Stabroek News (2020, March 22a). Gaskin says Mingo's Region Four figures don't add up. https://www.stabroeknews.com/2020/03/22/news/guyana/gaskin-says-mingos-region-four-figures-dont-add-up/

Stabroek News (2020, March 22b). Sir Shridath applauds Dominic Gaskin. https://www.stabroeknews.com/2020/03/22/news/guyana/sir-shridath-applauds-dominic-gaskin/

Stabroek News (2020, March 22c). Benn writes Top Cop over alleged threat by rank at GECOM HQ. https://www.stabroeknews.com/2020/03/22/news/guyana/benn-writes-top-cop-over-alleged-threat-by-rank-at-gecom-hq/

Stabroek News (2020, March 23). PPP/C urges Granger to instruct APNU/AFC candidate to withdraw challenge to vote recount. https://www.stabroeknews.com/2020/03/23/news/guyana/ppp-c-urges-granger-to-instruct-apnuafc-candidate-to-withdraw-challenge-to-vote-recount/

Stabroek News (2020, March 24a). Yesu Persaud urges President Granger to take steps to preserve democracy. https://www.stabroeknews.com/2020/03/24/news/guyana/yesu-persaud-urges-president-granger-to-take-steps-to-preserve-democracy/

Stabroek News (2020, March 24). Police force denies electoral interference. https://www.stabroeknews.com/2020/03/24/news/guyana/police-force-denies-electoral-interference/

Stabroek News (2020, March 26a). GECOM acquiesced in 2011 to APNU demand for SOPs. https://www.stabroeknews.com/2020/03/26/news/guyana/gecom-acquiesced-in-2011-to-apnu-demand-for-sops/

Stabroek News (2020, March 26b). GECOM says awaiting court ruling before any further actions. https://www.stabroeknews.com/2020/03/26/news/guyana/gecom-says-awaiting-court-ruling-before-any-further-actions/

Stabroek News (2020, March 27). GECOM Chair withdraws 'wrong' court affidavit. https://www.stabroeknews.com/2020/03/27/news/guyana/gecom-chair-withdraws-wrong-court-affidavit/

Stabroek News (2020, March 28). GECOM Chair deflects private sector request for SoPs. https://www.stabroeknews.com/2020/03/28/news/guyana/gecom-chair-deflects-private-sector-request-for-sops/

Stabroek News (2020, March 29a). Ministry asserts sovereignty over US 'summons'. https://www.stabroeknews.com/2020/03/29/news/guyana/ministry-asserts-sovereignty-over-us-summons/

Stabroek News (2020, March 29b). GHRA calls on GECOM Chair to proceed with recount. https://www.stabroeknews.com/2020/03/29/news/guyana/ghra-calls-on-gecom-chair-to-proceed-with-recount/

Stabroek News (2020, March 31a). Full Court temporarily stays recount case brought by APNU/AFC candidate. https://www.stabroeknews.com/2020/03/31/news/guyana/full-court-temporarily-stays-recount-case-brought-by-apnuafc-candidate/

Stabroek News (2020, March 31b). AFC now pressing for gov't of national unity. https://www.stabroeknews.com/2020/03/31/news/guyana/afc-now-pressing-for-govt-of-national-unity/

Stabroek News (2020, April 2). Commonwealth ministers call on GECOM to ensure right of people to duly elected gov't. https://www.stabroeknews.com/2020/04/02/news/guyana/commonwealth-ministers-call-on-gecom-to-ensure-right-of-people-to-duly-elected-govt/

Stabroek News (2020, April 3). GECOM agrees recount for all regions. https://www.stabroeknews.com/2020/04/03/news/guyana/gecom-agrees-recount-for-all-regions/

Stabroek News (2020, April 4). GECOM to recount all 10 regions. https://www.stabroeknews.com/2020/04/04/news/guyana/gecom-to-recount-all-10-regions/

Stabroek News (2020, April 6). Burnhamite faction has taken control of PNCR and will fight to stay in power – Jerome Khan. https://www.stabroeknews.com/2020/04/06/news/guyana/burnhamite-faction-has-taken-control-of-pncr-and-will-fight-to-stay-on-in-power-jerome-khan/

Stabroek News (2020, April 9). Lowenfield proposes 156-day vote recount. https://www.stabroeknews.com/2020/04/09/news/guyana/lowenfield-proposes-156-day-vote-recount/

Stabroek News (2020, April 10). GECOM gets 10-day plan for recount. https://www.stabroeknews.com/2020/04/10/news/guyana/gecom-gets-10-day-plan-for-recount/

Stabroek News (2020, April 17). Bar Council calls for GECOM to expedite process for accurate, transparent poll results. https://www.stabroeknews.com/2020/04/17/news/guyana/bar-council-calls-for-gecom-to-expedite-process-for-accurate-transparent-poll-results/

Stabroek News (2020, April 19). PPP asks GECOM Chair to reconsider recount proposal. https://www.stabroeknews.com/2020/04/19/news/guyana/ppp-asks-gecom-chair-to-reconsider-recount-proposal/

Stabroek News (2020, April 20). PPP rejects Nagamootoo limiting of recount hours. https://www.stabroeknews.com/2020/04/20/news/guyana/ppp-rejects-nagamootoo-limiting-of-recount-hours/

Stabroek News (2020, April 22). GECOM commissioners receive proposed recount order. https://www.stabroeknews.com/2020/04/22/news/guyana/gecom-Commissioners-receive-proposed-recount-order/

Stabroek News (2020, April 27). GECOM now major battlefront for free and fair elections – Ramkarran. https://www.stabroeknews.com/2020/04/27/news/guyana/gecom-now-major-battlefront-for-free-and-fair-elections-ramkarran

Stabroek News (2020, May 4). GECOM sets Wednesday for recount. https://www.stabroeknews.com/2020/05/04/news/guyana/gecom-sets-wednesday-for-recount/

Stabroek News (2020, May 5). Carter Center observer denied approval to fly to Guyana. https://www.stabroeknews.com/2020/05/05/news/guyana/carter-center-observer-denied-approval-to-fly-to-guyana/

Stabroek News (2020, May 11). APNU/AFC alleges 'clear pattern' of contamination of elections. https://www.stabroeknews.com/2020/05/11/news/guyana/apnuafc-alleges-clear-pattern-of-contamination-of-elections/

Stabroek News (2020, May 14). Golding exposes electoral fraud at OAS meeting. https://www.stabroeknews.com/2020/05/14/news/guyana/golding-exposes-electoral-fraud-at-oas-meeting/

Stabroek News (2020, May 22). Carter Center 'deeply disappointed' at not being able to return. https://www.stabroeknews.com/2020/05/22/news/guyana/carter-center-deeply-disappointed-at-not-being-able-to-return/

Stabroek News (2020, June 20). Ramjattan ready to accept recount results. https://www.stabroeknews.com/2020/06/20/news/guyana/ramjattan-ready-to-accept-recount-results/

Stabroek News (2020, June 23). Court of Appeal majority ruling on valid votes may have little impact. https://www.stabroeknews.com/2020/06/23/news/guyana/court-of-appeal-majority-ruling-on-valid-votes-may-have-little-impact/

Stabroek News (2020, June 24). OAS calls for end to elections using recount figure. https://www.stabroeknews.com/2020/06/24/news/guyana/oas-calls-for-end-to-elections-using-recount-figure/

Stabroek News (2020, June 30). Granger endorses Lowenfield chopping of 115,000 votes. https://www.stabroeknews.com/2020/06/30/news/guyana/granger-endorses-lowenfield-chopping-of-115000-votes/

Stabroek News (2020, July 31). Ralph Gonsalves: 'This soap opera has to come to an end and democracy has to prevail. It is self-evident'. https://www.stabroeknews.com/2020/07/31/news/guyana/ralph-gonsalves-this-soap-opera-has-to-come-to-an-end-and-democracy-has-to-prevail-it-is-self-evident/

Stabroek News (2020, October 13). Timeline of legal cases following the December 21, 2018 motion of no confidence. https://www.stabroeknews.com/2020/10/13/news/guyana/timeline-of-legal-cases-following-the-december-21-2018-motion-of-no-confidence/.

6

A New Beginning in a Turbulent World

If, like other poor countries we are to break the vicious circle of poverty we have to try to ascertain its root causes and to rely more heavily on our own internal resources, material and human. The job is difficult, but it is not beyond our capabilities, given good-will, cooperation, and hard work on all sides. CHEDDI JAGAN, 1964

When the PPP/C returned to office in 2020, it inherited an economy in distress, with all the key sectors paralysed due to the destructive policies of the APNU-AFC government. Unemployment was pervasive due to the collapse of the key sectors. The situation was further exacerbated by the COVID-19 pandemic and the election impasse following the March 2020 General and Regional elections. Adding to these challenges were the exceptionally high freight costs and a surge in consumer demand for goods that had been delayed during the COVID-19 pandemic, which further complicated the policy environment. Moreover, the global supply chain experienced significant disruption, resulting in further delays and shortages of consumer and producer goods globally. The cost of shipping escalated and combined with other global shocks to create a global cost-of-living crisis. Notably, in November 2020, three months after taking office, the freight cost for a 40-foot container surged by 75 per cent, thereby causing the cost of imported goods to rise sharply.

It was against this backdrop that the first budget of the newly formed government was framed in 2020. Specifically, the budget had to make provisions to control the spread of the COVID-19 pandemic while resuscitating the key sectors that came to a standstill in 2020 and faced the global supply chain disruption. The primary aim of the budget was to stabilise the economy while laying the groundwork for the full implementation of the transformative agenda outlined in the PPP/C's 2020 manifesto.

This chapter discusses some of the policies implemented by the PPP/C and the dividends that accrued from the same. It starts with a description of the policy environment and continues with an examination of the policies implemented between 2020 and 2025. The impacts of these policies are also discussed.

Reviving a stagnant economy in a turbulent world

The PPP/C returned to office in August 2020, when the economy was at a standstill due to the COVID-19 pandemic and a five-month election impasse. The latter resulted from the APNU-AFC's unwillingness to accept the results of the March 2020 national and regional elections, following their failed attempt to rig these elections. Due to pressure from our regional and international partners, however, the APNU&AFC agreed to recount the votes. Even after agreeing to the recount exercise, the APNU&AFC government attempted to derail the exercise. After five gruelling months and intervention by the courts, along with persistent pressure from our regional and international partners, the APNU&AFC finally conceded.

The COVID-19 pandemic made the situation worse, since there was a nationwide lockdown. During 2020, the non-oil sector contracted for the first time in more than a decade. With only a few months remaining in the year, the PPP/C government began preparing the national budget immediately. While the budget was being prepared, the PPP/C government engaged the commercial banks and the central bank to lower interest rates, extend the moratorium on loan payments, and waive bank charges for ATM transactions. The commercial banks also agreed to provide businesses with short-term working capital to meet payroll and other short-term funding requirements, as well as consumer loans of up to $10 million at a concessional rate. These measures provided relief to businesses and citizens, estimated at over $28 billion. Meanwhile, the central bank lowered the Reserve Requirements and Liquid Asset Requirements to boost liquidity in the system, estimated at $32.7 billion.

The government also commenced the distribution of a $25,000 cash grant to every household, where approximately $7.58 billion was placed into the hands of citizens across the country. The government simultaneously engaged several international agencies and bilateral partners to secure financial and other resources to curb the spread of the COVID-19 pandemic and minimise its impact on the local economy (GT, 17/08/2020).

In less than two months after assuming office, the PPP/C government prepared and presented its emergency budget. As promised in its manifesto, the PPP/C government removed the 200 punitive taxes imposed by the APNU-AFC on essential goods and services, which had increased the tax burden on ordinary citizens and crippled the productive sectors. To boost the disposable income of citizens, the government paid all public servants a one-off payment of $25,000, placing approximately $2 billion into their hands. The new government also paid a two-week bonus to members of the disciplined services and front-line health workers, placing approximately $1 billion into the hands of these public servants. These relief measures, which cost $2.1 billion, were implemented even as the government struggled to mobilise funds to procure vaccines, testing kits, sanitising materials, and personal protective equipment for citizens, all aimed at preventing the spread of the COVID-19 pandemic. To support vulnerable communities, the government distributed relief hampers, food items, and cleaning essentials at a cost of $906.6 million.

Unfortunately, the following year, the country experienced widespread flooding that affected more than 25,000 households in over 300 communities across regions 3, 5, 6, 7, and 10 (Floodlist, 2021). This flood had devastating effects on the productive sector in the affected regions.

Resuscitating the productive sectors and creating jobs

Even as the PPP/C government battled with various shocks, it remained steadfast in its commitment to fulfil its 2020 Manifesto promises. In this regard, the PPP/C government took decisive action to re-open the sugar estates within the first 100 days upon resuming office. These estates were not only shuttered but intentionally dismantled by the APNU-AFC government with the aim of annihilating the sugar industry permanently. In response to this unprecedented assault, the PPP/C government injected more than $17 billion into the sector to re-tool, revitalise, and consolidate the industry. Despite these investments, however, the sugar industry struggled to recover. Sugar production increased incrementally from 58,025.1 metric tonnes in 2021 to 60,203.5 metric tonnes by 2023, only to plummet to 47,103 metric tonnes in 2024 as the devastating effects of *El Niño* further stifled output. The sluggish rebound of the industry serves as a stark reminder of the deep wounds inflicted by the APNU&AFC on this industry, which supports the livelihoods of countless citizens in rural communities.

The rice industry, which was severely harmed by the 220 per cent increase in Drainage and Irrigation fees and 600 per cent increase in land rental fees, was granted relief in the first budget of the PPP/C government. In the 2020 budget, these fees were reversed, returning approximately $1.4 billion into the hands of rice farmers. To inject new life into this critical sector, the PPP/C government made significant investments in drainage and irrigation, farm-to-market roads, and removed the Value Added Taxes that were imposed by the APNU&AFC government on machinery, equipment, fertiliser, and pesticide. The sector also benefitted from access to seven new markets that motivated farmers to expand their operations.

The various measures, along with improved yields, contributed to the increased output of the rice industry between 2021 and 2024. The production of rice grains, which was 558,995 metric tonnes in 2021, increased by almost 30 per cent to 725,282 metric tonnes in 2024. This marks the highest production of rice grains since 1970 (see Figure 6.1). The foreign exchange earnings from rice exports also reached a historic level of US$254.8 million in 2024 (see Figure 6.1).

The PPP/C government took several bold steps to revive the fishery sector. In its first budget, the PPP/C government reverted to the 2014 licence fees and

Figure 6.1: Production and Export of Rice, 1991-2024

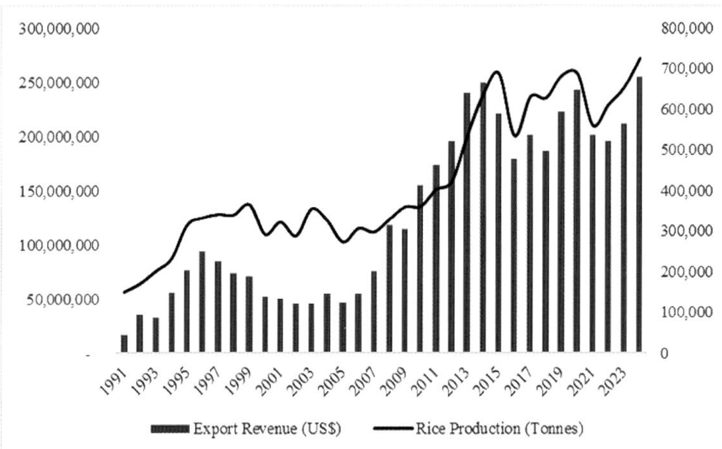

Source: Bureau of Statistics (Guyana)

zero-rated all fishing inputs. With the assistance of the FAO, the government also reviewed and updated the Inland Fisheries and Aquaculture Strategy (2021-2026), formulated an Aquaculture Bill and accompanying Regulations, and crafted a strategy for brackish shrimp. Additionally, the PPP/C government injected significant funds into the rehabilitation of ponds and the drainage and irrigation systems that support the aquaculture industry. These strategic measures yielded significant results, with fishery output soaring by 57.7 per cent, rising from 19,993 tonnes in 2020 to 31,526 tonnes by 2024.

The other crops sector also experienced significant transformation, fuelled by a raft of impactful initiatives implemented by the PPP/C Government to ensure that Guyana ultimately enjoys food and nutrition security and becomes a breadbasket in the Caribbean region. Among these initiatives was the large-scale cultivation of soybeans and corn in the intermediate savannah, which has already demonstrated remarkable success. The production of corn expanded by 293 per cent from 3,380 MT in 2020 to 13,291 MT in 2024, while soybean production grew by 1,669.6 per cent from 2022 to 2024. The production of niche vegetables such as broccoli and cauliflower also increased exponentially, from 624 MT and 750 MT in 2021 to 2,870 MT and 2,123 MT by 2024, due largely to the promotion of shade houses under the Agriculture and Innovation Entrepreneurship Programme.

Notable increases were also recorded for the production of coconut, root crops, spices, beans, and cereals. As shown in Table 6.1, the production of coconuts, root crops, spices, beans, and cereals for 2024 was 195.9 per cent, 73.2 per cent, 566.3 per cent, and 566.3 per cent higher than the levels in 2019. Meanwhile, livestock production (meat) almost doubled from 47,188 metric tons in 2020 to 87,056 metric tons in 2024. This growth was primarily driven by an increase in poultry production. The production of milk and table eggs also increased exponentially between 2020 and 2024.

The forestry sector, which collapsed with the exit of the two largest investors and was further crippled by higher taxes on machinery and equipment, as well as onerous fees and fines imposed by the APNU-AFC government, was resuscitated through various policy measures. In its first budget, the PPP/C government reversed the taxes, fees, and fines introduced by the APNU&AFC government. To enhance log production and promote value-added activities, the PPP/C established a $900 million revolving fund at the Demerara Bank and

Table 6.1: Other crops, 2015-2024 (MT)

Commodities	2015	2016	2017	2018	2019	2020	2021	2022	2023	2024
Other Crops	577,679	505,240	652,275	766,250	755,990	765,577	688,144	814,840	873,784	981,376
Coconut	24,263	22,737	30,356	31,007	28,712	30,503	36,544	49,138	73,924	84,946
Fruits	147,192	115,408	174,412	213,865	216,448	223,306	180,402	197,875	205,658	229,735
Root Crops	97,699	65,571	77,037	82,925	88,059	92,285	111,338	127,405	136,277	152,523
Spices	66,620	65,658	71,522	81,954	84,653	86,697	71,042	93,103	98,045	108,849
Beans & Cereals	5,407	2,660	3,633	2,891	4,003	4,214	6,887	11,354	13,930	26,674
Vegetables	232,775	230,898	293,023	351,277	325,998	327,555	279,253	330,493	340,635	373,250
Cole Crops	73	26	103	230	1,083	1,017	2,678	4,777	5,120	5,212

Source: Bureau of Statistics (Guyana)

issued concessions to both small and large-scale loggers. The PPP/C government also amended the log export policy to allow saw-millers to export logs. Between 2021 and 2024, the PPP/C issued over 150 small concessions and five large concessions. These measures, along with a surge in local demand for timber products driven by the construction boom, resulted in log production increasing to 483,000 cubic metres in 2024, up from 317,857 cubic metres in 2020, representing an increase of approximately 52 per cent (see Figure 6.2). Meanwhile, total employment, which had decreased from 22,000 in 2015 to 14,000 by 2020, surpassed 25,000 in 2024.

The bauxite sector was revived with the facilitation of the US$120 million investment by BOSAI Minerals Group in Linden. Under the APNU&AFC, production in this sector dwindled by 61.9 per cent between 2015 and 2020, and experienced a 50 per cent contraction in employment. The investment by BOSAI created more than 500 jobs and contributed to a more than threefold increase in production from 513,939 tonnes to 1,703,123 tonnes by 2024.

The construction sector has reported double-digit growth every year since 2021, averaging 31.1 per cent between 2021 and 2024. The growth in this sector has been due to various measures implemented by the PPP/C government, including the removal of Value Added Taxes on certain building and construction materials. Significant private investment in residential and commercial properties

Figure 6.2: Forestry product and growth in construction sector, 2015-2024

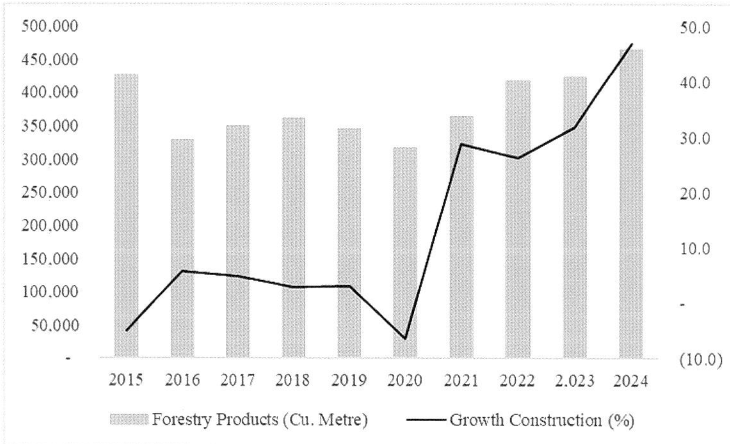

Source: Bureau of Statistics (Guyana)

and the bold Public Sector Investment Programme (PSIP) in the physical and social sectors also propelled the construction sector. The construction boom contributed significantly to the rapid expansion of the other mining subsectors. Sand declaration increased by more than four-fold, from 2,618,500 tonnes in 2020 to 12,618,998 tonnes by 2024. The declaration of crushed stone also grew more than four-fold during the same period, from 737,750 tonnes in 2020 to 3,338,760 tonnes in 2024 (Figure 6.3).

Meanwhile, the services sector has also experienced robust growth, benefiting from the positive spillover effects of growth in the oil and non-oil sectors. Between 2021 and 2024, the average growth rates approximated 15 per cent for the wholesale and retail sector, 14 per cent for transport and storage, 28 per cent for accommodation and food services, 10 per cent for information and communication, 9 per cent for financial and insurance activities, 30 per cent for professional, scientific and technical services and 14 per cent for administrative support services respectively. In addition to the buoyancy in the economy, the ICT sector benefitted significantly from the enactment of the Telecommunication Act No. 18 of 2016 in October 2020, which effectively liberalised this sector.

The successful revival of the productive sectors has ignited an unprecedented boost in non-oil GDP between 2020 and 2024. The non-oil GDP, which stood at $949.2 billion in 2020, rose by 48 per cent in 2024 to $1,405.2

Figure 6.3: Sand and crushed stone declarations, 2014-2024

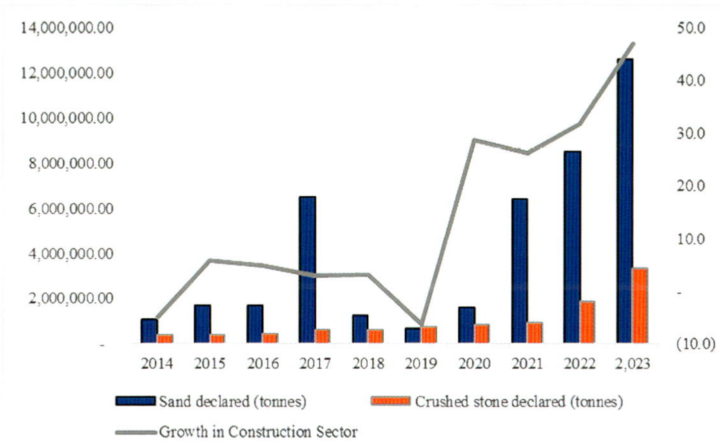

Source: Bureau of Statistics (Guyana)

billion. Even more remarkable is the fact that the growth in the non-oil sectors between 2021 and 2023 has outpaced the economic growth rates of many countries in the Caribbean and across the globe. In 2022, Guyana's non-oil GDP ranked it as the 11th fastest-growing economy in the world. In 2023, our non-oil GDP placed Guyana as the 3rd fastest-growing economy in the world, and the fastest in Latin America and the Caribbean. Figure 6.4 shows the annual real economic growth rates for Guyana *vis-à-vis* the global average and average for Latin America and the Caribbean (LAC). Based on the figure, the economic growth reported for Guyana was not only substantially above the global average and the average for LAC between 2020 and 2024 but is also projected to remain above these averages for the remainder of the decade (see Figure 6.4).

The oil and gas sector has also experienced significant growth. As of 2024, the ExxonMobil-led consortium has sanctioned six wells in the Stabroek Block, three of which are producing at a combined capacity of 650,000 barrels of oil per day. To date, the consortium has invested more than US$28.7 billion in the three developments. By 2027, the other three projects are expected to increase total investments to US$56.7 billion. This expansion has yielded significant fiscal benefits, with royalty earnings alone reaching nearly US$345 million in 2024. Also in 2024, an additional 5 new commercial discoveries were made, bringing the total number of discoveries to nearly 50 by the end

Figure 6.4: Real GDP growth (Annual per cent change), 2020-2030

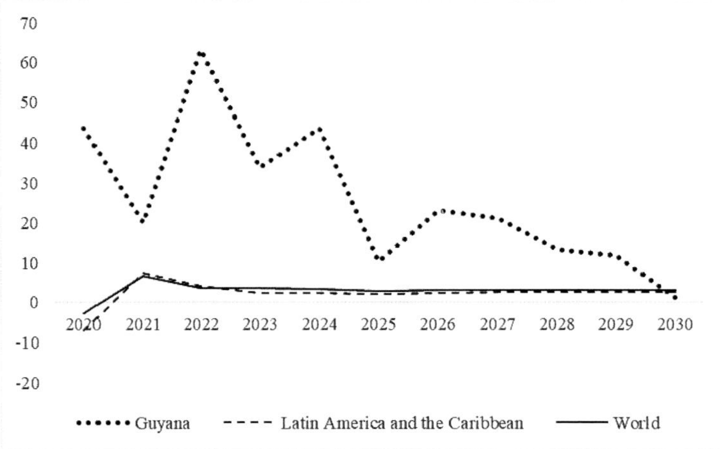

Source: IMF

of the year, and increasing the estimated recoverable resources to more than 11 billion oil-equivalent barrels, inclusive of 17 trillion standard cubic feet of gas. These developments have further solidified our position as a regional and global energy hub.

Recognising the risks often associated with rapid resource wealth accumulation and reaffirming our commitment to transparency, accountability, and sound resource governance, the PPP/C government repealed and replaced the 37-year-old Petroleum Exploration and Production Act with the Petroleum Activity Bill. The PPP/C government also developed and introduced a new fiscal regime that see all discoveries outside of the Stabroek block being subjected to a 65 per cent cost recoverable ceiling, 10 per cent royalty, 10 per cent tax paid by the operator and a 50/50 profit share, all carefully calibrated to maintain Guyana's global competitiveness in the sector.

Despite all the excitement in the oil and gas industry, we will not be able to boast that the true benefits of the industry are realised if citizens and local businesses do not benefit from opportunities along the value chain of the industry. To this end, the PPP/C has been diligently working to ensure that every Guyanese and business, regardless of geography, size, or sector, benefits from the new oil and gas sector.

A key innovation in this regard is the Local Content Act, which has enhanced procurement transparency and accountability among operators and contractors. The success of the Local Content Act is evident. The procurement of goods and services from local companies exceeded US$612 million in 2024, and exceeded more than US$1.5 billion since 2022. This has led to an increase in local capacity, with Guyanese firms now providing advanced services, including sub-sea services, the manufacturing of premium downhole drilling accessories, and even the supply of Multi-Purpose Support Vessels (MPSVs). As of 2024, there are over 6,500 Guyanese employed in the industry. In 2025, the expectation remains the same. We expect the total number of Guyanese working in the industry to exceed 7,000, with nearly 900 new hires anticipated during the first quarter of 2025. Additionally, total procurement opportunities for local companies are projected to exceed US$650 million.

Addressing the infrastructure gap to catalyse development

Upon returning to office in 2020, the PPP/C government embarked on an ambitious Public Sector Investment Programme (PSIP) aligned with its 2020 Manifesto. Consequently, the capital expenditure increased from $66.3 billion in 2020 to $737.9 billion in 2024. The increase in capital spending has stimulated the construction sector (see Figure 6.5) and has laid the groundwork for sustainable development and the provision of world-class social services by 2030 and beyond.

Since our independence, our country has been grappling with an infrastructure deficit that has constrained the private sector and hindered efforts to ensure balanced development due to weak transport links between the coastal and hinterland regions and the rest of the world (Wenner and Bollers, 2018). To close the gap, the country would have to invest between US$9.4 and US$23.8 billion across several sectors, including transport (US$6.2 to US$11.5 billion), electricity (US$900 million and US$2.4 billion), telecommunications (US$81 to US$221 million), flood protection (US$417 to US$680 million), water and sanitation (US$474 to US$783 million) and trade infrastructure (US$532 to US$959 million) by 2030 (IDB, 2023).

Since 2020, the government has allocated $735.7 billion to rehabilitate, upgrade, and expand the country's transport infrastructure. Of this amount, more than $651.8 billion has been allocated for roads and bridges, and in excess of

Figure 6.5: PSIP ($ billion) and growth (percentage change) in the construction sector, 2015-2024

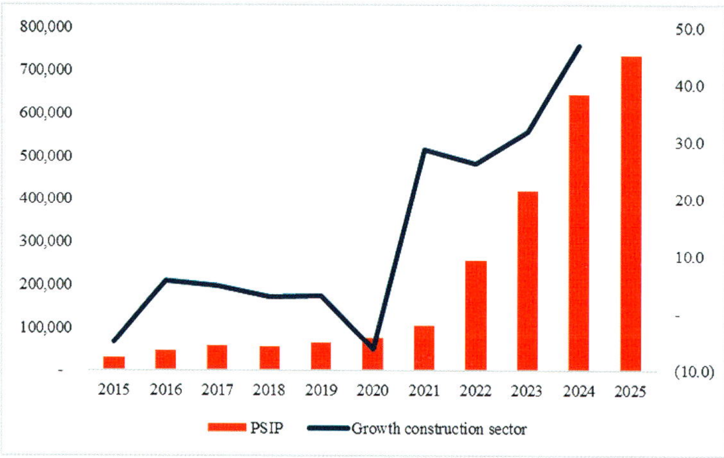

Source: Ministry of Finance and Bureau of Statistics (Guyana)

$30.4 billion and $ 19.1 billion for river transport and air transport infrastructure, respectively.

Consistent with its 2020 Manifesto, the government initiated several transformative infrastructure projects, including a new four-lane high-span bridge over the Demerara River to improve connectivity between the two most populous regions (Regions 3 and 4), the Wismar-McKenzie Bridge and the Linden-Mabura Road that will unleash the trade potential between the state of Roraima in Brazil, and Guyana, and road links from Parika to Goshen and Timehri to Bartica to facilitate smoother and more efficient movement of goods, services and commuters. In the 2025 Budget, the government allocated funds for the Corentyne Bridge and Berbice Bridge to facilitate efficient trade between Suriname and Guyana.

Additionally, construction has begun on new highways, such as Sheriff Street to Orange Nassau, Schoonord to Crane, and Ogle to Eccles, and the upgrade of the road between Grove and Timehri on the East Bank of Demerara into a four-lane highway as well as the Linden-Soesdyke Highway. Apart from enhancing connectivity and reducing travel time costs, these projects will open land for industrial, commercial, and residential development.

Over the past five years, the government has also allocated significant resources to rehabilitate hinterland airstrips and expand the CJIA. As a result

Table 6.2: Budgetary allocations for infrastructure projects, 2021-2025 ($ billions)

Sectors	2020	2021	2022	2023	2024	2025
Road and bridges	na	25.6	76.7	136.1	204.1	209.3
Air transport	na	3.1	2.6	1.6	2.3	9.5
River transport	na	4.6	3.1	4.7	8.1	9.9
Total	34.4	33.3	82.4	142.4	214.5	228.7

Source: Budget Speech (various years)

of the upgrade of the hinterland airstrips, reversal of VAT of hinterland travel, and an upsurge in economic activities in the hinterland regions, internal air travel has risen to unprecedented levels. The river transportation infrastructure has also benefitted from significant budgetary allocations to construct and rehabilitate stellings, wharves, and ferries, as well as build and rehabilitate ocean-going passenger and cargo vessels. Together, all the infrastructure projects will position Guyana as a logistics hub in South America and the Caribbean.

In our effort to make Guyana's energy secure, the government has embraced an energy mix that will see Guyana transition from energy generation based on fossil fuels to renewable sources, such as solar, hydro, and wind. Since returning to office in 2020, the government installed 201.2 megawatts of additional power generation capacity to the Demerara Berbice Interconnected System (DBIS) to meet the growing demand for electricity.

The PPP/C administration has also invested in thirteen solar farms and nineteen mini solar grids, resulting in a 224 per cent increase in electricity from PV technology, from 5.35 megawatts before 2020 to 17.37 megawatts in 2024. The government's commitment towards greening the energy sector is underscored by its ongoing investments in solar farms at Mahdia (0.65 megawatt), Wakenaam (0.75 megawatt), Leguan (0.6 megawatt), roof-top solar systems for government buildings, and 2.2 megawatts of new hydropower capacity at Moco Moco and Kamu. Distributions of 30,000 Solar PV Home Energy Systems procured for the Hinterland and Riverine communities added 4.8 megawatts across the ten administrative regions.

The Government also commenced work on several small hydro projects, including the construction of a 1.5-megawatt (MW) hydropower Plant at Kumu, Region 9, and the rehabilitation of the hydropower plant at Moco Moco. It also continued work on a 150-kW Hydropower Station at Kato, Region 8. Meanwhile, three new generators were installed and functioning: Lethem (900kVA), Mabaruma (900kVA), and Port Kaituma (625kVA). The investment in the sector has led to an increase in electricity generation of almost 50 per cent, from 902.6 thousand MWh in 2020 to 1,348.8 thousand MWh in 2024 (Table 6.3).

In line with its 2020 Manifesto commitment, the government commenced work on the transformative Gas to Energy (GtE) project, which will add an additional 300 megawatts to the national grid. This initiative is projected to yield a 50 per cent reduction in the cost of electricity and is expected to propel manufacturing activities. To support the GtE project, the government started work on the construction of 46 km of 69 kV and 24 km of 230 kV transmission lines. An Expression of Interest (EOI) for another 250 megawatts from gas, as part of phase 2 of the GtE project, was also launched.

To bolster the country's resilience to climate change, the government has allocated $199.2 billion to upgrade and expand the national drainage and irrigation system from 2020 to 2025 (see Table 6.4). These allocations have facilitated the installation of high-capacity drainage pumps and financed the construction of three new major outfall channels in Regions 3, 5, and 6. These investments were complemented by the strengthening of the country's sea and river defence system throughout the country, with a budgetary allocation of $30.1 billion from 2020 to 2025 (see Table 6.4).

Between 2020 and 2025, the government allocated $75.6 billion to the water sector (see Table 6.4). As a result of these allocations, the water distribution system was expanded, with over 60 communities benefitting from potable water for the first time. New water treatment plants were also constructed, while

Table 6.3: Investment in Energy Sector, 2020-2025

Sectors	2020	2021	2022	2023	2024	2025
Energy Generation (MWH)	902.6	958.8	1,030.3	1,179.9	1,348.8	na
Budget ($ billion)	na	1.54	33.32	45.1	95.7	88

Source: Budget Speech (various years)

Table 6.4: Budgetary allocations for D&I, Sea & River Defence, Sanitation, ICT

Sectors	2020	2021	2022	2023	2024	2025
D&I	9	12	13	19.7	72.3	73.2
Sea & river defence	-	5.1	5.0	4.9	6.9	8.2
Water	2.8	4.6	4.9	17.7	22.5	23.1
Sanitation and solid waste management	0.6	1.1	1.4	1.9	2.6	13.2

Source: Budget Speech (various years)

existing facilities were upgraded. To ensure that residents in hinterland and riverine communities benefit from access to potable water, new wells were constructed in these communities, benefitting over 35,000 residents. The proportion of the hinterland community with access to water also improved from 31.4 per cent in 2018 to 75 per cent by 2022, due to these investments. Today, more than 97 per cent of the population has access to potable water.

To ensure that citizens have access to sanitation services, the government allocated $20.8 billion to implement its integrated sanitation management programme aimed at enhancing sanitation and waste management across the country (see Table 6.4). These budgetary allocations catered for the upgrade of existing disposal sites, the development of new sanitary landfill sites and to finance solid waste disposal programmes. The percentage of the population with access to basic sanitation services improved to 91 per cent due to the government's investments in sanitation services (FAO, 2025).

Two months after assuming office in August 2020, the government liberalised the telecommunication sector to unleash the vast transformative potential of this important sector. Since then, the government has facilitated the growth in the sector through budgetary support and various initiatives, such as the phased digitisation of government to government, and government-to-citizen services, Safe Country initiative, modernising the identification system and services, creation of a digital platform, implementation of the Education Management Information System, and operationalisation of telemedicine sites to support healthcare access to hinterland communities.

Promoting private sector investment

Apart from the strategic investment that encouraged private investment, the government has implemented various measures that have resulted in the rapid expansion in both domestic and Foreign Direct Investment (FDI). Among the measures implemented are:

(i) adjustments to the tax regime to improve the investment climate. These include restoring VAT Zero-Rating on basic food items and household necessities, rolling back freight costs to pre-pandemic levels, reducing excise taxes on gasoline and diesel, adjusting the income tax threshold, and others.
(ii) Easy monetary policy, such as the lowering of the Reserve Requirements and Liquid Asset Requirements, to boost liquidity.
(iii) Monetary policy to contain inflation and promote a stable exchange rate, to empower investors to make informed decisions and plan effectively for the future.
(iv) Counter cyclical policies to foster viable business opportunities.
(v) Initiatives to promote political, social, and economic stability to engender investors' confidence.

Between 2020 and 2024, credit to the private sector increased by approximately 73 per cent, more than three times the growth rate reported under the APNU-AFC (see Table 6.5). The rapid expansion in credit to the private sector has not been restricted to any specific economic sector. Indeed, all major economic sectors registered growth in credit to the private sector during the four years ending 2024, reflecting widespread confidence by domestic investors. The highest growth in credit to the private sector was recorded in the other services sector (134 per cent), followed by agriculture (128 per cent), construction and engineering (120 per cent), manufacturing (91 per cent), and distribution (10 per cent).

The renewed confidence in the economy can also be observed in the unprecedented surges in Foreign Direct Investment (FDI) since returning to office in 2020. Between 2021 and 2024, the country attracted more than US$25.2 billion in FDI, more than six times the level reported under APNU&AFC from 2016 to 2020 (see Table 6.6). Increases in FDI inflows were registered in all the

Table 6.5: Credit to Business Enterprises ($ millions)

	2016	2017	2018	2019	2020	2021	2022	2023	2024
Private Sector Credit	219,092	224,192	233,562	253,584	259,794	286,876	328,868	376,118	450,575
Agriculture	11,172	11,359	13,285	13,408	13,832	16,520	19,081	21,892	31,576
Manufacturing	16,841	14,195	14,481	14,914	12,021	14,787	19,499	21,564	22,984
Construction & Engineering	11,866	10,327	9,978	10,954	9,254	12,239	17,253	20,999	20,348
Distribution	32,977	34,920	38,358	38,990	37,233	40,074	44,258	41,008	40,785
Personal	32,584	33,507	34,774	36,637	36,843	38,910	42,218	41,270	51,367
Mining	4,172	5,348	5,130	4,431	4,756	4,231	4,513	5,327	5,803
Other Services	29,108	30,953	31,403	42,314	50,322	61,842	73,718	92,169	117,085
Real Estate Mortgages	74,542	77,894	81,771	87,391	90,639	95,620	104,992	128,647	155,771
Other	5,830	5,689	4,382	4,545	4,894	2,653	3,336	3,242	4,856

Source: Bank of Guyana

Table 6.6: FDI Inflows, 2015-2024

Sectors	2015	2016	2017	2018	2019	2020	2021	2022	2023	2024
Forestry	-	-	-	-	-	-	-	-	-	0.2
Agriculture	19.6	5.8	23.9	0.1	1.2	(2.4)	1.7	2.9	16.4	19.4
Energy	3.0	19.7	87.9	1,090.9	2,400.8	1,972.0	4,399.7	4,269.1	28.0	8,972.6
Information & Telecommunic-ation Technology	2.8	3.5	-	-	2.3	31.7	9.3	7.2	25.8	24.4
Mining & Quarrying	36.7	15.3	49.5	47.3	25.9	(33.1)	13.3	72.9	7,080.2	53.9
Manufacturing & Distribution	12.5	4.3	1.9	5.9	16.0	26.4	43.5	39.6	13.7	98.1
Tourism and Hospitality	13.4	0.9	16.8	0.9	3.5	0.3	0.6	1.7	33.9	-
Transport & Tele-communication	0.5	0.3	23.8	10.6	-	-	-	-	-	-
Others	33.3	8.2	8.3	76.1	240.6	78.9	-	-	-	-
TOTAL	121.7	58.0	212.2	1,231.8	2,690.3	2,073.8	4,468.1	4,393.4	7,197.9	9,168.6

Source: Bank of Guyana

major sectors, including agriculture, energy, information and telecommunication technology, mining and quarrying, manufacturing and distribution, tourism and the hospitality sectors. The notable increases in FDI in every sector is a clear indication that Guyana is rapidly emerging as an investment hub in Latin America and the Caribbean.

Between 2021 and 2024, the influx of FDI in the mining and quarrying sector was US$138 million, more than 52 times higher compared to the 2016-2019 period. This is due to the efforts of the PPP/C to make the bauxite sector, which was previously damaged by the APNU&AFC, more attractive to foreign investors. The information and telecommunication sector attracted FDI to the tune of US$66.7 million between 2021 and 2024, almost 12 times the level reported from 2016 to 2019. This was attributed to the liberalisation of the sector by the PPP/C government. As a result of the attractive business climate and incentives offered by the PPP/C, the manufacturing & distribution sector also benefitted from FDI to the tune of US$194.9 million during the four years ending 2024, almost seven times the US$28.1 million recorded under the APNU&AFC between 2016 and 2019. The energy sector, which benefitted from the largest influx of FDI, approximately US$17.7 billion during the period 2021-2024, reflects the burgeoning oil & gas sector that was catalysed by policies and initiatives of the PPP/C to grow this new sector. According to ECLAC (2024), Guyana attracted the highest FDI inflow in the Caribbean between 2021 and 2023, and in 2022, it was also ranked as the sixth-largest recipient of FDI inflows in the entire Latin America and the Caribbean.

The growth in both domestic and foreign investment is not coincidental but can be attributed to the favourable business environment and climate created by the government's policies. These included counter-cyclical policies aimed at resuscitating key non-oil sectors, as well as prudent monetary and fiscal policies to contain inflation at low single-digit levels and promote exchange rate stability. Improvement in governance, coupled with the deliberate efforts of the government to promote social and political stability, also inspiring greater confidence among investors.

The robust economic growth, as well as social and political growth, also inspired greater confidence among investors, while the successful implementation of the government's strategic investments also attracted additional investment.

Preserving real wages and boosting disposable income

Faced with the global cost of living crisis caused by the disruption in the global supply chain and the Russia-Ukraine war, the government implemented numerous initiatives to preserve the real wages of citizens. Through effective monetary policy, inflation was contained at low single-digit levels, well below the global average and the average inflation rate for Latin America and the Caribbean between 2020 and 2024 (see Table 6.7). This is remarkable, given the rapid pace at which the local economy expanded.

The low inflation rate may also credited to fiscal measures such as the reversal of the VAT basic food and household items imposed by the previous administration, adjustment of the excise tax on fuel and the rolling back of the freight charges to pre-pandemic levels, which blunted the impact of volatile fuel prices and surge in commodity prices globally. The fiscal measures implemented by the government to ease the cost of living pressures have translated into savings for citizens estimated at approximately $100 billion annually.

Furthermore, to boost the disposable income of citizens, the government distributed several targeted cash transfers, including a $25,000 COVID-19 cash grant to each household and a one-off $25,000 bonus to public servants. These targeted cash transfers, which cost the government close to $10 billion, were applauded by the IDB (GT, 28/12/2022). To preserve the disposable income of citizens against inflationary pressures, the government also granted wage increases to public sector employees of 7 per cent in 2021, 8 per cent in 2022,

Table 6.7: Annual Inflation Rate (%), 2015-2024

	2020	2021	2022	2023	2024
The World	2.9	6.3	8.8	6.0	4.9
Advanced Economies	0.5	5.3	7.3	3.1	2.5
Latin America and the Caribbean (LAC)	6.4	11.7	14.9	17.2	12.1
Guyana	0.9	5.7	7.2	2	2.9

Source: IMF

6.5 per cent in 2023, 10 per cent in 2024, and 8 per cent in 2025. The across-the-board increases consistently exceeded the annual inflation rate. Some categories of workers, such as healthcare workers, teachers, and members of the discipline services, benefited from adjustments to their salaries. Additionally, the income tax threshold was progressively increased from $65,000 in 2022, then to $85,000 in 2023, $100,000 in 2024, and $130,000 in 2025. As part of its commitment outlined in the 2020 Manifesto, the government restored the one-month tax-free bonus for members of the disciplined services. Bonuses were also paid to healthcare professionals in 2020, 2021, and 2022.

In fulfilment of its manifesto commitments, we restored the *Because We Care Cash Grant*. This cash grant was not only increased from $19,000 in 2020 to $50,000 but also extended the direct cash transfer to students attending private schools. Additionally, the government restored the water and electricity subsidy, doubled the Old Age Pension, and increased Public Assistance by more than 144 per cent. Other direct transfers paid by the government include a cash grant of $600,000 to help dialysis patients, a one-off cash grant of $100,000 to children with disability, $3,000 vouchers to school children and pensioners for eye tests, and $15,000 vouchers for spectacles. To alleviate the impact of the rising cost of living, the government launched a part-time job initiative that benefits over 10,000 citizens in Regions 2, 3, 5, 6, 9, and 10, thereby improving the disposable income of their households. In 2024, the government implemented a $100,000 cash grant, which is expected to benefit more than 600,000 citizens aged 18 and older, at a cost of over $60 billion.

Despite the various initiatives to preserve the real disposable income of citizens and the ambitious capital budget implemented by the government, no new taxes were imposed, and fiscal discipline was maintained. Indeed, the ratio of tax revenue to GDP has declined continuously, from 20.0 per cent in 2020 to 8.2 per cent in 2024, reflecting the lower tax burden on consumers and businesses.

Although the government initiated several proactive countercyclical policies, the ratio of fiscal deficit to GDP remained in the low single digits throughout the four years leading up to 2024. The ratio of debt to GDP was also contained below the acceptable threshold of 50 per cent (IMF, 2023) and among the lowest in Latin America and the Caribbean in 2024 (see Figure 6.6). These outturns underscore the prudent approach to fiscal management by the PPP/C government since 2024.

Table 6.8: Old Age Pension, Public Assistance and *Because We Care Cash Grant*, 2014-2025

Period	Old Age Pension	Public Assistance	Because We Care
2014	13,125	5,900	0
2015	17,000	6,500	0
2016	18,200	7,500	0
2017	19,000	8,000	0
2018	19,500	8,000	0
2019	20,500	8,000	0
2020	20,500	9,000	0
2021	25,000	12,000	15,000
2022	28,000	14,000	25,000
2023	33,000	16,000	35,000
2024	36,000	19,000	40,000
2025	41,000	22,000	50,000

Source: Ministry of Finance

Figure 6.6: ratio of debt-to-GDP, 2024

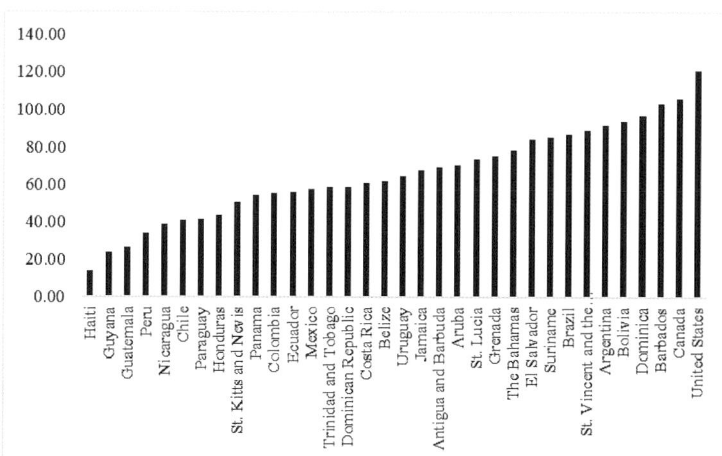

Source: IMF

The prudent fiscal policy implemented by the PPP/C did not go unnoticed. International agencies, such as the International Monetary Fund (IMF), commended the government for its fiscal strategy, which it described as sustainable. In its recent Article IV report, the IMF applauded the government for:

- Addressing the country's development needs through capital spending.
- The accumulation of Gross International Reserves and improved import cover.
- The unprecedented economic growth that it attributed to the government's modernisation plans.
- Maintaining debt sustainability and balanced growth path through its fiscal policies while simultaneously addressing the country's development needs.
- Its commitment to fiscal discipline that would allow for a balanced growth path.
- Strengthening the AML/CFT, governance, and anti-corruption framework.
- Its progress in strengthening the management of oil wealth and its fiscal transparency.
- Climate efforts implemented through the LCDS 2030.
- Its efforts to maintain financial stability and asset quality reviews, progress in conducting stress test exercises, and strategies to promote financial inclusion.

The IMF presents a striking departure from academic and technical analyses of the pre-1992 era, when the PNC resorted to accumulating debt, printing money, and imposing burdensome taxes on the citizens to sustain its bloated and inefficient bureaucracy.

Providing world-class social services to citizens

Guyana's improved creditworthiness with bilateral and multilateral partners, coupled with increased revenue from its new oil and gas sector, enabled the government to accelerate its investments in the social and economic sectors. For instance, the government made substantial investments to rehabilitate, upgrade, and construct new health facilities across the country. The government also upgraded the health centres in all ten regions, as well as those in Linden, Mabaruma, Leonora, and the Diamond Diagnostic Centre.

For the first time, twenty-four remote health centres have been equipped to offer telemedicine, and several hospitals linked to the GPHC have been equipped to offer teleradiology and teleophthalmology programmes. Six new regional hospitals (Regions 2, 3, 4, 5, and 6), plus the Bartica Regional Hospital, along with a Paediatric and Maternal Hospital at Ogle, and new hospitals in Moruca, Kamarang, Kato, Lethem, the Lusignan Diabetic One-Stop Specialist Centre, will modernise healthcare beyond anything we have seen before in Guyana. The investments in the health sector are already delivering enormous benefits, as evident in the provision of specialised surgeries, such as cardiac, paediatric cardiac, cataract, knee, and hip replacement, as well as complex and less complex brain surgeries, now averaging 22,000 annually. The capital investment in the health sector has been accompanied by increased budgetary allocations to recruit, train, and retain healthcare workers. Consequently, the number of Physicians per 10,000 population increased from 11.2 in 2020 to 20.6 in 2024 (see Table 6.9).

An extensive overhaul of the education system is underway. This is evident in physical infrastructure, curriculum, and pedagogy reform, as well as administration and teacher training. Since 2020, the PPP/C government has invested substantial resources to maintain 350 nursery schools, 440 primary schools, and 115 secondary schools across the country. More than 20 SMART classrooms were established at secondary and primary schools by integrating ICT into the teaching and learning process. These investments are being complemented with the training of more than 4,000 teachers to deliver the new

Table 6.9: Selected social indicators, 2020-2024

Indicators	2020	2021	2022	2023	2024
Number of physicians per 10,000 Population	11.2	13.0	12.5	13.7	20.6
Number of Hospital Beds per 10,000 Population	23.4	22.0	25.8	25.8	36.0
Trained Teachers Across the Education Sector (%)	71.0	69.0	72.0	72.0	86.0
Gross Enrolment Rate at Tertiary/ TVET Institutions (%)	5.0	5.0	5.0	10.0	11.0

Source: Budget Speech 2024

curriculum. Consequently, the percentage of trained teachers in the school system increased from 71 per cent in 2020 to 86 per cent in 2024 (see Table 6.9). To improve student attendance and performance, the government has allocated $8 billion to procure textbooks and a school feeding program that is benefitting 101,991 students. The government also fulfilled its promise to reintroduce and increase the *Because We Care Cash Grant*, placing billions into the hands of parents of school children attending public and private schools. To ensure that education is free from nursery to university, the government commenced the write-off of loans taken by students to pursue programmes at the University of Guyana (IN, 27/09/2024), implemented free University education from January 1, 2025 (GC, 23/04/2025), while awarding more than 30,000 scholarships to students to pursue various programmes under the GOAL scholarship programme (DPI, 09/06/2025).

A similar transformation is also taking place in the housing & water sector. In support of expanding home ownership, the government has allocated more than 50,000 house lots across the country, exceeding its Manifesto's target (DPI, 31/05/2025). Lower interest rates and the increase in mortgage ceiling from $8 million to $20 million in 2023 have been negotiated. Value-Added Taxes on locally produced building and construction materials were removed, and the government increased the Mortgage Interest Relief (MIR) from $15 million to $30 million. Additionally, the government implemented the cement and steel subsidy home construction assistance programme and restarted the Young Professional housing development and turnkey home programmes.

To improve access to potable water, thirteen new water treatment plants have been constructed in Regions 2, 3, 4, 5, and 6, bringing the total number of water treatment plants nationwide to 41. The water distribution system has been expanded with an investment of $15.4 billion, providing access to water for the first time to 60 communities. Furthermore, a 5 per cent reduction in water tariffs has been implemented, saving consumers $260 million annually. As a result of these investments, more than 98 per cent of the population had access to potable water in 2024, with over 91 per cent of hinterland and riverine communities now benefiting from it, compared to 46 per cent in 2020 (DPI, 02/01/2025).

Given the positive returns on investment in the health and education sectors, the Human Development Index (HDI) surged from 0.708 points in 2019 to 0.776 points in 2023, the highest value since 1980 (see Figure 6.7). The upward

Figure 6.7: Human Development Index (HDI), 1980, 1990, 2019-2023

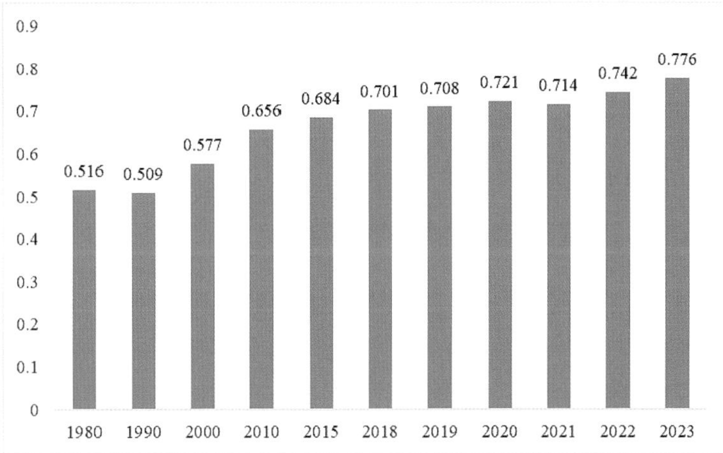

Source: The Global Economy.com, Worrel (2024), World Development Report (various years)

trajectory of the HDI since 2020 stands in stark contrast to the low HDI score of 0.516 in 1980 due to the collapse of the social sector and the score of 0.509 recorded in 1990, when Guyana's HDI was the lowest in the Caribbean (Worrel, 2024). The relatively improved HDI score in 2023 not only improved Guyana's ranking to 89 out of 193 countries but also placed our country in the High Human Development category.

The improvement in the HDI since 2019 can be attributed to increases in life expectancy at birth, expected years of schooling, mean years of schooling, and GNI per capita (2021 $) between 2019 and 2023. The life expectancy increased from 69.1 years in 2019 to 70.2 years by 2023, while the expected years of schooling and mean years of schooling increased from 12.9 years and 8.6 years in 2019 to 13.0 years and 8.7 years, respectively, during 2023 (see Table 5.9). The GNI increased from $12,838 in 2019 to $46,959 in 2023, representing a 265.8 per cent change (see Table 6.10).

Table 6.10: Life Expectancy at birth, Expected years of schooling, Mean years of Schooling and GNI, 2019-2023

Period	Life expectancy at birth	Expected years of schooling	Mean years of schooling	GNI per capita (2021 $)
2019	69.1	12.9	8.6	12,838
2020	67.8	13.0	8.6	18,424
2021	64.3	13.0	8.7	21,902
2022	69.9	13.0	8.7	35,506
2023	70.2	13.0	8.7	46,959

Source: Human Development Reports

Conclusion

Notwithstanding the challenges created by the COVID-19 pandemic, supply chain disruption, the Russia-Ukraine war, and a major flood, the PPP/C has been able to fulfil its manifesto promises successfully. My government revived the productive sectors that had stagnated under the APNU&AFC government. We have also created jobs for citizens while providing world-class social services across sectors. Our achievements have also been lauded by objective observers, placing Guyana as a trailblazer on the international stage in areas such as climate change, biodiversity, and food security. This is in striking contrast to the pre-1992 era, when we were bankrupt and among the poorest in the world.

Since returning to office in 2020, the PPP/C government has tirelessly worked to establish a strong foundation for sustainable development that extends well into the future, beyond 2030. Yet, a formidable challenge looms in the form of the divisive politics practiced by the PNC-led APNU and its opportunistic ally, the AFC. Unless we come together as one nation, the dream of prosperity for all citizens will remain elusive. It is with this understanding that *Vision 2030* was formulated to create a unified country where every Guyanese can live, work, and retire with dignity. This vision not only embodies the pursuit of material wealth but also emotional and spiritual richness, ultimately leading to a cohesive and harmonious society.

REFERENCES

Department of Public Information (2024, January 2). Guyana takes up membership of the United Nations Security Council. https://dpi.gov.gy/guyana-takes-up-membership-of-the-united-nations-security-council/

Department of Public Information (2025, May 31). Promise fulfilled: Over 50,000 house lots allocated so far. https://dpi.gov.gy/promise-fulfilled-over-50000-house-lots-allocated-so-far/

Department of Public Information (2025, January 2). GWI records 98.3% coverage as Guyana improves access to potable water. https://newsroom.gy/2025/01/02/gwi-records-98-3-coverage-as-guyana-improves-access-to-potable-water/#:~:text=Guyana's%20population%20now%20has%2098.3,Incorporated%20(GWI)%20in%202024.

Economic Commission for Latin America and the Caribbean (ECLAC), Foreign Direct Investment in Latin America and the Caribbean, 2024 (LC/PUB.2024/8-P), Santiago, 2024.

FAO (2025). Global Report on Food Crises (GRFC). https://www.fao.org/brussels/events/events-detail/2025-global-report-on-food-crises-high-level-launch-event/en

Floodlist (2021, June 8). Guyana – 25,000 Households Affected by Floods. https://floodlist.com/america/guyana-floods-update-june-2021

Guyana Chronicle (2021, January 17). Guyana completes successful chairmanship of G77 & China. https://guyanachronicle.com/2021/01/17/457633/

Guyana Chronicle (2023, September 12). Commonwealth looks to Guyana for 'blueprint' on forest conservation. https://guyanachronicle.com/2023/09/12/commonwealth-looks-to-guyana-for-blueprint-on-forest-conservation/

Guyana Chronicle (2024, April 23). Free tuition takes effect at University of Guyana. https://guyanachronicle.com/2025/04/23/free-tuition-takes-effect-at-university-of-guyana/

Guyana Times (2020, August 17). *President Ali engages IDB on COVID-19 financing, other key sectors*. https://guyanatimesgy.com/president-ali-engages-isdb-on-covid-19-financing-other-key-sectors/

Guyana Times (2022, December 28). Targeted cash transfers in Guyana right decision – IDB. https://guyanatimesgy.com/targeted-cash-transfers-in-guyana-were-right-decision-idb/

IDB (2023). IDB Group Country Strategy with Cooperative Republic of Guyana (2023-2026).

iNews Guyana. Govt aims to write-off further $5B in student loans by year-end. https://inewsguyana.com/govt-aims-to-write-off-further-5b-in-student-loans-by-year-end/

International Monetary Fund (2023, October 23). Staff Report for the 2023 Article IV Consultation – Debt Sustâinability Analysis.

International Monetary Fund. Western Hemisphere Dept. "Guyana: 2025 Article IV Consultation-Press Release; Staff Report; and Statement by the Executive Director for Guyana", IMF Staff Country Reports 2025, 103 (2025), accessed June 7, 2025, https://doi.org/10.5089/9798229008860.002

Ministry of Foreign Affairs and International Cooperation (2023, June 23). https://www.minfor.gov.gy/newsroom/guyana-secures-seat-inter-american-commission-human-rights

OilNow (2024, January 3). Ali assumes CARICOM chairmanship, vows regional development and peace. https://oilnow.gy/featured/ali-assumes-caricom-chairmanship-vows-regional-development-and-peace/

OilNow (2022, July 22). Strengthening Guyana's relationship with the United States. https://oilnow.gy/featured/strengthening-guyanas-relationship-with-the-united-states/

Wenner, M. D., & Bollers, E. (2018). Development Challenges in Guyana. https://doi.org/10.18235/0001135

Worrel, D. (2024). Development Performance and Economic Policy in Guyana, 1990-2021. In: DaSilva-Glasgow, D., Khemraj, T., Thomas, D. (eds) Economic Challenges in Early 21st Century Guyana. Palgrave Macmillan, Cham.

7

One Nation, One Vision: Guyana's Future Unveiled

I am aware of the changes that are still necessary for the people of Guyana, because I look at them with the eyes of the people and not with the privileged eyes of the privileged few who have always had things easy and so did not want a change. CHEDDI JAGAN

The time has come for the lives of all Guyanese to be transformed. For generations, Guyanese have long yearned to be part of a nation where progress and prosperity are no longer a distant hope but a living and shared reality. In 2020, after five years of economic stagnation, astute and visionary leadership rekindled this hope. Standing firm on the progress made in office since 2020, Guyana has now solidified its position as one of the fastest-growing economies in the world and is expected to continue on this remarkable trajectory over the next decade.

Vision 2030 presents an ambitious roadmap to transform our nation into a diversified, inclusive, and sustainable economy, providing a high standard of living for all citizens while positioning the nation as a regional leader in food security, energy security, environmental stewardship, and social equity. This chapter provides a detailed discussion of *Vision 2030.*

Pillars of *Vision 2030*

As noted earlier, *Vision 2030* aims to achieve sustainable and inclusive economic growth, improve living standards for every Guyanese, promote social and economic development through innovation, economic diversification, and responsible governance. This blueprint rests on the following core pillars:

- Human Transformation
- Economic Transformation/Diversification
- Infrastructure Transformation

- Cultural and Social Transformation
- Technological Transformation
- Protection of vulnerable groups
- Positioning Guyana as a global leader

Human Resource Transformation

EDUCATION: Guyana's future requires a workforce equipped with the technical skills and know-how to manage and operate world-class industries. As the country advances, key sectors such as Agro-processing, petrochemicals, renewable energy (solar and wind), manufacturing, and technology will play a vital role in shaping our economic future. Our future human resource base will exemplify self-improvement and professional excellence and be equipped with technical competencies and internationally recognised certifications to compete effectively at both regional and global levels. This would allow us to enhance national productivity and the responsiveness of service delivery.

In this regard, *Vision 2030* seeks to establish a more inclusive and equitable educational system – one that focuses not only on academic excellence but also on equipping students with the technical skills, adaptive mindset, cognitive flexibility, and competency to adapt and thrive in a rapidly growing service economy. To achieve this, the PPP/C will significantly increase its investment in the education sector, focusing on curriculum reform, digital infrastructure, and expanding access to vocational and tertiary education.

A key pillar of this strategy involves the targeted training of over 1,000 healthcare professionals annually, thereby enabling us to address both current and projected human resource gaps in the healthcare industry. By 2028, it is anticipated that both the new Dental Technician Training Programme and the University of the West Indies Medical School Campus will become operational. This would enable us to strengthen our local healthcare capacity while advancing the country's strategic positioning as a regional hub for medical expertise and professional training.

Sustained investment in education is also critical to meeting the anticipated surge in demand for skilled labour, particularly in the fields of construction and engineering. This growth will be further propelled by the establishment of Guyana's first Artificial Intelligence Data Centre and ExxonMobil's initiative to develop the Guyana Technical Training College Inc. into a global hub for Floating Production, Storage, and Offloading (FPSO) skills training. These developments, among others, will create additional job opportunities for our people in innovative industries. Such developments are aligned with our overarching vision of establishing Guyana as a leading educational hub within the region.

To ensure equitable access to education, targeted measures will be implemented to guarantee that both girls and boys have access to complete, free, and high-quality education at the nursery, primary, and secondary levels. Having achieved universal primary education and being on track to attain universal nursery and secondary education by 2025, one of the goals of *Vision 2030* is to ensure that every child has access to an educational institution within a 20-minute commute from their residence by 2030. This would help reduce travel time for our students, alleviate financial burdens on families, and enhance parental confidence in the accessibility and reliability of the education system.

Moreover, by 2030, every student graduating from secondary school will possess proficiency in at least one sport, one musical instrument, one foreign language, and one Technical and Vocational Education and Training (TVET) discipline, alongside a strong sense of civic responsibility through volunteerism. Maintaining low school dropout rates will remain a priority for this government. To achieve this, we will continue to introduce targeted programs to ensure that socioeconomic disparities do not hinder access to quality education. The *Because We Care Cash Grant* will continue to be provided to every child enrolled in both public and private schools, reinforcing educational equity. Our National School Feeding Programme will be expanded to target students' overall health, cognitive development, and academic performance. These initiatives will continue to have a positive impact on school dropout rates.

Increasing student matriculation rates will necessitate a multifaceted approach that effectively addresses academic, social, and economic barriers to education. By 2030, our goal is to achieve a 75 per cent matriculation rate, thereby fostering a well-educated and highly skilled population. Efforts will also be directed toward equipping 65 per cent of our adult population with marketable competencies, including Technical and Vocational Education and Training (TVET), to enhance employability, facilitate access to decent jobs, and support entrepreneurial ventures within Guyana's evolving industrial landscape.

To further enhance educational and employment opportunities, the government will continue to implement and expand key initiatives such as the Guyana Online Academy of Learning (GOAL) and the Guyana Reinvestment in Opportunities for Work (GROW) program. By 2030, Guyana aims to establish the University of the West Indies (UWI) School of Medicine and the Guyana Law School. This is crucial in achieving our national goal of ensuring that every household has access to a university education.

By 2030, the full integration of Information and Communication Technology (ICT) into the education sector will drive an innovative, equitable, and inclusive approach to learning. Investments in digital infrastructure will be prioritised to support the effective utilisation of technology in education. The development of the Guyana Digital School will serve as a cornerstone for promoting e-learning and distance education, offering interactive multimedia content and supplementary learning tools that equip students with the skills required to navigate an increasingly digitised world. Simultaneously, the expansion of the Learning Channel and EdYou FM will provide extensive educational access to students across Guyana, particularly in remote and hinterland communities, ensuring that all learners benefit from high-quality instructional content.

In keeping with *Vision 2030*, the PPP/C is committed to fostering a more educated, innovative, and adaptable society – one that is equipped to navigate future challenges and capitalise on emerging opportunities. A central component of this strategy is sustained investment in Science, Technology, Engineering, Arts, and Mathematics (STEAM) education. To facilitate experimental learning, we will upgrade all secondary schools to ensure that science laboratories are equipped with state-of-the-art resources. Simultaneously, ongoing investments will be allocated to teacher training, with a focus on expanding opportunities for online professional development. The overarching goal is to achieve a 100 per cent trained teaching workforce by the end of 2025 while ensuring that by 2030, at least 85 per cent of educators hold graduate-level qualifications.

To enhance professional standards in the education sector, we will introduce a teacher licensing system that mandates ongoing professional development to maintain certification. This initiative will help maintain high teaching standards, thereby improving the quality and effectiveness of classroom teaching. We will also focus on improving the teacher-student ratio to meet national standards. This will create a more supportive and engaging learning environment.

Additionally, the PPP/C will continue to invest heavily in the construction and modernisation of schools nationwide by:

- Developing modern, conducive learning environments to support a holistic education.
- Integrating digital learning resources and modern technology.
- Constructing more user-friendly school facilities for students with disabilities, allowing for an equitable educational environment.
- Incorporating environmentally sustainable practices, such as establishing green learning spaces, contributes to climate resilience and environmental consciousness.

Physical education (PE) will remain a fundamental pillar of student development, recognising its role in fostering not only physical well-being but also mental, social, and emotional health. The government will upgrade school tarmacs nationwide to provide safe and accessible spaces for sports and recreational activities. In addition, inclusive PE programs will be developed to incorporate diverse activities, ranging from traditional sports to dance and yoga, while simultaneously emphasising the importance of proper nutrition and overall wellness in students' daily lives.

Addressing the current labour shortage is also on the government's agenda. We will examine targeted policies to transform the traditional brain drain into a brain-circulation economy. The aim is to attract highly skilled individuals who can contribute to national development while leveraging the opportunities available in Guyana. This process is already underway, particularly within the construction industry, where a diverse workforce from across the Caribbean, South America, Africa, and Asia is actively participating in Guyana's economic modernisation.

Vision 2030 envisions an economy with the productive capacity of a three-million-person workforce. While, of course, this figure does not reflect the resident population, it represents the level of human capital required to optimise Guyana's economic potential. Strategic investments will continue in education, labour market expansion, and infrastructure development to ensure that Guyana remains well-positioned to sustain long-term economic growth, innovation, and global competitiveness.

HEALTH CARE: *Vision 2030* not only aspires to empower our citizens with the skills required by the labour market but also ensure a healthy population. To achieve this, the PPP/C will develop a globally respected healthcare system that addresses existing gaps in service delivery while ensuring that people benefit from universal coverage and access to affordable, high-quality healthcare services. Over the past five years, Guyana has made significant strides in enhancing its healthcare infrastructure, workforce capacity, and medical services. To build on this success, the PPP/C will expand the country's healthcare capacity by constructing 12 additional hospitals by 2030. These facilities will increase bed availability by approximately 1,326 beds and provide comprehensive medical services, including

- ✔ Internal Medicine, General Surgery, Obstetrics and Gynaecology (OBGYN), Paediatrics.
- ✔ Advanced diagnostic services, including CT scans and teleradiology, were previously available only at Level 4 healthcare facilities.

To address the growing burden of cancer, the PPP/C will intensify its focus on early detection, treatment, and providing specialised care, by constructing an Oncology Centre, continue the Comprehensive Cervical Cancer Programme, expand the Breast Cancer Programme and Prostate Cancer Screening programme, and train more health workers to support the delivery of specialised care. Additionally, the PPP/C will invest more resources to combat infectious diseases, with the aim of eliminating several diseases by 2030. These include Neglected Tropical Diseases (NTDs), such as Leishmaniasis, Lymphatic Filariasis, Chagas Disease, and Leprosy; Malaria, Tuberculosis (TB), and HIV/AIDS. To mitigate viral infections and enhance public health resilience by expanding the Immunisation Programmes.

Vision 2030 also aims to establish biomedical hubs nationwide, with a specific focus on the manufacturing of pharmaceuticals, vaccines, medical devices, and essential medical supplies to reduce the country's dependence on imports while simultaneously strengthening our supply chain of medical products. This will be done through Public-Private Partnerships and the involvement of international stakeholders.

Additionally, *Vision 2030* will focus on developing Guyana as a premier medical tourism hub within the Caribbean and South America. Through strategic partnerships with the private sector, the country will expand its capabilities to provide world-class healthcare services, including:

- ✔ Organ transplantation services
- ✔ Advanced surgical interventions
- ✔ Dialysis treatment
- ✔ Comprehensive laboratory and pharmaceutical services.

Continuous investment in our healthcare infrastructure, focusing on specialised healthcare services and medical innovation, will enable us to build the foundation for a modern, resilient, and patient-centred healthcare system that ensures equitable access and improved health outcomes.

HOUSING: To ensure that our population continues to benefit from adequate shelter, *Vision 2030* aims to build on the success of the previous PPP/C government in establishing sustainable, resilient, and smart communities across the country. As part of this national agenda, the PPP/C is committed to allocating a minimum of 5,000 house lots annually through 2030 to meet the growing demand for housing and ensure equitable access to homeownership. The PPP/C will also continue to collaborate with other public sector agencies to ensure that communities have access to modern roads, drainage systems, and social services, including education, healthcare, recreational facilities, and water and sanitation.

To address informal settlements in an organised and systematic manner, legislation will be developed to address squatting, while a new Housing Policy will be developed and implemented to address housing issues generally, taking into consideration the local and international context.

An important cornerstone of the government's housing programme over the next five years is Silica City. This will be Guyana's first smart and sustainable urban development. Earlier this year, the completion of its city's master plan marked a significant milestone in the country's urban development agenda. This comprehensive blueprint, developed in partnership with the University of Miami (UM), lays the groundwork for a resilient, technologically advanced, and environmentally sustainable urban centre. Silica City is envisioned as a beacon of innovation, sustainability, and smart infrastructure, poised to drive economic diversification, promote environmental stewardship, and redefine modern urban living in Guyana. Specifically, the city will incorporate green infrastructure, climate-resilient construction, renewable energy, and smart technology, reflecting Guyana's commitment to developing forward-thinking and smart cities.

A pivotal feature of Silica City is the Innovation Village, a cutting-edge innovation district designed to foster entrepreneurship, research, and technological advancement. This district will serve as a hub for business incubation, education, and healthcare integration, creating a dynamic ecosystem where businesses, academia, and industry leaders can collaborate to drive economic transformation.

The private sector is expected to play a critical role in funding the Innovation Village, with investments expected to commence once the necessary public infrastructure is in place. These investments will facilitate the development of state-of-the-art facilities and resources, generating employment opportunities and positioning Guyana as a global leader in innovation.

The Innovation Village will not only symbolise Guyana's commitment to sustainable development but will also catalyse long-term socio-economic progress, ensuring that innovation remains at the heart of the nation's development strategy.

WATER AND SANITATION: To satisfy the growing demand for water and Sanitation, the PPP/C will prioritise the implementation of the projects outlined in the 2026-2030 Strategic Plan for the Water and Sanitation Sector. The implementation of the plan will also help Guyana to achieve the United Nations Sustainable Development Goal (SDG) 6. The key priorities of the plan include:

1. **Expanding Access to Potable Water Supply and Improving Water Quality**
   - ✔ Construction of new water treatment plants and expansion of potable water infrastructure.
2. **Development of Wastewater Treatment and Sewerage Networks**
   - ✔ Establishment of modern wastewater treatment facilities.
   - ✔ Expansion of Georgetown's sewerage system to cover the entire city.
3. **Investments in Renewable Energy for the Water Sector**
   - ✔ Adoption of alternative energy solutions, such as solar-powered water supply systems, to improve efficiency and sustainability.

4. **Building Climate-Resilient Water Infrastructure**
   - ✔ Implementation of flood-resilient designs to enhance water security in vulnerable regions.
5. **Asset Management and Infrastructure Renewal**
   - ✔ Upgrading and replacing ageing water distribution networks to improve reliability.
6. **Integrated Water Resources Management (IWRM)**
   - ✔ Implementing comprehensive water governance strategies to ensure sustainable resource utilisation.
7. **Human Resource Capacity Building**
   - ✔ Strengthening technical expertise within the water sector workforce through training and development programs.
8. **Ensuring the Financial Viability of Water Utility**
   - ✔ Sustainable financing strategies to enhance the financial resilience of GWI.

Economic Transformation/diversification

Guyana's economy is not merely expanding; it is undergoing a structural reconfiguration that shifts the nation beyond the traditional paradigm of raw material extraction and exportation. *Vision 2030* focuses on value creation within national borders, ensuring that every resource – whether oil, agricultural produce, minerals, or timber – generates sustained economic benefits through local processing, manufacturing, and technological innovation. The aim is to maximise our economic return from every sector: oil, agriculture, mining, forestry, manufacturing, and services.

This vision extends beyond conventional economic growth metrics. It is about expanding our value creation model, ensuring that every sector, worker, and enterprise reaches new heights. A truly transformative economy enables individuals at all levels to transform professionally, where a graduate teacher sees a clear trajectory toward becoming an expert educator, and a nurse has avenues to specialise and advance within the healthcare system, thereby contributing to improved national health outcomes. This approach ensures that Guyana's national development is inherently linked to the individual growth and aspirations of its people.

Vision 2030 is about building a prosperous nation – one where every citizen has the opportunity to thrive, where economic opportunities are abundant and sustainable, and where environmental stewardship is a key pillar supporting national development. This approach is crucial if we are to ensure that the wealth generated in this country translates into significant enhancements in the quality of life for all citizens of Guyana.

While hydrocarbons, mining, forestry, and agriculture currently serve as the backbone of the economy, the next phase of national development will be defined by strategic expansion into emerging sectors. These include digitalisation, ecotourism, sports and medical tourism, as well as advanced service industries spanning education, healthcare, security, and research and development.

To facilitate this level of economic transformation, our financial sector must evolve, allowing for easier access to affordable capital and modernising business registration and insolvency frameworks. Concurrent enhancements to the stock exchange will establish a dynamic and competitive corporate environment, foster investor confidence, and accelerate capital formation. These reforms will play a pivotal role in strengthening the business climate, ensuring that both established and emerging enterprises can thrive within an efficient and transparent regulatory framework.

CONSTRUCTION SECTOR: A cornerstone of *Vision 2030* is redefining our construction practices to be more sustainable and resilient through the use of advanced methodologies, such as 3D printing and Building Information Modeling (BIM), to reduce costs, minimise carbon emissions, and enhance project execution. Green and renewable materials will also be used to help meet evolving industrial standards and facilitate the development of a sustainable construction sector. This will be achieved through the development of a National Strategy for Sustainable and Resilient Construction, ensuring that climate resilience and environmental sustainability are integrated into construction standards and urban planning. This approach will enable the introduction of a new building code that is durable, cost-effective, and environmentally friendly, particularly suited to Guyana's climatic conditions.

MANUFACTURING: By 2030, we envision a fully operational network of industrial estates across Guyana strategically developed based on comprehensive needs assessments. Emphasis will be placed on the completion and operationalisation of the Wales Development Authority and the Gas-to-Energy Project, both of which will help reduce electricity costs while enhancing the competitiveness of the manufacturing sector. Lower energy costs would likely make Guyana a more attractive destination for large-scale manufacturing and value-added production. In the medium term, Crab Island will also be developed as an important industrial hub.

A critical component of Guyana's industrial strategy is the National Quality Infrastructure (NQI) Project, which is in its final phase of development. This project intends to enhance innovation and competitiveness within the manufacturing sector. Key aspects of this project include:

- The construction of a state-of-the-art metrology laboratory for the Guyana National Bureau of Standards (GNBS), ensuring that local products meet international quality benchmarks.
- The finalisation and implementation of a National Quality Policy that will facilitate the standardisation of products, thereby strengthening their competitiveness in global markets.
- Technology transfer initiatives aim at integrating advanced manufacturing techniques within local industries.
- Development and enforcement of industry standards, ensuring that Guyanese products are synonymous with high quality and reliability.
- Strategic marketing and export promotion, positioning locally manufactured goods in regional and international markets.

These initiatives will allow Guyana to develop a more competitive and dynamic manufacturing sector. This transformation will position the country as the industrial capital of the Caribbean, driving economic diversification and increasing value-added production within national borders.

Additionally, the Government is committed to fully operationalising all call centres, maximising their potential, and creating sustainable employment opportunities for 1,500 to 2,000 individuals. These initiatives not only contribute to long-term economic growth and job creation across multiple regions but also expand the service sector as a whole.

In the area of trade facilitation, the goal is to significantly reduce both costs and processing time by 2030, thereby increasing efficiency and accessibility for businesses. The modernisation of trade processes will enhance transparency, coordination, and regulatory efficiency across various sectors, reinforcing Guyana's integration into the global economy. This would further stimulate demand for logistics, financial services, and Information and Communication Technology (ICT), creating a more favourable business environment and improving the overall ease of doing business in the country.

SERVICES: In alignment with *Vision 2030*, the Government will prioritise the development of key sub-sectors within the services sector, including: Tourism and Hospitality, Entertainment and Sports Tourism, Health Tourism, Logistics and Financial Services, Information and Communication Technology (ICT).

These emerging industries seek to enhance economic resilience, create sustainable employment opportunities, and foster innovation in both the public and private sectors. This comprehensive strategy is designed to unlock the full potential of Guyana's national resources, positioning the country as a key player in the global market while ensuring that its local industries and communities benefit equitably from economic growth.

To drive long-term economic prosperity, the Government will develop strategic economic zones in various regions, including Palmyra, Lethem, Mahdia, Mabaruma, and Port Kaituma.

Among the most transformative initiatives currently under consideration is the construction of an Economic Zone in the Berbice Region, envisaged as a catalyst for industrialisation and commercial growth. This initiative aims to:

- ✔ Unlock significant opportunities for economic development and regional transformation.
- ✔ Foster private sector growth, supporting both domestic enterprises and attracting much-needed Foreign Direct Investment (FDI). At the core of this vision is the strategic development and monetisation of natural gas, which will reinforce Guyana's position at the forefront of the energy transition and industrial diversification. The Berbice Free Zone is envisioned as a vital platform for industrial activity, attracting investment in sectors such as:

- ✓ Power generation, petroleum refining and storage, and advanced manufacturing, positioning Guyana as an energy and industrial hub.
- ✓ Agriculture and agro-processing, including fruit and vegetable processing, leveraging the region's agricultural strengths to support value-added production and export expansion.
- ✓ Logistics, cold storage, and aggregate storage, strengthening supply chains, supporting local construction projects, and facilitating new international trade flows.

Beyond Berbice/New Amsterdam, the economic benefits of this Free Zone will extend to Lethem, Linden, and Northern Brazil, enhancing regional integration and economic inclusivity. The Berbice Free Zone will serve as a conduit for cross-border trade, industrial innovation, and investment partnerships, positioning Guyana as a strategic player in regional and global markets.

The Free Zone will provide local entrepreneurs and small businesses with opportunities to collaborate with established foreign companies, enabling them to integrate into global supply chains and expand their operations. By offering a competitive international business environment, the Free Zone will foster innovation, skill development, and sustainable employment across multiple industries, contributing to widespread community upliftment and economic empowerment.

With natural gas as the focal point, Guyana is taking bold steps toward energy self-sufficiency and sustainability. This initiative aligns with the broader Energy Transition Strategy, ensuring that the country reduces its reliance on any single sector while building a robust, multi-faceted economy. The Government remains committed to ensuring that the wealth generated from these Free Zones and industrial projects benefits all Guyanese, fostering broad-based prosperity and intergenerational wealth creation.

TOURISM AND HOSPITALITY DEVELOPMENT: Since taking office in 2020, my administration has worked to increase visitor arrivals by more than 268 per cent while introducing 50 new 'tourism experiences'. Notably, in recent years, Guyana has received several awards and nominations for its tourism products. Additionally, by 2030, an additional 15 new hotels are expected to come on stream.

The PPP/C is aware that establishing a year-round sports and entertainment ecosystem will require a robust hospitality infrastructure to accommodate the influx of tourists, athletes, and event organisers. As such, the expansion of hotels, restaurants, transport systems, recreational spaces, and historical landmarks to meet the demands of international sporting and cultural events will be prioritised. By integrating sports tourism with heritage tourism, Guyana can create immersive experiences that appeal to a diverse audience, further strengthening its appeal as a global destination.

To achieve this, the National Strategic Tourism Action Plan will be updated to make Guyana the number one tourism destination in the Caribbean. In so doing, the number of tourism experiences will be doubled, and all tourism businesses will be certified. Furthermore, new tourism niche areas and circuits will be developed in Regions 1, 5, 6, 8, and 10.

AGRICULTURE: The PPP/C is committed to establishing a sustainable food system that ensures food security, environmental protection, and economic growth. Central to this vision is achieving self-sufficiency while positioning Guyana as a regional exporter of key agricultural commodities, including poultry, animal feed (corn and soybeans), black-eyed peas, high-value crops, honey, coffee, cocoa, and hatching eggs. By 2030, agricultural output is projected to increase by over 30 per cent, driven by technological advancements, climate-smart practices, and value-added processing.

By the end of this decade, Guyana's agricultural sector will be fully modernised and diversified, with strategic initiatives such as the Wales Development Project playing a pivotal role in reducing fertiliser imports and production costs. The adoption of climate-smart agriculture will be central to this transformation, incorporating:

- ✔ Hydroponics and shade-house farming to enhance productivity while reducing environmental impact.
- ✔ Precision agriculture and climate-smart technologies to improve resilience to climate change.
- ✔ Sustainable land management and soil conservation practices to ensure long-term agricultural viability.

By 2030, Guyana will establish a robust food processing industry centred on sugar, rice, coconuts, cassava, fruits (for juice production), livestock, and aquaculture. This industrial expansion will:

- Enhance value-added production to reduce reliance on raw material exports.
- Diversify agricultural outputs, making Guyana a key supplier of processed agricultural products.
- Increase agricultural exports by 30 per cent, particularly in high-value markets.

To further stimulate growth, the establishment of Export Promotion Zones (EPZs) will enhance market access and trade efficiency. A key component of this strategy is the creation of food hubs targeting regional markets such as the Caribbean and Northern Brazil. By 2030, Guyana aims to:

- ✔ Establish 10 fully operational food hubs and agro-processing centres, serving over 10,000 farmers.
- ✔ Position these hubs in strategic regions, ensuring direct access to export markets in the Caribbean Community (CARICOM), North America, Europe, and Asia.
- ✔ Develop a comprehensive transport and logistics network that integrates cold chain infrastructure to maintain the quality and shelf life of perishable goods.

By 2030, Guyana will adopt advanced agricultural solutions to ensure greater affordability and accessibility of high-quality, low-cost technologies, thereby boosting farm productivity and food production. This will include:

- ✔ Significant investments in biotechnology, enhancing crop and animal breeding programs to improve disease resistance, climate resilience, and productivity.
- ✔ A 15 per cent increase in agricultural mechanisation, ensuring efficiency and sustainability across farming operations.
- ✔ A transformation of the rice industry, achieving 55 per cent full

mechanisation by 2030, modernising rice farming practices, and improving sustainability.

The production of animal-based protein will continue to be a key driver of economic growth and improved farmer livelihoods. To support the sustainability and efficiency of livestock farming, Guyana will commence domestic vaccine production for livestock. This initiative will:

- ✔ Reduce dependency on imported animal healthcare products while lowering costs for farmers.
- ✔ Enhance disease control and animal health to ensure overall agricultural productivity.
- ✔ Strengthen Guyana's livestock industry to ensure resilience and sustainability in meat and dairy production.

Given the pivotal role of poultry production in Guyana's agricultural sector, the Government will introduce new fiscal incentives in the next fiscal year to drive investment in this industry. Specifically, the introduction of accelerated depreciation rules for capital investments by poultry farmers will:

- ✔ Lower the effective cost of investment so as to incentivise the expansion and modernisation of poultry farms.
- ✔ Encourage increased production capacity to ensure Guyana meets both domestic and regional poultry demand.
- ✔ Position Guyana as the premier poultry meat producer in the Caribbean, solidifying its role as a regional hub for poultry exports.

Infrastructure Transformation

Our vision is that by 2030, connectivity throughout Guyana will be significantly enhanced, with a strong emphasis on linking the hinterland regions, improving river crossings, developing railway systems, revitalising waterfronts, and upgrading critical roadways and aerodromes.

The PPP/C strategic investment in the transport infrastructure aims to foster economic growth, enhance regional integration, and create a seamless transportation network across the country, ensuring that no region is left behind. To ensure that hinterland communities are better connected, several key road links are in the pipeline. We plan to establish direct connections between Region 8 and Region 9, as well as link Mabaruma to Port Kaituma and Matthews Ridge, and connect Kwakwani to Orealla and Linden to Kwakwani. Additionally, a critical road link between Lethem and the villages in the Deep South will enhance access to remote areas, ensuring that residents in these communities can enjoy improved access to essential services, markets, and economic opportunities.

Recognising the importance of efficient river transport, our 2030 agenda includes constructing pivotal bridges across Guyana's major rivers. These projects include a bridge over the Berbice River and another spanning the Corentyne River, which will facilitate better trade with Suriname. The Essequibo River will see two key crossings: one at Kurupukari, improving connectivity with the interior, and another from Fouls Mouth to Bartica. To further ease transport flows, a pontoon crossing across the Demerara River, linking Timehri to Sand Hills, will be established, enhancing the movement of people and goods along the river.

The PPP/C will also invest in railways to boost cargo movement and passenger travel. A light railway line from CJIA to Ogle will facilitate passenger transport, while a cargo railway from Linden to Lethem will create a crucial logistics corridor. Waterfronts will see a transformation with development projects in Charity, Parika, Vreed-en-Hoop, Stabroek, and Wismar, alongside the rehabilitation of all landing facilities along the Demerara and Berbice Rivers.

In road infrastructure, new projects include the Schoonard to Parika 4-lane Highway, the Parika to Goshen Road Link, and the paving of the Mabura Hill to Kurupukari to Lethem Road, enhancing access to key economic zones and facilitating the efficient movement of goods and people. We also plan to develop the Berbice Deep Water Development, which is critical for boosting trade. Meanwhile, upgrades to aerodromes, including the Lethem Aerodrome and Hinterland Airstrips, will ensure that air travel remains a viable option for accessing remote communities.

This comprehensive plan aims to ensure that Guyana's transport network is resilient, efficient, and capable of supporting our economic and social development goals, bringing the benefits of progress to every region and community by 2030. In essence, our Infrastructure Master Plan 2030 is literally "paving the way to a future of limitless potential."

ENERGY: *Vision 2030* ensures an energy-secure Guyana, where the expected surge in energy demand will be met primarily from natural gas, alongside renewable sources such as wind, solar, and hydro. By 2030, 27 per cent of Guyana's electricity demand will be met using renewable energy sources, and 47 per cent will come from natural gas, based on a gas strategy designed to provide low-cost electricity for onshore industrial development while also commercialising gas for export in the medium term. By converting natural gas into electricity, the country can supply large mining operations in the hinterland, replacing diesel-based generation with a more cost-effective and environmentally friendly alternative.

To reinforce the country's shift toward a sustainable energy future, the PPP/C will pursue 165 MW Amaila Falls Hydropower plant and initiate Phase 2 of the Gas-to-Energy project will include a 300-megawatt (MW) combined cycle power plant and a Natural Gas Liquids (NGL) facility with a capacity to produce approximately 5,800 barrels per day (b/d), of which 80 per cent will be exported. This strategic move will transform Guyana from a net importer to a net exporter of NGLs, strengthening its position in global energy markets and increasing foreign exchange earnings.

By 2030, the two Gas-to-Energy facilities will be operationalised, further strengthening Guyana's energy resilience and economic diversification. These facilities will be accompanied by the development of a fertiliser plant and related industries, capitalising on natural gas resources to enhance agricultural productivity and food security.

Looking ahead to 2040, when peak electricity demand is projected to reach 1,326 megawatts (MW), the majority of power generation is expected to be sourced from renewable sources. In line with its commitment to regional energy security, Guyana is pursuing collaboration with Suriname, Brazil, and French Guiana to develop a 3,000 MW power interconnection system. This initiative underscores the government's long-term vision for energy cooperation, creating a regional power network that fosters stability, promotes energy trade, and facilitates economic integration.

Vision 2030 also envisions a fully operational Smart Grid by 2030, incorporating a Distribution Management System (DMS), advanced metering infrastructure, and smart distribution equipment. The Smart Grid initiative will significantly reduce the frequency and duration of outages, improve service restoration times, and enable real-time fault detection up to the customer's metering point, managed from the new Guyana National Control Centre. Additionally, these improvements will result in reduced operational costs and significant reductions in system losses, ensuring a more reliable and cost-effective power supply for businesses and households.

Cultural and social transformation

There has not been a better time for culture and creativity in Guyana than the present. We can start with a cultural policy. A critical starting point is the establishment of a comprehensive cultural policy. In this regard, a revised draft of the Framework National Cultural Policy will be put into public consultation in the new year. This policy will not only focus on the fundamental issues of integrating culture into development, heritage preservation, and the growth of creative industries, but will also examine more recent concerns, such as the impact of the digital ecosystem on culture and the dangers (and opportunities) posed by generative artificial intelligence.

We have not waited for the implementation of the policy to act on areas that are immediately actionable. The reinstatement and upgrading of the Guyana Prize for Literature, making it an annual event and expanding the categories for submissions, have resulted in the recognition and reward of home-grown literary talent across all genres, unequalled in the history of this prestigious award.

Finally, looking to the very near future, my administration has begun laying the groundwork to establish a world-class film production environment in Guyana, one that draws upon the tremendous working talent available in the industry across the diaspora and the burgeoning creative talent here. Also, through the Ministry of Culture, Youth and Sport, we are currently negotiating a co-production agreement with one of our key international partners. This agreement will facilitate the establishment of a National Film Commission.

The PPP/C has already initiated the development of an integrated sports economy, designed as a dynamic and multifaceted ecosystem that leverages the synergies between sports, entertainment, and culture. This ambitious initiative aims to position Formula 1 racing, horse racing, athletics, cricket, and cycling as core sporting attractions, strategically coupled with entertainment and cultural experiences. By leveraging the unique attributes of each sport and event, this integrated approach fosters a year-round destination that stimulates economic growth through tourism, media, and local employment.

The creation of a diversified sports economy extends beyond the direct benefits of hosting events; it contributes to the broader economic landscape by enhancing infrastructure development, creating jobs, and fostering global brand recognition. Furthermore, it serves as a vehicle for social transformation, fostering community pride, cultural exchange, and sustainable development. This initiative aligns with Guyana's long-term economic vision, ensuring that sports and entertainment act as pillars of national progress and resilience. Significantly, this vision encompasses initiatives that would ensure that youths are provided with opportunities to acquire life skills, have access to sports and recreational facilities, are gainfully employed, and are afforded avenues to pursue careers in sports.

By serving as a convergence point between sports, culture, and commerce, the sports economy drives comprehensive regional development and strengthens Guyana's position as a premier destination for international sporting events. In support of this vision, a new National Cricket Academy will be created in Good Hope, as well as a Stadium in Region 3. Additionally, sustained investment will be directed toward maintaining and enhancing sports facilities nationwide, ensuring broad-based access and long-term viability.

The sports economy is not only an economic driver but also a tool for social transformation, fostering increased participation in sports and physical activities. The establishment of grassroots programs and youth sports initiatives will encourage community engagement while promoting health and wellness. Moreover, hosting international sporting events will facilitate cultural exchange, fostering global interaction and intercultural understanding. These events enhance national identity and pride, galvanising social unity and strengthening community bonds.

A thriving sports economy will generate significant employment opportunities across multiple sectors, including event management, hospitality, security, media production, and sports facility maintenance. To ensure that the local workforce is adequately prepared, vocational training centres will be established, equipping individuals with specialised skills necessary to support the growing sports industry. These initiatives will empower local communities by creating sustainable career paths within the sports, entertainment, and tourism sectors. Under the Department of Youth, 50,000 youths will be trained in soft, technical, and vocational skills. Furthermore, the President's Youth Arm of the Republic of Guyana will be relaunched, and 8,670 youths will be engaged in fourteen (14) skills areas in regions 2, 3, 4, 5, 6, and 10.

The broadcasting rights for international sporting events such as Formula 1, cricket, and concerts present a lucrative opportunity to generate substantial revenue and attract global media coverage. The expansion of digital media infrastructure, including high-quality broadcasting studios, digital streaming platforms, and augmented reality experiences, will elevate Guyana's visibility on the global stage. By positioning "Brand Guyana" as a key player in the international sports and entertainment market, this initiative will drive investment, enhance diplomatic partnerships, and elevate the country's international profile.

The development of a modern sports economy presents an opportunity to align with global sustainability goals. The PPP/C is committed to implementing eco-friendly initiatives, including:

- Green transportation solutions, such as cycling lanes and electric shuttles for Formula 1 events.
- Renewable energy integration in stadiums and sports venues.
- Implementing waste reduction and recycling programs to minimise the environmental impact of large-scale sporting events.

These initiatives will not only reduce the carbon footprint of sporting events but also attract environmentally conscious investors and tourists, reinforcing Guyana's commitment to sustainable development.

The integration of sports, culture, and entertainment will further enhance the economic and social impact of this initiative. Cultural tourism will be promoted through events that incorporate traditional festivals, food fairs, and art exhibitions, offering visitors a comprehensive entertainment experience. By merging sports tourism with cultural tourism, Guyana will attract a diverse range of visitors, from sports enthusiasts to cultural tourists.

As part of this initiative, the PPP/C is developing a state-of-the-art museum and national zoo, which will preserve the country's rich history while showcasing its future potential. Additionally, the establishment of a cultural market in

Palmyra, Berbice, will serve as a permanent hub for young artists, culinary entrepreneurs, and local artisans, further strengthening the nation's cultural identity and expanding economic opportunities for creatives. A Cultural and Creative Industries Grant and Emancipation Grant will also be launched to provide additional sources of funding for creatives. A programme to subsidise the cost of artists for recording their music and participating in national events will also be launched.

The convergence of sports and entertainment will drive significant economic gains by attracting diverse audiences to major events. The inclusion of concerts, music festivals, and performing arts showcases within sports venues – a strategy successfully implemented in global stadiums and arenas – will enhance the overall economic impact of each venue. By creating a multi-purpose entertainment landscape, Guyana will maximise revenue generation and tourist engagement, ensuring that each sports facility serves as a continuous economic driver.

Sports have emerged as a powerful driver of economic and social transformation in Guyana, not only fostering a culture of athletic excellence but also promoting public health and well-being. As the sports industry expands, it encourages greater community participation in physical activities, contributing to healthier lifestyles and reducing the national burden of non-communicable diseases such as diabetes and hypertension. This, in turn, contributes to reduced healthcare expenditures, enhanced population productivity, and a measurable improvement in overall quality of life.

In parallel, the rise of sports as an economic pillar is driving corporate involvement in workplace wellness programs, reinforcing the link between physical activity and workforce productivity. Businesses are recognising the value of integrating fitness into corporate culture, leading to healthier, more engaged employees and reduced absenteeism.

Simultaneously, sports technology and innovation are unlocking new economic opportunities. The growing demand for smart stadiums, digital ticketing systems, and advanced training equipment is fostering the development of a technology-driven sports industry. These innovations are not only modernising sports infrastructure but also driving growth in tech-based industries, positioning Guyana as a hub for sports innovation and technological advancement.

Guyana's tourism potential is unparalleled, with the capacity to rival the world's most iconic destinations, from the Pyramids of Giza to the opulence of Dubai. The nation's economic vision extends beyond traditional industries, embracing transformative and sustainable sectors such as ecotourism, sports and entertainment tourism, health tourism, and business tourism. These industries are not just engines of economic growth but also pillars of environmental stewardship, cultural preservation, and social inclusivity.

A significant milestone in this vision is the ongoing discussions with Kent and Abercrombie, one of the world's leading eco-tourism hotel operators, to establish operations in Guyana. This potential partnership is a clear signal that Guyana's tourism product is gaining international recognition and attracting high-value investments.

With an ambitious target of three million visitors by 2030, Guyana is investing in critical infrastructure and human capacity development to accommodate and capitalise on this influx of visitors. Key initiatives include:

- ✔ Training of over 8,400 tourism stakeholders.
- ✔ Constructing the Hospitality Technical Training Institute.
- ✔ Exploring the development of key aviation infrastructure, including:
  - ❍ A second terminal at Cheddi Jagan International Airport (CJIA).
  - ❍ A domestic airport in Berbice.
  - ❍ A new international airport in Lethem to enhance regional connectivity.

Protection of Vulnerable Groups

WOMEN: Women have long been at the forefront of Guyana's development, shaping its economy, society, and governance through activism, entrepreneurship, and leadership. Recognising their invaluable contributions, the government is committed to fostering greater economic independence for women, ensuring they play a central role in shaping Guyana's future.

By 2030, at least 50 per cent of newly established agribusiness ventures will be led by women and youth, solidifying their role as key contributors to the food economy. This strategic focus will empower women through entrepreneurship, skills development, and financial inclusion, enabling them to become economic drivers within their communities. Aligned with this goal, a framework will be created to provide support to women, youths, and persons with disabilities to access funding for entrepreneurial activities, training, and markets for their products and services.

Through the expansion of the homestead project, additional single mothers will be empowered by being provided with the opportunity to own their homes and finance them from the income generated from climate-smart agriculture activities, specifically shade house farming. Additional initiatives to support women include:

- Increase in the *Because We Care Cash Grant.*
- Continue to empower women, youths, and individuals with determination through scholarships and other educational opportunities, enabling them to actively contribute to and participate in the development of our country.
- Continue the National Pathway Workers Project to empower women and vulnerable households.

ELDERLY: Guyana's elderly population represents a reservoir of wisdom and experience, having laid the foundation for national progress. As the nation evolves, it is essential to ensure that seniors can retire with dignity and continue to be active participants in society.

Vision 2030 places a strong emphasis on dignified elderly living, which goes beyond satisfying the physical needs of our senior citizens to recognise their worth, while creating an environment where they can lead safe, fulfilling, valued, and engaged lives. The 2030 Vision for elderly welfare includes:

- Doubling the Old Age Pension and Public Assistance.
- Continued home-based care for senior citizens to increase their access to healthcare.
- Increasing the electricity and water subsidy for the elderly
- Providing Senior Entrepreneurship Support, offering training and financial incentives to older adults who wish to establish businesses or social enterprises.

- ✔ Combating Loneliness and Social Isolation by promoting social interaction through the establishment of senior centres, community gardens, and intergenerational activities where the elderly can engage with younger citizens.
- ✔ Development of Age-Friendly Communities, incorporating accessible transportation, pedestrian-friendly infrastructure, and recreational spaces to enhance mobility and social participation, thereby ensuring that public spaces enhance the mobility and social participation of senior citizens.
- ✔ Promote research and development in the use of robotics and AI-driven solutions for elderly care, such as robotic caregivers, AI companions, and automated medication dispensers.
- ✔ Ensuring that government, banking, shopping, transportation, and other services are user-friendly for the elderly with interfaces that are simple, intuitive, and user-friendly for the elderly.
- ✔ Launching Volunteer and Mentorship Programs, which encourage seniors to share their knowledge and skills with younger generations.
- ✔ Digital Literacy Programs to equip seniors with skills to navigate modern technology, ensuring they remain connected and engaged.

INDIGENOUS COMMUNITIES: Guyana's Indigenous communities hold a unique and invaluable place in the nation's heritage, with their ancestral knowledge, cultural traditions, and sustainable practices shaping the country's environmental and social landscape. *Vision 2030* envisions a future where Indigenous communities benefit equally from the country's patrimony and development, and enjoy food and nutrition security, energy security, modern infrastructure, world-class education, healthcare, and retire with dignity. The vision for inclusive development prioritises:

- ✔ Food security, energy security, modern infrastructure, world-class education, and healthcare parity for hinterland and Indigenous communities.
- ✔ Enhancement of healthcare facilities in the hinterland to ensure equal access to medical services as in coastal regions.

- Expansion of technological integration, including the establishment of remote learning centres, enhanced internet connectivity, and digital access initiatives.
- Enhance vocational and technical training programs to equip youth and adults with practical skills relevant to local industries.
- Development of local sports infrastructure, training community-based sports coaches, and bridging the sports accessibility gap between the hinterland and the coastland.
- Promotion of climate-smart agriculture, developing sustainable markets for Indigenous products, and revitalising interest in agricultural livelihoods.
- Facilitation of eco-tourism investments, recognising the untapped potential of Guyana's pristine natural landscapes.
- Construction of an international airport in Lethem.
- Expansion cultural programs, increasing funding for the preservation of Amerindian heritage sites, traditional festivals, and Indigenous art forms.
- Strengthening of local governance, equipping village councils with administrative and resource management training to empower communities.
- Provision of training and resources to village councils to enhance governance and administrative capabilities, as well as to empower them to manage resources and advocate for their communities effectively.

A nation poised for global leadership

We no doubt live in a world dominated by the Great Powers. However, through hard work, we have succeeded handsomely in making our mark. It takes courageous and insightful leadership, built on strong and enduring commitments to democratic values, for our foreign relations to be successful. The world is watching as this small and beautiful country transitions from relative obscurity to becoming a catalyst for economic development, a leader in climate change, and a beacon of hope for the Caribbean.

In addressing the pressing planetary issues of climate change and food security, we have deepened and broadened our innovation to the point where

Guyana is now recognised as a top-tier global leader. In the realm of diplomacy, we have established a vast network of reciprocal relationships that will not only bolster our national interests but also those of the Americas and beyond.

We need to lead boldly and constructively. Guyana is moving forward at full force at the bilateral, regional, and multilateral levels. Our foreign policy must establish us as a leading light in defence of the core principles of the UN Charter, of international law, human rights, human dignity, and of those who by no fault of their own, face unbearable suffering in a world where the cries of freedom can still be heard but continue to go unanswered. This country stands resolute in its commitment to:

- ✔ International security and global peace, based on the rule of law
- ✔ Global governance based on expansive multilateralism and universal principles of equality and equity
- ✔ Democratic governance at home and abroad
- ✔ Economic development based on comprehensive environmental and ecological sustainability
- ✔ Robust regionalism in the Caribbean Basin and the Americas, and
- ✔ The defence of the most vulnerable populations with particular emphasis on the rights of Indigenous populations, women, and young people, beginning here in Guyana.

In the international arena, Guyana has called for a global coalition focused on advancing biodiversity conservation, supported by the launch of the Global Biodiversity Alliance Summit in the first quarter of 2025. Focus Areas of the Alliance include:

- ■ Creating a Market for Biodiversity Credits: Develop a marketing framework targeting biodiversity credits so as to enhance the value of biodiversity while promoting sustainable practices.
- ■ Scaling Biodiversity Conservation Debt Swaps: Implement a scalable structure for biodiversity conservation debt swaps so as to allow countries to exchange national debt for commitments to protect biodiversity.

- Accelerating Biodiversity Bonds: Promote the issuance of biodiversity bonds for emerging markets linked to specific conservation objectives and targets.
- Blueprint for Biodiversity Taxonomies: Establish a blueprint for biodiversity taxonomies that will guide investment and policy decisions to ensure alignment with conservation goals.
- Promoting Nature-Positive Actions: Encourage nature-positive actions that align biodiversity conservation with carbon neutrality objectives, contributing to a sustainable future.

The Blavatnik School of Government at the University of Oxford will collaborate with the Guyana Bankers Association to develop the financing models and mechanisms outlined above. The vision of the Global Biodiversity Alliance is to unite large stakeholders worldwide in a concerted effort to preserve and restore biodiversity for future generations. This collaboration would further protect and enhance biodiversity on a global scale.

Additionally, Guyana's LCDS has become a global trademark, demonstrating the country's commitment to sustainable development and biodiversity conservation. The Global Biodiversity Alliance will enhance this strategy, positioning Guyana as a leader in biodiversity conservation and sustainable finance.

Over the past four years, the PPP/C has risen to the formidable challenge of restoring our nation's image on the world stage, achieving remarkable success. Our accomplishments shine as testaments of our success, marked by numerous unprecedented milestones, which include:

- ✔ Election of Guyana, for the first time, to serve on the United Nations Security Council for two years.
- ✔ Election of Guyana to serve on the Executive Council of the World Meteorological Organisation (WMO) for the first time.
- ✔ Attaining membership in the Inter-American Commission for Human Rights (IACHR), which is mandated to promote and protect human rights throughout the Americas, is another notable achievement.

- ✔ Hosting major meetings, including the CELAC Ministers of Agriculture Meeting, the 12th ILO Meeting of Caribbean Ministers of Labour, and the itinerant sitting of the Caribbean Court of Justice.
- ✔ Hosting high-level officials, diplomatic, economic, and technical delegations from the United States (US), India, Saudi Arabia, Qatar, the Republic of Ghana, the United Arab Emirates (UAE), Brazil, and several Caribbean Leaders.
- ✔ Engaging global leaders such as H.H. Sheikh Tamim bin Hamad Al Thani, Emir of the State of Qatar, H.E. Xi Jinping, President of the People's Republic of China, Prime Minister Boris Johnson, His Excellency William Nana Addo Dankwa Akufo-Addo, President of the Republic of Ghana, Rwanda's President Paul Kagame, and Prime Minister Shri Narendra Modi.
- ✔ Signing of several MoUs, Service Agreements, and a joint Communiqué with our counterparts from these countries.
- ✔ Securing visa-free travel to the UAE and UK.
- ✔ Providing global and regional leadership in the areas of forest conservation and climate finance, open innovation, dedication to inclusive development, and food security.
- ✔ Recognition of our leaders for positioning Guyana as global trailblazer for forest conservation and climate finance, open innovation, dedication to inclusive development (for example, Sustainable Development Leadership Award by Vice President, Dr Bharrat Jagdeo, the Global Leadership Award by HE Dr Mohamed Irfaan Ali for his contribution for environmental conservation and sustainability through pioneering initiatives such as advancing mechanism for carbon trading and efforts to establish an International Centre for Biodiversity, the Caribbean Global Leader 2024 by the Caribbean Global Awards for his dedication and leadership in advancing Guyana's interest while fostering regional cooperation, the Wilson Centre Latin America award in recognition of his contribution to biodiversity and climate change efforts, the Global Africa Leadership Award for his dedication to inclusive development through his One Guyana philosophy, the Pravasi Bharatiya Samman in recognition of his contribution in Politics/

Community Welfare and Order of Freedom of Barbados for his strong commitment to enhance cooperation to achieve regional cooperation and collaboration particularly in relation to Food and Nutrition Security).
- ✔ Established new Missions in Guyana, Belize, Dominican Republic, UAE, Qatar, and France.

Additionally, the PPP/C has preserved Guyana's territorial sovereignty and territorial integrity through a diverse array of strategic collaborations and partnerships, while working through various agencies, including the International Court of Justice (ICJ), the United Nations (UN), the Commonwealth, the Organization of American States (OAS), and CARICOM.

Guyana's development trajectory is one of transformation, inclusion, and sustainability. With strategic investments in tourism, sports, technological innovation, gender equality, elderly welfare, and Indigenous empowerment, the nation is solidifying its position as a global leader in sustainable economic growth.

The government's commitment is clear: to build a Guyana where every citizen, regardless of background or geography, enjoys the full benefits of national development. This vision is not just aspirational – it is the blueprint for a thriving, equitable, and forward-thinking Guyana.

Continuing along this trajectory, the PPP/C government will:

- Collaborate with various international agencies, including the United Nations, the Commonwealth, the Organization of American States, and CARICOM, to promote awareness and support for Guyana's territorial integrity.
- Strengthen our partnership with the United States, Canada, South American neighbours, and members of CARICOM to protect our territorial integrity.
- Collaborate with our allies on military training, intelligence sharing, and defence planning, while avoiding escalation of tensions with our continental neighbours.
- Enhance air, land, and sea operations to fortify our presence along our borders, while deploying cutting-edge surveillance technology that provides real-time monitoring and rapid reaction times in various settings.

Technological transformation

Guyana is no longer confined by geographic limitations or the constraints of the past. The government is spearheading the transition to a digitally advanced nation, one that embraces technology to foster innovation, economic expansion, and social progress. The Digital Guyana vision aims to create a thriving, citizen-centric digital ecosystem that enhances education, fosters innovation, promotes digitisation, and promotes equity. It seeks to deliver secure, inclusive, and accountable digital services across all sectors, ensuring Guyana remains globally competitive while driving sustainable economic and social development. This transformative agenda focuses on six key pillars:

1. Digital Education – Expanding Technological Literacy and Access to Digital Learning.
2. Digital Incubation – Creating an ecosystem that enables start-ups and entrepreneurs to thrive.
3. Digital Transformation – Modernising industries, government services, and financial systems.
4. Digital Leadership – Positioning Guyana as a leader in AI, fintech, and digital governance.
5. Digital Sovereignty and Citizenship – Empowering citizens with secure access to digital public services.

The PPP/C has already begun implementing nationwide digital education initiatives, ensuring access to cutting-edge learning opportunities. Key programs include:

- ✔ One Guyana Digital Initiative (1GD): A collaboration with Toronto Metropolitan University, providing over 2,000 Guyanese with training in front-end and back-end technologies. Participants will be equipped with job-ready skills, enabling them to earn approximately USD 100,000 per annum while residing in Guyana.
- ✔ 150K Guyana Coders Initiative: A partnership between the Governments of the United Arab Emirates and Guyana, training youth in programming fundamentals, data science, and Android development at no cost.

- Guyana Coursera Platform: Launched in March 2024, this initiative offers 400,000 citizens free access to over 6,000 courses, with the government investing approximately US$1.46 million annually.
- GOAL Scholarship Program: Over 29,000 online scholarships have been awarded through this initiative in the past three years, valued at $2.9 billion, benefiting 21,000 women and 8,500 men.

To ensure nationwide access to quality education, the government is establishing the Guyana Digital School. This AI-enhanced learning platform will provide every student – regardless of location – with the same high-quality teaching and educational materials. The digital school will feature:

- An online curriculum from nursery to Grade 12.
- Digital textbooks and teaching resources.
- AI-powered tutors and assessments.
- Virtual parent-teacher associations (PTAs) and extracurricular activities.
- Specialised training in entrepreneurship, cultural studies, nursing, and accounting.
- Remedial education for adults, as well as assessments for the NGSA and CXC examinations.

To ensure inclusivity, the Get Safe Online initiative provides fundamental digital literacy training to individuals who may not have had the opportunity to complete formal education. Meanwhile, continued investments in teacher training, ICT tools, and curriculum reforms will ensure that every classroom is equipped for the digital future.

The government is committed to nurturing a culture of innovation, with the expertise of global industry leaders such as John Chambers (former CEO of CISCO Systems) and the Haas School of Business (University of California) guiding its strategy. Key initiatives include:

- Providing funding, training, and market access for young people, women, and persons with disabilities to launch digital enterprises.

- ✔ Developing Smart Villages, leveraging digital infrastructure for economic and social growth.
- ✔ Engaging local financial institutions to expand access to capital for digital entrepreneurs. This will include establishing innovation funds to encourage students and entrepreneurs to think creatively.
- ✔ Establishing centres of excellence to foster collaboration between diverse stakeholders, including start-ups, corporations, academia, investors, and government bodies.
- ✔ Prioritising Science, Technology, Engineering and Mathematics (STEM) fields to ensure that the school system provides a continuous stream of skilled individuals who can drive innovation.
- ✔ Ensuring that our country has the digital infrastructure, such as cloud computing, data analytics, and quantum computing, as well as reliable high-speed internet access, that would allow start-ups and researchers to scale up faster.
- ✔ Providing tax incentives for Research and Development grants, research entities, and innovative start-ups.
- ✔ Establishing an Innovation Village that would incubate new ideas, drive technological advancements, and integrate healthcare, education, and entrepreneurship.
- ✔ Developing an artificial intelligence eco-system to empower industries, from agriculture to public safety, will position Guyana as a leader in AI Innovation and Digital Leadership.

This approach will position Guyana as a hub for digital start-ups, enabling businesses to scale both domestically and internationally.

Guyana is actively integrating advanced technologies to enhance productivity, create employment opportunities, and promote sustainable growth. The adoption of smart technologies in agriculture will allow farmers to increase yields through precision farming. *Vision 2030* also aims to create a vibrant, citizen-centric digital ecosystem that leverages digital technology and innovation to enhance the lives of our citizens and improve the quality and accessibility of government services throughout Guyana. High-speed internet access will be provided to all Guyanese, regardless of whether they reside in urban, rural, or hinterland communities. By facilitating access to high-speed internet throughout

Guyana, *Vision 2030* will enable every citizen to engage with E-government services and empower them to participate fully in an increasingly digital world. In furtherance of this vision, we will:

- ✔ Establish the Guyana Digital School to create a new and innovative learning environment for our students across the country.
- ✔ Digitise public services so that citizens can access government services from the comfort of their own homes.
- ✔ Modernise the financial services sector by promoting digital banking and adopting suitable financial technology.
- ✔ Create an artificial intelligence ecosystem that empowers industries from agriculture to public safety.
- ✔ Create a digital incubation platform that enables SMEs to benefit from the expertise of experts worldwide.
- ✔ Develop a real-time data analysis Centre of Excellence in Agriculture.

Healthcare is also undergoing a digital revolution, with e-health systems ensuring universal access to advanced medical services. AI-powered diagnostics, robot-assisted surgeries, and telemedicine applications such as tele-ophthalmology, teleradiology, and telepathology will enhance healthcare outcomes. By 2025, all medical imaging will be digital, and the disease surveillance system will be fully digitised.

In fiscal governance, the Guyana Revenue Authority (GRA) is implementing AI-driven tax administration with:

- Reduced human discretion in tax processing.
- Automated trade and border laws administration.
- Enhanced transparency and efficiency in revenue collection.

The Guyana School of Agriculture, in collaboration with IICA, is being transformed into a Centre of Excellence for real-time agricultural data analysis. This hub will provide specialised training in precision farming, agribusiness, and digital agriculture, equipping young people with skills for the future of farming.

Guyana is leveraging data-driven approaches to sustainable natural resource management. The forestry sector already employs one of the most advanced monitoring systems globally, ensuring that harvesting rates remain among the lowest worldwide. In financial services, *Vision 2030* aims to modernise banking through:

- ✔ Expansion of digital banking and fintech innovation.
- ✔ Strengthened e-commerce infrastructure to connect businesses and consumers.
- ✔ The launch of a National Support Services Platform, enabling citizens to report poor-quality government services via a centralised digital hub under the Office of the President.
- ✔ Integrate eID for access to government services across the country.
- ✔ Expand the Safe Country programme across all regions.
- ✔ Expand the Safe Road Intelligent System Programme to all major highways.
- ✔ Expand Border Control and e-passport facilities across the country.
- ✔ Continue expanding the fibre optic cable network in Regions 2, 3, 4, 5, 6, 7, and 10.
- ✔ Establish an innovation village to incubate new ideas, drive technological advancements, and integrate healthcare, education, and entrepreneurship.
- ✔ Strengthen the digital logistics networks and e-commerce infrastructure to connect businesses and consumers.
- ✔ Deploy digital solutions to improve the sustainable management of our natural resources.

To cement its status as a leader in digital governance and artificial intelligence, Guyana is investing in:

- ✔ AI-powered public safety, agriculture, and industrial automation.
- ✔ A groundbreaking mineral mapping project utilising AI and traditional techniques to identify critical minerals such as lithium.
- ✔ The development of an AI Data Centre, leveraging Guyana's abundant energy resources to power global AI computing demands.

The AI Data Centre will:

- ✔ Attract foreign investment, creating a ripple effect of economic growth.
- ✔ Position Guyana as a strategic hub for AI infrastructure, catering to global companies seeking reliable hosting solutions.
- ✔ Generate high-quality jobs that foster local expertise in AI development.

Educational institutions and research organisations will benefit from this initiative, which integrates AI-driven tools into classrooms and laboratories, thereby upskilling the next generation of digital leaders.

As we look beyond our borders, we see the potential to become an international AI leader, offering excess computing capabilities to our trading partners right here in the Region, thus further enhancing our position as leaders.

This data centre will position Guyana as a key player in the global tech ecosystem, enhancing our international reputation and allowing us to forge strategic partnerships with other nations, tech companies, and research institutions. Such collaborations will open doors to new markets, ideas, and innovations, further strengthening our economy and technological capabilities.

In the era of digital transformation, data sovereignty is a fundamental pillar of national security and economic independence. Establishing robust legal and technological frameworks to protect and manage Guyana's data within its borders is imperative to safeguarding sensitive information, digital assets, and proprietary knowledge. To achieve this, the government has engaged with leading satellite providers, including Hispasat, Viasat, and Starlink, to assess the feasibility of securing satellite infrastructure that guarantees the security and autonomy of national data. This strategic initiative will ensure that Guyana retains control over its digital resources, reducing dependencies on external entities and strengthening national cybersecurity measures.

Moreover, as digital systems expand, cybersecurity must remain a top priority. The government is investing in a comprehensive cybersecurity strategy to fortify critical national infrastructure, protect citizen data, and mitigate cyber threats. This initiative will ensure that Guyana's digital economy is resilient against emerging cyber risks, fostering a secure and stable digital ecosystem that enables trust in e-governance, digital finance, and national defence systems.

The evolving global security landscape necessitates the modernisation of national defence systems through the use of digital technologies. *Vision 2030* establishes a security architecture that is adaptive, intelligence-driven, and leverages the capabilities of cutting-edge technologies. Importantly, *Vision 2030* aims to establish a responsive security architecture that can readily adapt to an evolving security landscape.

Guyana will integrate advanced digital tools to enhance national security capabilities, ensuring the nation remains prepared for contemporary and future security challenges. By leveraging artificial intelligence, data analytics, and secure communication networks, the government will enhance border security, disaster response mechanisms, and intelligence operations, thereby reinforcing national resilience in an increasingly digitalised world. To achieve this goal, the PPP/C government will:

- ✔ Expand the Safe Country Initiative throughout the country.
- ✔ Automate citizen reporting platform, regional police dispatch, and fleet management system while digitising case management that will allow for real-time data collection and analysis by the Guyana Police Force (GPF).
- ✔ Implement an AI-driven automated system that leverages emerging satellite technologies and utilises existing and new radar technology for the surveillance of all aspects of our borders.
- ✔ Improve our intercept capability through continued investments in our maritime, aerial, and terrestrial assets.
- ✔ Increase personnel and provide training to support the technological systems.
- ✔ Construct new barracks and modern headquarters to support the operational functions and well-being of the ranks.
- ✔ Construct fire stations in hinterland areas.
- ✔ Increase the marine capabilities of the Guyana Fire Service.
- ✔ Provide GFS officers with advanced training in industrial fire hazards.
- ✔ Prioritise the digital transformation of the GFS, interstation connectivity, and expand rank structures.
- ✔ Upgrade the infrastructure of the Guyana Prison Service.

- ✔ Introduce a modern prison management system.
- ✔ Invest in rehabilitation programs for inmates and provide training to officers in areas such as human rights and advanced prison management.
- ✔ Enhance data analytics.
- ✔ Invest in advanced surveillance tools.
- ✔ Strengthen recruitment and provide trained officers with continuous training.

A digitally empowered citizenry is essential for the successful implementation of Guyana's technological transformation agenda. The PPP/C will continue to promote digital literacy programs, ensuring that all Guyanese – regardless of geographic location or socio-economic background – can participate fully in the digital economy. Through targeted initiatives in education, workforce development, and public engagement, digital literacy efforts will prepare individuals to navigate, contribute to, and benefit from the expanding digital landscape.

This strategy is more than just a development plan – it is the blueprint for Guyana's future. A future where digital transformation fuels innovation, economic diversification, and national prosperity. A future where every citizen has equitable access to digital opportunities. A future where Guyana emerges as a technological leader, not just within the Caribbean but on the global stage.

Guyana's vision for digital transformation is rooted in sustainability, security, and inclusivity. As the nation embarks on this journey, it remains committed to ensuring that technological advancements contribute to economic empowerment, environmental preservation, and societal progress. The foundation for Digital Guyana is being laid today, and through collective effort, the country will emerge as a model of innovation, resilience, and sustainable development in the digital era. Together, we will shape a future where every Guyanese thrives in a technology-driven world.

Vision 2030 aims to establish a vibrant, citizen-centric digital ecosystem that leverages digital technology and innovation to enhance the lives of our citizens and improve the quality and accessibility of government services throughout Guyana. A key objective of this digital transformation agenda is to provide high-speed internet connectivity to all citizens – regardless of geographic location – ensuring that residents in urban centres, rural communities, and hinterland regions alike are fully integrated into the digital economy. By facilitating access to high-speed internet throughout Guyana, *Vision 2030* will enable every citizen to engage with E-government services and empower them to participate fully in an increasingly digital world.

Maintaining our environmental credentials and providing global leadership in the area of climate change

Vision 2030 seeks to hasten the implementation of the Low Carbon Development Strategy 2030 (LCDS 2030). Central to *Vision 2030* is a commitment to expand the protected area system for preserving our forests and biodiversity. *Vision 2030* also encompasses the transition to renewable energy, the promotion of adaptation strategies to mitigate adverse climate events, and the development of sustainable cities. To this end, we will:

- ✔ Increase Guyana's protected areas system to at least 30 per cent by 2030.
- ✔ Establish an International Centre for Biodiversity Research.
- ✔ Collaborate with local organs and other entities to prepare sustainable urban development plans for Guyana's urban areas and their environs, including the capital city, eight towns and Silica City.
- ✔ Accelerate the transition to renewable energy, including the construction of the Amaila Falls Hydropower Project, and the installation of solar and wind projects.
- ✔ Completion of the hope-like canals in Regions 3, 5 and 6.

The integration of sustainable artificial intelligence (AI) will enable the country to harness clean energy solutions to power its technological advancements. The utilisation of natural gas from Guyana's oil fields to generate electricity for the national data centre exemplifies a balanced approach to economic growth and environmental stewardship. By leveraging these resources responsibly, Guyana can minimise its carbon footprint while simultaneously fostering innovation and the development of digital infrastructure.

Furthermore, as the data centre expands, additional renewable energy sources will be incorporated to further reduce the environmental impact. This initiative aligns with Guyana's commitment to sustainability, reinforcing the nation's role as a global leader in environmentally conscious technological advancement. The strategy ensures that Guyana's digital transformation does not come at the expense of environmental integrity but rather complements efforts to build a resilient, low-carbon economy.

Recognising the critical role of technology in conservation, Guyana will deploy digital tools to monitor and manage its vast carbon resources, thereby advancing global efforts to promote sustainability. Through the integration of digital carbon management systems, the country will enhance its forest conservation initiatives, strengthen carbon trading mechanisms, and make significant contributions to climate mitigation strategies. This initiative underscores Guyana's commitment to conserving its natural resources while maximising the economic benefits of carbon sequestration and emissions reduction.

Defending Sovereignty: Guyana's Stance on the Essequibo Region

The Bolivarian Republic of Venezuela continues to fuel controversy over the Essequibo region – an area that is indivisible from Guyana's territorial integrity and fundamental to our national sovereignty. This is a persistent challenge to our border regional stability.

As a nation committed to peace and diplomacy, Guyana firmly upholds the principles enshrined in the United Nations Charter and remains resolute that international law must be the ultimate instrument for dispute resolution. There is no viable alternative to the rule of law, and all diplomatic engagements must adhere to the established protocols of the international legal order.

Guyana has consistently reaffirmed the sanctity of the 1899 Paris Arbitral Award, which conclusively settled the boundary between Guyana and Venezuela. This ruling remains legally binding and internationally recognised, yet Venezuela persists in disregarding its legitimacy. Guyana maintains that the International Court of Justice (ICJ) is the rightful and final authority to adjudicate this matter, as it operates within a framework of legal neutrality, fairness, and global consensus. History has demonstrated that geopolitical brinkmanship rarely yields the desired outcomes, and any attempt to undermine the international judicial process serves only to isolate those who reject its jurisdiction.

Guyana's foreign relations are rooted in strong alliances and enduring diplomatic partnerships with powerful friends and formidable allies. The unwavering support of the international community reinforces our commitment to safeguarding our territorial sovereignty. Let there be no miscalculation – Guyana stands firm in its resolve to defend every square mile of its 83,000 square miles, ensuring that the Essequibo remains an integral part of our nation, now and forever.

Our investments in human resources, technology, infrastructure, and training have bolstered Guyana's position as a regional leader in security and defence. We will continue to build on these successes, ensuring that the safety and sovereignty of our nation remain a top priority.

Vision 2030 focuses on safeguarding our sovereignty and protecting our territorial integrity. As such, we will collaborate with various international agencies, including the United Nations, the Commonwealth, the Organization of American States, and CARICOM, to promote awareness and support for Guyana's territorial integrity. Our focus will also be on strengthening our partnership with the United States, Canada, our South American neighbours, and members of CARICOM to protect our territorial integrity. We will work with our allies on military training, intelligence sharing, and defence planning, all while avoiding the escalation of tensions with our continental neighbours.

Furthermore, air, land, and sea operations will be enhanced to fortify our presence along our borders, while deploying cutting-edge surveillance technology that will provide real-time monitoring and rapid reaction times in various settings.

REFERENCES

Bae, S. H., & Yoo, K. (2015). Economic modelling of innovation in the creative industries and its implications. *Technological Forecasting and Social Change, 96*, 101–110.

Agenor, P., & Neanidis, K. C. (2015). Innovation, public capital, and growth. *Journal of Macroeconomics, 44*(3), 252–275.

Hysa, E., Kruja, A., Rehman, N. U., & Laurenti, R. (2020). Circular Economy Innovation and Environmental Sustainability Impact on Economic Growth: An Integrated Model for Sustainable Development. *Sustainability, 12*(12), 4831. https://doi.org/10.3390/su12124831

International Monetary Fund (2025). IMF Executive Board Concludes 2025 Article IV Consultation with Guyana. https://www.imf.org/en/News/Articles/2025/05/07/pr-25132-guyana-imf-executive-board-concludes-2025-article-iv-consultation

UNDP. (2022). Human Development Report 2021/2022: Shaping our future in a transforming world. https://hdr.undp.org/system/files/documents/global-report-document/hdr2021-22reportenglish_0.pdf

8

Concept of the One Guyana Vision

Regardless of race or ethnic origin, let us consolidate our forces, win new support and march forward to victory ... Racism is the greatest curse of our land ... anyone who spreads racial propaganda must be severely dealt with. Such a person is an enemy to himself and his country. CHEDDI JAGAN, 1965

The *One Guyana* theme is a vibrant, dynamic, and empathetic approach, grounded in the principles of cooperation, unity, hard work, visionary thinking, people-centred politics, and a free-thinking society aimed at addressing the contemporary social, economic, and environmental challenges plaguing our nation.

As your President, I am committed to building a Guyana where true prosperity is accessible to all, regardless of ethnicity, religion, race, gender, or creed. It is my firm belief and conviction that if we can move forward together as one people, as a united nation with a shared destiny, then our potential will become boundless.

The concept of *One Guyana* can be imagined as a tree, as depicted on the following page, one that is rooted in Guyana being a nation of one people, united by a common purpose and destined for a prosperous future. Like any tree, its growth is dependent on the nourishment it receives. Nurturing the *One Guyana* vision by investing in the Guyanese people, cultivating a society where moral fortitude and ethical and good governance are its cornerstones, valuing and embracing its rich cultural heritage, respecting religious freedom, embodying a spirit of dignity and national pride, championing equality and social justice, and promoting social harmony, would result in the growth, actualisation and reproduction of this vision. In so doing, the fruits of equality, trust, social harmony, togetherness, and a strong democracy will be born.

As a nation, that which unites us is greater than the forces that seek to separate us. It is my sincere hope and intention that the vision of One Guyana

The One Guyana Concept
Social Harmony
Trust
Togetherness
Equality
Strong Democracy
ONE GUYANA
Threats
Ethnic Polarization
Inequality
Social Exclusion and Marginalisation
Corruption
Misinformation
Climate Change
Foundational Drivers
Investing in our People
Morals and Ethics
Good Governance
Cultural Heritage
Religious Freedom
Dignity and Pride
Equality and Social Justice
Social Harmony and Togetherness
One People, One Purpose, One Prosperous Future

will become our national vision – embraced, owned, and brought to life by all our people.

It is essential that we understand the principles of this vision and what is required to achieve it. Achieving this vision requires, first and foremost, the recognition that the Guyanese people possess the capacity to become world-class experts, excelling in any field, once provided with the requisite resources, training, and sustained investment.

Investing in our people

Empowering our people is fundamental to national progress. A people empowered is a people equipped for transformation. Our citizens must remain at the heart of all developmental initiatives. To advance as a nation and equitably benefit from the wealth and resources at our disposal, we must prioritise the development of human capital. This is not only essential for fostering inclusive economic growth and structural transformation, but it also has significant implications for social equity and general welfare. In an era of rapid technological advancements, investment in human capital has become more critical than ever.

As our nation moves forward, the Guyanese people must be at the forefront of this development, gaining invaluable knowledge, skills, and competencies that will position them as leaders in their respective fields. Our development trajectory requires a knowledge base that is skilled in the areas of science, technology, engineering, arts, cultural competence, and mathematics. One that possesses not only the certifications but also the functional experience in operating world-class industries.

Our transition towards knowledge-intensive industries presents an opportunity to enhance female participation in the workforce and reduce gender disparities. Achieving this requires a steadfast commitment to providing high-quality education and skills development. My government sees our people as our greatest asset, and we are committed to harnessing this asset efficiently to enhance productivity, stimulate creativity, and overcome mediocrity. As Malcolm X aptly stated, "Education is the passport to the future, for tomorrow belongs to those who prepare for it today." Having a knowledgeable and skilled populace resulting from investments in our people is only part of what is required to achieve the *One Guyana* vision.

Morals and ethics

Moral principles and ethical integrity must be the cornerstones of our society. We must cultivate an environment where collective success is not only possible but actively encouraged – one in which every individual has the opportunity to achieve their aspirations. *One Guyana* must be built on a foundation of moral fortitude and ethical governance, fostering a society that values collaboration over competition, integrity over self-interest, and collective prosperity over individual gain.

Our emphasis on morality and ethics is not merely philosophical; it is a pragmatic approach to improving the lives of our people. Ethical leadership should not only strive for virtue in the abstract but should also recognise the interconnectedness of fundamental values such as friendship, justice, honour, virtue, and even economic well-being. A well-rounded ethical framework requires us to develop not only an understanding of what is right but also the wisdom to apply these principles in ways that are contextually relevant.

Practical wisdom cannot be acquired solely through theoretical instruction; rather, it must be cultivated through experience, social engagement, and ethical practice. This entails developing the deliberative, emotional, and social competencies necessary to apply moral reasoning in ways that are meaningful and impactful. Our goal is not simply to adhere to rigid moral doctrines but to integrate ethical decision-making into our daily lives, ensuring that our actions consistently reflect our shared commitment to justice and equity.

Furthermore, there are some common values in our belief system that we must inculcate if we are to build a stronger Guyana that will bring prosperity to all.

- ✔ We must celebrate each other's accomplishments.
- ✔ We must be open and transparent in the ways we relate to each other,
- ✔ We cannot love God and hate each other,
- ✔ We cannot love Guyana or be part of the *One Guyana* family by sowing seeds of division and divisiveness.
- ✔ We must avoid planting and cultivating too many thorns in the bosom of society.
- ✔ We must value education, health, justice, freedom, equality, and respect, by ensuring equitable access, fairness, and investment that will allow all our people to benefit.

The Dalai Lama, Tenzin Gyatso, refers to trust as the glue that holds society together. Trust cements relationships by allowing people to live and work together, feel safe, and engender a sense of belonging. Therefore, *One Guyana* must be premised on trust, including trust in leaders, family members, friends, and co-workers. Fostering trust further requires effective communication, respect, transparency, engagement, and credibility. The only way we can be trusted and be part of a trusting system is if this foundation is firmly knitted to the principles that guide us in our religious contexts.

It is trust that will make every one of us as Guyanese engender a shared purpose and a willingness to depend on each other. Through trust, we will willingly contribute what is needed, not just by offering our presence, but also by sharing our dedication, talent, energy, and honest thoughts on how we can achieve our one goal as a nation. Under the One Guyana umbrella, we remain committed and willing to fulfil our obligations.

As part of my plan to build trust among all Guyanese, I propose holding regular high-level consultations with representatives from the private sector, trade unions, religious bodies, and other civil society groups to address key issues confronting our nation. I also intend to directly engage with communities and community leaders across every village, building trust and deepening relationships to the benefit of the people in those spaces.

Partnership is always crucial. We must know how to select our partners. We have to know who has our best interests at heart. We must be honest with our partners, and we also need to ensure that we reciprocate with honesty and trust. Therefore, our relationship should be based on fairness, on equity, and mutual interests. The watchword for the governance of our country must be partnership. As Nelson Mandela reminded us, "Trust is not something that can be demanded or imposed. It must be earned through consistent actions and a genuine concern for the well-being of others." These words serve as a powerful reminder that trust is the foundation upon which we must build our nation.

With morals and ethics as pillars of my vision for a *One Guyana*, good governance of the nation's patrimony then becomes an integral part of the discourse. Without good governance, the prospects of achieving transformation across all sectors of our Guyanese society remain a distant hope.

Good governance

The governance of a nation's systems and resources to actualise forward movement is key in my vision for a *One Guyana*. There is absolutely no place for a governance system that prioritises the personalisation of power, disregards human rights, promotes corruption, and has an unelected and unaccountable government. Instead, our governance system must be one that is for the people, by the people, and is in alignment with what former United Nations Secretary General, Kofi Annan describes as good governance, that is, one that ensures respect for human rights and the rule of law, one that seeks to strengthen democracy while promoting transparency and accountability in public administration (Weiss, 2000).

As aptly put by the United Nations Human Rights Office of the High Commissioner (OHCHR), United Nations (n.d.), "The true test of 'good' governance is the degree to which it delivers on the promise of human rights: civil, cultural, economic, political and social rights." Therefore, the focus of governance in *One Guyana* must be people-centric, ensuring all Guyanese are afforded more than just the basic inalienable rights, resulting in a higher quality of life for all.

This form of governance is critical not only at the central government level but also at the level of the private sector. Governance at every single layer of national life, whether at the CDC, the NDC, the RDC, or the National Toshaos Council (NTC). Our laws must reflect the direction and development trajectory of the country. Therefore, we must continue to modernise and organise the legislative and judicial branches of the Government to meet the new demands of the future.

If we are to ensure that political, civil, and human rights are protected, if our one Guyana is to prosper, then we must preserve and strengthen our democracy. The governance system of a One Guyana nation must be efficient, reliable, trustworthy, accountable, simple, responsive, and flexible to the global environment in which we operate.

As Cheddi Jagan articulated in his book *A New Global Human Order*:

> Democracy is a vital ingredient of development. It must be representative, consultative and participatory. The people,

> especially women, must be fully empowered. The goal of democracy must be, as the American Declaration of Independence stipulated: "life, liberty and the pursuit of happiness."

We must appreciate the fact that the dimensions of good governance are centred on the importance of the rule of law, protecting the means of expressing our people's voice, holding the government accountable, preserving political stability, and eliminating all forms of violence. In his book, *Long Walk to Freedom*, Nelson Mandela stated:

> To be free is not merely to cast off one's chains, but to live in a way that respects and enhances the freedom of others.

Our governance system must also recognise the cultural nuances of our uniquely Guyanese society. A people-centric governance approach acknowledges and promulgates the nation's cultural heritage, mainstreaming culture into developmental initiatives.

Cultural heritage

Cultural heritage is the bedrock of cultural identity and, therefore, must be safeguarded. We must not lose who we are as a people in achieving the vision of a *One Guyana*, but maintaining this identity is part and parcel of what it means to be One Guyana. It is our cultural heritage that connects past, present, and future generations of Guyanese, shaping their uniquely Guyanese identity.

As Sabine von Schorlemer opined, "cultural heritage not only bundles the collective memories of humanity and the expressions of our ancestors. It also positively represents the dignity, uniqueness, and identity of humans, peoples, groups, and communities living today" (Ebers, 2022). Therefore, this dignity must permeate all aspects of our developmental agenda and not just be something we reference in passing.

Throughout the lands of what is now the Americas – from Canada in the North to Argentina in the South – the Indigenous people suffered historic injustices, including colonisation by European nations, dispossession of their lands, and prevention from developing in accordance with their particular needs and interests.

In our *One Guyana*, the Amerindian community occupies a special place as our First Peoples. This is a circumstance we must never forget and must always honour. They deserve the respect of all of us for their Indigenous knowledge, culture, and traditional practices, which contribute to the sustainable development and informed management of the environment that we all share and from which we all benefit.

Over the next five years, as this government is tasked with managing our country's affairs, we are determined to improve the lives of our Amerindian-Guyanese communities through a range of measures that we will implement.

These include updating the Amerindian Act after consultation with every Amerindian community, as well as improving education, healthcare facilities, housing, and infrastructural development in the areas where they live. The culture of the Amerindian Guyanese is a golden thread in the rich tapestry of the common civilisation that we have collectively woven over almost two centuries. We should all be proud of it, treasure it, and celebrate it.

As present-day Guyanese, it is our responsibility to preserve our sense of identity and pass down our cultural heritage to future generations. Cultural heritage is an important driver in enhancing social cohesion, fostering community identity, and promoting social inclusion. The immense social capital within our communities builds networks, relationships, and trust, fostering social cohesion.

Religious freedom

The One Guyana vision is founded on respect for religious freedom. This right is enshrined in Article 145 of our Constitution, which states:

> ... except with his or her consent, no person shall be hindered in the enjoyment of his or her freedom of conscience.

Our Constitution also affirms the right of all religious communities to provide religious instruction to their adherents. It prohibits a person from being compelled to take an oath that is contrary to their religion or belief. Religious heritage is an integral part of Guyana. It is enshrined in the Constitution, and it is protected. Respect for religious freedom remains a core value of the *One Guyana* vision.

So why is this important? If we are to respect religious freedom, then we must understand that it is closely tied to national and political freedom. Religious freedom is related to democracy. We cannot separate the two. That is why our congregation must understand that they are part of the national values of freedom as well.

The religious community plays a role in resolving conflicts within our society. It provides care and support to the needy and the destitute. It supports the poor and attends to the sick. Therefore, it must be free from prejudice and strife. Religious leader to condemn those who foment hatred and prejudice. The religious community plays a vital role in helping to create conditions that will allow us to realise the vision of a United *Guyana*.

Dignity and pride

When we speak of the *One Guyana* vision, we must do so with pride and dignity, not merely as rhetoric, but as a reflection of our deep-rooted commitment to national identity and collective progress. We must stand tall, confident in our heritage, and let the world recognise our unwavering pride in being Guyanese. To be Guyanese is to embody dignity, honour, and prosperity, values that define not only who we are as individuals but also the character of our nation.

Pride does not mean you must be arrogant, but that you must lift your head high, knowing that you're Guyanese and wanting the world to know that you're proud of being Guyanese. Being Guyanese is about having dignity, being prosperous, and deserving honour. What is noteworthy about us as Guyanese is that we will always bear with dignity whatever fortune sends and will always make the best of our circumstances.

We, the people, are the ones who give life to this country, Guyana. If we want the character of Guyana to be positive, then we must examine our character as a people. As the Universal Declaration of Human Rights puts it (Parr, 2021):

> ... recognition of the inherent dignity and of the equal and inalienable rights of all members of the human family is the foundation of freedom, justice, and peace in the world.

Equality and social justice

The hallmark of a productive society in which individuals thrive both individually and collectively rests on the foundation of equality. I have cherished the ideal of a society in which all persons live in harmony and with equal opportunities. It is an ideal under the *One Guyana*, which I hope to achieve, deepen, and live for.

As Guyana continues its upward trajectory towards increased prosperity, every Guyanese must be afforded the opportunity to lead productive, successful, and happy lives and to make the most of their talents. *One Guyana* cannot be achieved if inequality continues to permeate Guyanese society. Inequalities that exist in access to education at all levels, access to proper and adequate healthcare services, employment opportunities that correspond to educational levels attained, income, and justice will be addressed at the policy level.

Equality must also extend to our women in all aspects of their lives, and as such, we must all continue to work with immediacy and urgency to reduce the inequalities that disadvantage our women and deny them the dignity to which they are entitled.

From the level of Government there are several underlying themes in relation to what we want to achieve for women's advancement including greater participation, empowerment, enhanced livelihood options, a more secure environment in which they can live, stronger families and, ensuring that our national institutions address, in a holistic manner, the challenges of women.

This government is committed to not being distracted from the goal of building a *One Guyana* in which all our people enjoy equality of opportunity and a pathway to prosperity. This is a Guyana in which all races and persons are equal, with common rights, entitlements, and shared benefits. This government is committed to ensuring that every citizen is accorded a dignified existence, with due respect for their rights, and with equality before the law. The goal is One Guyana, One people, One nation in which all races and all persons are equal with common rights, common entitlements, and shared benefits. And my administration will fervently pursue this goal. That is why I have resolved that we live in One Guyana, as One People with no group more entitled than another, and no individual more deserving than any other except by virtue of diligence, manifest talent, and commitment to the national good. I will continue to lead the struggle that will bring an end to racism in this country with courage, compassion, and an unwavering commitment to social justice and equality. In *One Guyana*, there is absolutely no place for racial or ethnic prejudice, hatred, incitement, and violence.

Social harmony and togetherness

There is no space for division based on race or ethnicity; racism and racial discrimination have no place in a *One Guyana* nation. As one people, we cannot advance our country and improve our lives until we do it together. As one people, we should aspire to live in a society that is free of racism, discrimination, and violence; one that is firmly set on the path of harmonious relations and equity for all Guyanese.

My government's guiding principle in rising to this challenge of creating a *One Guyana*, is the same guiding principle that influences everything this government does: my unshakeable belief that the people of Guyana working together – as *One Guyana* – have the skills, the ingenuity and the experience to create a better country of which we can all be proud. Working together, we can transform our country without leaving any area of our country or segment of our people behind. We can become an ever more attractive place for investors and for our diaspora to choose to come home. And we can look after all our people by generating the resources to care for the most vulnerable and provide help when people need support that only the state can offer.

I urge, instead, that all Guyanese strive to eliminate the practice of defining ourselves by race and by politics and usher in a new era where we are defined more by our nationality and by our common love for each other, for our country. This is a critical prerequisite for us to improve our collective fortunes and leave a legacy of unity and prosperity for those who follow.

In this aspect of a *One Guyana* nation, the religious community plays a crucial role. The religious community is the custodian of morality and can help people to appreciate their moral and social obligations. The religious community must lead the way in promoting social harmony, particularly by encouraging greater tolerance and understanding, as well as respect for our multicultural diversity, since religious texts often speak to the values of equality and forgiveness. Further, the underpinnings of all religions should have no room for hate but should be based on love and respect for one another. Because under no banner of religious belief can you hate; under no banner can you discriminate; under no banner can you not be tolerant to each other. In the words of Nelson Mandela (Koomson, 2016, 45):

> No one is born hating another person because of the colour of his skin, or his background, or his religion. People must learn to hate, and if they can learn to hate, they can be taught to love, for love comes more naturally to the human heart than its opposite.

Our cultural heritage must also be safeguarded. We must not lose who we are. We are not a country that is only rich with oil and gas. That is not who we are. We are a country with people who are humble, hospitable, and love the world equally. While we must be willing to shed bad habits, we must also hold fast to the core values and enduring principles that define us as Guyanese.

REFERENCES

Ebers, T. (2022). Philosophy and Cultural Heritage. An Approach to Philosophy in Museal Contexts. *Ibero-American Journal of Culture and Though*t. 10. 55-57.

Government of Guyana. Constitution.

Koomson, K.W. (2016). Discrimination Experiences of Dreadlocked People in Ghana - A Case Study of Winneba. *Journal of Culture, Society, and Developmen*t, 23, 45-48.

Lin, T. (2018). Incorporating Social Activism. *Boston University Law Review*, 98(6), 1535-1605.

United Nations (n.d.). About good governance – OHCHR and good governance. https://www.ohchr.org/en/good-governance/about-good-governance#:~:text=In%20summary%2C%20good%20governance%20relates,economic%2C%20political%20and%20social%20rights.

Parr R. The Universal Declaration of Human Rights. In: *Citizens of Everywhere: Indian Women, Nationalism and Cosmopolitanism, 1920–1952*. Global South Asians. Cambridge University Press; 2021:165-172.

Weiss, T. (2000). Governance, good governance and global governance: conceptual and actual challenges. *Third World Quarterly.* 21 (5). 795-814.

Index